ETERNAL LAWYER

THE MACMILLAN COMPANY
NEW YORK · BOSTON · CHICAGO
DALLAS · ATLANTA · SAN FRANCISCO

MACMILLAN AND CO., LIMITED
LONDON · BOMBAY · CALCUTTA
MADRAS · MELBOURNE

THE MACMILLAN COMPANY
OF CANADA, LIMITED
TORONTO

Rostra from which Cicero Spoke
Restoration of ca. 1906

ETERNAL LAWYER

A Legal Biography of Cicero

BY

ROBERT N. WILKIN

He was, of course, middle-class, a little excessively, perhaps, which is called prosy. But at great moments, the commonplaces of honesty, virtue, justice, and the like are very big words indeed. His life and his death prove that he actually believed in them. For the rest, if on a horse in white armor in the Campus Martius, he was not in his place, why, he was not a soldier at all, but a lawyer.

—William Bolitho, "Twelve Against the Gods"

THE MACMILLAN COMPANY · NEW YORK

1947

Second Printing

PRINTED IN THE UNITED STATES OF AMERICA
BY THE VAIL-BALLOU PRESS, INC., BINGHAMTON, N. Y.

To NORMA

INTRODUCTION

JUDGE Wilkin has done us a great service. He has convinced us that Cicero was not, after all, a political opportunist, a trimmer, but a Roman patriot whose attitudes and actions were invariably determined by his legal training. He was always the lawyer.

As an orator, he was supreme. Oratory is the art of persuasion and Cicero spoke on almost numberless occasions with almost invariable success. Even after nearly two thousand years, the best of his speeches still stir us with the majesty of their diction and their appeal to the deep laid foundation of human rights—that beacon light of Cicero's life—the *ius gentium*.

As a correspondent, Cicero has served as a model for countless generations of letter writers. The great man at ease is still great—perhaps a little querulous as age and failure confront him—but still witty and kindly.

His philosophical paraphrases of Plato are worthy of the great originals. To him, and not to the Greeks, we owe our philosophic terminology. And as a teacher of rhetoric and oratory, he is still the final authority. One may well apply to him as the author of the *de Oratore*, Dante's description of Aristotle—the "Master of them that know."

No man has ever touched the keys that control the cadences of the monumental Roman speech as has Cicero. Words, phrases, clauses and sentences fall into place at his touch, and the sentences that they build rise into paragraphs that in their orderly sequence have the purposeful directness of the straight and level Roman roads, the sta-

and serene dignity of the Roman temple. And it is no tribute to the abiding influence of Cicero's person- that the editor of a great newspaper and a federal Judge of the United States should be his two most recent biographers.

All this may fully be granted Cicero. But till I read Judge Wilkin's book, I was not satisfied with Cicero the politician—the man of affairs. I found him short-sighted and unstable. I could not see in his career any consistent activating motive. This is partly due, I suspect, to the fact that my work on Cicero has centered around the Catilinarian conspiracy. In collaborating on a "Third Year Latin Book," I was forced to devote much space to the oration against Catiline, and the volume I was asked to write for the Loeb Library contains seven orations, all dealing more or less directly with the episode of this conspiracy. For it was really an episode, not a paralytic seizure, as Cicero thought. It was only one of the concomitant symptoms of the mortal disease that was destroying his Republic. That Caesar understood this and that Cicero did not, is perhaps the best measure of the difference between the patriot and the statesman.

Judge Wilkin has shown clearly that even in this crisis, Cicero was true to the deep devotion to the Republic that motivated all his actions. He has pointed out for the first time, I think, that Cicero was first, last and all the time a lawyer. His legal training under the great Roman jurists was never forgotten. It never failed to supply him with a basis for judgment, with a reason for his course of action. It was this grounding in the law and this reliance on the eternal verities that led him to defy Sulla's henchmen, to resist Catiline, to execute the conspirators, to hurl his Philippics at the coarse and sullen Antony and at the last, calmly to offer his neck to the sword of his murderers. To have portrayed Cicero as always the lawyer has been a great service to Cicero's memory.

No effort is made to minimize Cicero's faults, "His excessive display of sarcastic wit" is recognized. His "lack of modesty" is freely admitted. These defects Judge Wilkin does not condemn, but in explaining that quality of Cicero's mentality which led him so often to express his self-adulation he has shown a rare—an almost unique—understanding of the sensitive legal mind.

Not only has Judge Wilkin given us an adequate outline of Cicero's life but he has also added a masterly analysis of his philosophy of life, of government and of law. In this final chapter he has, it seems to me, attained that goal so earnestly sought by all biographers and so seldom attained—a complete and sympathetic understanding of the mind of his hero.

Judge Wilkin is not a pessimist but he is profoundly dissatisfied with the world of things as they are. Like other thoughtful historians, he sees in the life of Cicero's age, many a parallel to present conditions and many a warning that what once has been again may be. Cicero the eternal lawyer thus becomes Cicero the prophet. It will not be Judge Wilkin's fault if Cicero's voice is "the voice of one crying in the wilderness."

Louis E. Lord

Scripps College,
October 22, 1946

PREFACE

THE lawyer in any period occupies a peculiar position in human affairs, and from that position stem certain common experiences. The lawyer stands on middle ground. His sphere is swept by all the currents of life, especially its cross-currents. He is brought into contact with all kinds of people. He is the private go-between, the public intermediary, the international diplomat. The boundaries of his influence overlap the boundaries of all classes, all trades, and all professions. He is doctor and priest, yet he is necessarily more of a philosopher than the doctor of medicine and more of a scientist than the priest of religion. In analyzing human emotions he is a psychologist; in playing upon human emotions he is an artist; in marshaling facts to the support of his thesis he is a logician. In business he is a statesman; in statecraft he is a business man; in politics he is a humanist. In all things he is a moralist. But in adjusting his principles to the arts of his profession he is a consummate sophist. He is a philosopher gone to market; a poet gone to court; a mental warrior fighting for peace.

Always he is the champion of his client—and what client needs not a champion? The more despicable, the greater the need! And for his client he will practice mental quirks and moral quibbles which he would not indulge for himself. Although he is a minister of justice, it is not for him to judge. He knows that the manifestations of right and wrong in life are not so clear as their names in theory, and for that reason his first loyalty must be to his client, whatever his private conviction. But no matter how artful the practices of the lawyer, he is still the avowed defender of law and order. He is the self-constituted oracle of liberty and equality. Though conceited and contentious, his sense of right is the needle of his life's compass and its magnetic pole is Justice.

Cicero lived at a time when the talents of a lawyer were given the freest play and his virtues and foibles the severest tests. His words and deeds have been subjected to history's searchlight. In his day the world's stage was set for great drama, and the cast of characters had great historic significance, containing such names as Caesar and Pompey, Cato and Catiline, Antony and Brutus, Cleopatra and Clodia. On that high stage of history Fate assigned Cicero the part of Lawyer—and he played the part in a lawyerlike way.

This work does not presume to compete with the many distinguished biographies of Cicero already on the world's shelves. It is not so much a chronicle of a person or a period as a consideration of Cicero's particular character and significance as lawyer. Yet an absolutely detached analysis of his legal efforts would hardly be either fair to him or of interest to modern readers. It has therefore been necessary to repeat the essentials of Cicero's life story. In order to appreciate the man and his accomplishments even as lawyer it is necessary to see him in relation to the people and the circumstances of his time. The book was written with the hope that a professional interpretation might reconcile some of the diverse opinions concerning Cicero's influence and worth. It was further hoped that such a study might arouse an interest in the history of law and the purpose of the legal profession. The trends and problems of constitutional government today require a more thorough understanding of the evolution of our law and the function of lawyers. The brief flare of the Roman Republic may be illuminating, and its tragic fate may be a timely warning if considered in the light of Cicero's counsel.

During recent years many considerations regarding Cicero and his times have arisen which schoolday studies had not suggested. Such reflections prompted the thought that Cicero's life more than that of any other man summed up and emphasized the essential hopes, aims, problems and experiences of lawyers of all times. When viewed in the light of many years of experience at the bar and an association with all kinds of lawyers, Cicero seemed to be the epitome of all the vanities and virtues, aspirations and failures, contrasts, compromises and accomplishments of the legal profession generally.

No doubt the historians and critics will say this is a very one-sided portrait. True; but it is a side that has not heretofore been portrayed. It would be necessary of course for one making a thorough study of Cicero and his times to supplement this work with the work of other biographers: Plutarch, Forsyth, Strachan-Davidson, Boissier, Delayen, Sihler, and the chapters dealing with Cicero in Volume IX of the Cambridge Ancient History. A recent biography by an American newspaper editor, H. J. Haskell, presents the opposite profile from the view presented here. That author's point of view is revealed in the title: "This Was Cicero: Modern Politics in a Roman Toga." To consider the man as lawyer now seems only fair—and timely.

The Roman lawyer and the Roman Republic, because of the similarity of their problems to the problems of today, will repay a great deal of attention. In Cicero's time, mainly in his life, what Von Jhering has referred to as the "Struggle for Law" was presented on the City-

State stage. During the eighteenth and nineteenth centuries that struggle was presented on the national stage. And now in our time it is being presented in full panoply and panorama on a world stage. We can better comprehend the issue if we review the struggle in its earlier and simpler form.

CONTENTS

ETERNAL LAWYER

1

YOUTH AND EDUCATION

Legal Inclination

Before Cicero was born, the waves of civilization had moved about the eastern Mediterranean, and the crest of human endeavor had appeared in Egypt, in Asia, in Greece. Now the high-water mark of achievement was at Rome. Egypt had developed papyrus, pen, and ink—a system of writing. Phoenicia had given the world its commerce; Greece had endowed the world with philosophy and art; and Rome had now established its system of law. The civil administration, which had been extended by her legions into all lands, was directed and controlled by Rome. But poor Roma, like the goddess of justice, was blind. She was an indulgent mother whose wealth exceeded her wisdom. Though empress of the world, she was merely mistress of the world. Though she ruled the world, she was in turn ruled by her children. She was weakened, racked and ruined by their avarice, lust and cruelty. She was bullied and beaten in turn by her populace and her military commanders. And into this maelstrom of law and licentiousness; civil order and individual indulgence; devotion to state and self-aggrandizement; patriotism, conspiracy and tyranny; where the glory of citizenship contrasted with the misery of slavery; where fabulous fortunes were won and lost by barter and trade, chicanery, and means even more violent and foul; where ambition clashed with ambition for supreme command; where the government of a city became the government of the world and a republic became an empire—into this ruck of humanity and reel of affairs came Cicero the Lawyer.

Marcus Tullius Cicero was born one hundred and six years before the beginning of our Christian era, in a humble farmhouse which his grandfather had built on the banks of the Liris near Arpinum, a town of the New Latium. His mother, Helvia, was of the noble Helvius family, and his father of the Tullius family, of good middle or equestrian rank. The son could claim no higher rank than the father. Whether, as Pliny thought, the name Cicero was given to this branch of the family because it was noted for the cultivation of the vetch (*cicer*), as Fabius, Lentulus and Piso had their names from beans, tares, and peas, or whether, as Plutarch thought, it came from the fact that one of Cicero's forebears had a flat excrescence on the top of his nose which resembled a vetch, we do not know. But we do know that when early in life Cicero was advised by his friends to drop the appellation, it called forth a display of the pride and ambition that vitalized his whole life. "I decline to drop the name," he said; "not only will I keep it but I will make it glorious!"

How he would make it glorious he indicated at an even earlier stage of life. The bent of Cicero's nature, the very purpose of his existence, was revealed in his boyhood play. Apparently he did not romp with the boys of his age in the usual pranks and athletic games. Instead he held mock court with the older boys, preferring for himself the role of attorney for defense. These mimic trials would be staged in the porch of some private house or the portico of some less used public building, in order to have the setting of the open Roman Forum. A bundle of sticks with projecting axehead would serve the purpose of the *fasces,* the emblem of authority of the higher magistrates—and lately the emblem of Fascist rule in Italy. The acting *praetor,* the Roman judge, would be seated upon an improvised curule chair, that glorified campstool which, having its origin in the military history of Rome, came in time, like the English "Bench," to signify the majesty of law. There would be of course the conventional attendants, the lictors, armed with wooden shield and sword, who performed the functions of the English bailiff and sheriff. The praetor, probably almost lost in the folds of a borrowed *toga praetexta,* the purple-edged garment of the Roman dignitary, would hear the accusations and the defense. If the verdict of the judices, the Roman jury, should be against the accused, the praetor would then pronounce the sentence, and the lictors would solemnly lead the condemned lad to some adjacent dark room which served the purpose of the famous Roman Tullianum, or dungeon. In such mimes as these the youthful and ungainly Cicero first gave vent to his imagination in faltering bursts of oratory and learned the power of his personality to impassion and persuade. Thus the bent of the twig indicated the inclination of the tree.

Education was a tradition in Cicero's family and he was therefore sent to school at an early age. When six years old he was placed under Archias, the Greek poet, who remained his lifelong friend. At the age of eight years he with his brother Quintus was removed from the austere simplicity of the country home, where rural life was still preserving the ancient virtues that were the strength and honor of the Republic, and sent to Rome in order that his future training might be free from the crudities of provincial life. There he studied under Philo, the academician philosopher who was loved for the wisdom of his conduct, under M. Licinius Crassus and Marcus Antonius, both noted orators, and under Scaevola the pontiff and his cousin Mucius Scaevola, an eminent and learned lawyer and president of the Senate. M. Scaevola was admired by his contemporaries for his bravery, justness and gentle character, and is remembered by us as the author of a treatise which first arranged and classified the law according to the nature of its subjects.

Cicero's education led him into that disappointment which has marked the inception of so many legal careers. Proper training for the bar * is, and always has been, necessarily of such character that it overtrains the receptive youth. Society is right in demanding that those who would practice law should be learned in the law; that those who are responsible for the administration of justice should have some conception of the ideals of justice. But one of the results of such training is that the responsive youth will form the belief, subconscious, deep-seated, that the law is an exact science, and that every judgment is the consummation of justice. Then when he comes to the bar, and to grips with its problems, he learns to his bitter sorrow that the law, no matter how exactly stated, cannot be exactly applied, because human relationships and the conditions of life are always varying and seldom foreseen, and because its application is dependent on human agencies, also varying and full of error. The youthful spirit is shocked, if not blighted, to learn that the practice of law is only an approximation to justice, that government is only a game of expediency, that the forum is crowded with shysters and mountebanks, and that even those in high places will sometimes tamper with the scales of jus-

* The word "bar" is used to signify the legal profession generally, but there was of course no Latin equivalent because there was no actual bar in the Roman forum.

tice for personal gain. It is only the strongest character that is not bid down by such experiences to the practices of the opportunist and the demagogue.

Cicero, who had entered upon his legal studies with the highest hopes, was profoundly disappointed by what he saw when he entered public life. At Rome as elsewhere the practice of law was not the exclusive prerogative of the ablest and best characters. In the wake of several great political orators was a mob of attorneys who made much of their pretended political influence and used it to their own advantage. But "the mediocre character of these ranters, who sprang up like mushrooms in the Forum," was apparent to Cicero. Their rabid speechifying, with which they would defend the worst felons against honest men, won for them the name of "spouters" or "barkers." They seemed particularly abominable to Cicero because they not only accepted such cases but also received fees for them and were in that respect lawbreakers themselves.

At the inception of the profession the acceptance of fees was considered unconscionable. This was probably in part due to the fact that the relationship of attorney and client was associated in men's minds with the relationship of patron and client which imposed upon the Roman *patroni* the obligation of protecting their dependent clients, and partly because it had been for a long time the religious obligation of the pontifices to give legal advice and instructions (*responsa*) without charge. In any event it seemed against public policy to allow men to be paid for their public influence and knowledge of law and custom, for fear such practice might lead men to sponsor unjust causes merely for gain. Men of outstanding position and honor considered it an obligation to the state to instruct their less fortunate neighbors and to assist in the administration of justice. The law of Romulus on patronage and clientage had forbidden the giving of fees, and the more recent law of Cincius had imposed a more rigorous inhibition against payment for legal services. It was not until a later date that the acceptance of an honorarium was permitted and the maximum amount was limited by law. In Cicero's day reputable lawyers had to be men of some independent means.

When Cicero began his public life he had some land which he had received from his father, and he obtained some compensation from public offices which he held. Since the practice of the profession was still supposed to be political and not commercial, it was with apprehension that Cicero saw those things being done which tended to dishonor his calling. He saw moreover not only his profession being degraded to a trade, but also the ancient order of the Republic being destroyed by civil wars, and the rights of its citizens being subverted by military dictators. The magistrates were frequently subsidized and more frequently intimidated.

After a year's apprenticeship Cicero left the Forum with bitterness. In spite of the efforts of his master, Scaevola, to restrain him, he abandoned the bar and entered upon a military career. He first served in the Social War under Pompeius Strabo, father of the great Pompey, and later in the Marsian War under Sulla, the future dictator. That such military excursions from the bar are not unusual is attested by the great number of military titles among the members of the legal profession. Is there a bar anywhere or anytime that does not have its captain or major or its colonel? Our Chief Justice Marshall was first Captain Marshall, and the late Justice Holmes was a distinguished captain in the Civil War. The two world wars have drawn heavily from the legal ranks.

But Cicero's military experience served only to teach the truth of the statement which Caesar wrote to him in later years: "Better to extend the boundaries of the mind than to push back the frontiers of the empire." Cicero found that there was as much dishonesty, selfishness and greed for glory and power in warfare as in the practice of the law. Weary of the sham and pretense practiced in the forum, and bitterly disappointed over the frequent miscarriage of justice, he had turned to the military life with the expectation that it would be more forthright, more vigorous, more honest. He had thought the battle of arms would bring him more definite and lasting peace of mind than the battle of intellects. But his cultured sensibilities were terribly wounded by the brutality of war, his spirit which longed for order and harmony in men's relationships could find no rest in warfare. The true lawyer can never be long content with military life. He prefers the toga to the sagum. He loves law and order and is shocked at the ruthlessness of military force. He is devoted, not to the assertion of arbitrary will, but to the establishment of social welfare. His battleground is the human mind; his only force is the force of reason; his ideal conquest is the conquest of human emotions; and his grand triumph is to bring the passions of the human heart to the bar of justice and make them disciplined subjects of a high state of society. So Cicero by the force of his own nature was led back to the forum. He returned to his profession with greater determination than ever to make men listen to the voice of reason and order their lives according to the higher law of their nature.

First Public Case

Before entering into active participation in the public affairs of the Forum proper, Cicero practiced for some time before the praetors in matters pertaining to their civil jurisdiction. At an earlier time one praetor had been sufficient for Rome, but by Cicero's time the population had so increased and legal business had so expanded that at least two praetors were engaged in the hearing of civil cases while others presided over the criminal courts.

The praetor's judicial authority (*jurisdictio*), as distinguished from administrative power (*imperium*), enabled him to direct the ordinary course of procedure in civil cases. In the first instance he performed much the same function as the officer of a modern court who develops and determines the issue. He determined whether there was a justiciable question, and if so, gave permission to bring the cause into court. He then appointed an arbitrator and stated the issue to be determined. He also stated the law and applied it to the case. Finally he gave effect to the decision of the arbitrator by entering judgment. In addition to these duties under the formulary system, the praetor also personally made investigation of facts and issued decrees in certain cases. He had what we would term equitable jurisdiction, power to determine in what cases strict law was to give way to natural justice (*naturalis aequitas*), and also a general authority to determine certain public considerations (*publica utilitas*).

Cicero's early practice therefore led him into trials involving contracts, possession of personal property, title to land, determination of damages. He assisted in settling estates of decedents, involving questions as to heirship or rights of legatees under a will. If some minor under twenty-five had entered into an imprudent bargain, Cicero would present the case to the praetor and ask for a decree avoiding the contract. Or he may have sought redress for those who had been deprived of their property by fraud or force. In addition to such active service he was called upon by numerous clients for advice. He instructed the ignorant and directed the doubtful. But he no doubt learned, like the priest, the physician, and all who give counsel, that his greatest service to the troubled mind was in disposing it aright toward its problems. Injuries which he could not redress he taught his clients to bear with patience and fortitude.

The young lawyer's private civil practice afforded him an excellent experience. He learned how to analyze a case into its essential legal features and to state the facts in concise and convincing form. He developed a skill in analyzing the human mind, and learned to frame questions with penetrating insight. He learned to apply his knowledge of the law to any set of circumstances with logical power. His analytical skill and logic were supported by the emotional force of his strong personality. But he had a propensity for irony and sarcasm, the most dangerous weapon in the lawyer's mental equipment.

His reputation grew to such extent that he was soon marked for more conspicuous service in the public Forum. Fate was pressing him forward. His feet were in the Sacred Way that led to the Capitol. Soon his voice would be heard from the Rostra, the Roman orator's goal. This speaker's stand was originally a pedestal of tufa in the form of a square slightly curved and elongated in front and was located at the southern limit of the Comitium. It was higher than a man and was mounted by steps at one side. Its protruding circular part, the front of the pulpit, was ornamented with six beaks or rostra of captured ships, from which it took its name. By Cicero's time the speaker's platform was a more spacious structure of tufa blocks and was decorated with monuments as well as rostra. To the south of it lay the Forum, which was an open space, 100 feet wide at the north end. This Forum and the Comitium which it supplanted since B.C. 145 as the scene of the legislative assemblies, had been the principal meeting place since the time that the Sabines and Romans met there at the head of the valley between their respective hills and formed the community. The space was bordered on the north and east by the Sacra Via, the most famous street of Rome, if not of the world. The most important buildings, the Capitol, the Senate House, and many temples and shops faced upon this open court. This Forum was the center of a government and a power such as no other city has ever afforded. It must have been an inspiring place when the crowds assembled there for a great public trial! Around the Rostra would move a sea of auditors, the dignitaries of Rome and distinguished men from all the world, deputations from the provinces, delegations from all Italy, and members of every section of the Roman dominion. What an orator said in that Forum was echoed to the four corners of the world.

Cicero's first appearance in that rostrum, his first public case, the defense of Sextus Roscius, affords an admirable example of a lawyer's courage. In order, however, to understand the courage that Cicero exemplified, it is necessary to recall the political conditions that existed at the time. We must bear in mind the ruthlessness of the military commanders of that day and the general disregard of the sanctity of human life.

During the whole period of Cicero's young life the Roman world had been in civil strife. The sword had been playing the decisive part in Roman politics. During the last decade Rome had been divided into bitter factions by the warfare between Marius and Sulla. Between the years 87 and 82 B.C., Rome witnessed such scenes as were never forgotten by those who had survived them.

When Marius took Rome he turned his released soldiers and liberated slaves against his enemies, real or supposed, in order to gratify the lust for vengeance that was then consuming him. Octavius, the consul, was publicly butchered and the Rostra in the Forum was decorated with the heads of senators. For five days and nights there was unrestrained carnage. The bodies of the murdered became carrion in the streets, because friends and relatives dared not appear in order to give them burial.

Soon thereafter Marius died. His adopted son and his followers were unable to hold Italy long against Sulla with his veterans from the East, and the Romans who had taken refuge in Greece to await their time of attack. When Marius the younger saw that Rome could not be held, he gave orders that all prominent citizens who had been suspected of friendly inclinations toward Sulla should be murdered before the city was evacuated. One of the numerous victims of this atrocity was Mucius Scaevola, the noted instructor of Cicero in the science of law. His gentleness, his courage, his knowledge of law, could not save him.

The bloody battle of the Colline Gate and the fall of Praeneste placed Sulla in complete control of Italy. The Marians were then dispatched or dispersed. Sulla's acts of reprisal were worse than the vengeance of Marius. His cruelty set a high-water mark of atrocities for Rome. The monuments of the triumphs of his enemies were overthrown. The burial places of his deceased enemies were desecrated. Their living relatives were publicly slaughtered. M. Marius Gratidianus, who had twice been praetor, was dissected piecemeal. The captured prisoners were murdered by the thousand. Whole garrisons were slaughtered without mercy.

For some time thereafter Italy endured terrible political

sufferings through the proscriptions of Sulla. All who were even suspected of aiding the Marians were listed as outlaws, and rewards were offered to those who murdered or betrayed any on the proscribed lists. And those who befriended or concealed them were liable to the severest penalties. The property of the victims was confiscated and their descendants were excluded forever from public office. The equestrian order, to which social class Cicero's family was assigned, was the object of Sulla's special hatred because that order had generally been opposed to his class, the nobles. That these times had deeply impressed the mind of Cicero is evidenced by the fact that in later letters he frequently referred to the terror of the *Sullanum regnum.*

The arbitrary and cruel will of Sulla did not vent itself only against his enemies. When one of his military commanders, Ofella, aspired to public office and refused to withdraw when ordered to do so by Sulla, the dictator had him murdered in the Forum. Sulla's epitaph, which he is said to have composed himself, proclaimed that men had never known a truer friend or a more remorseless enemy. But so intense was his cruelty that it was thought at the time that he considered all mankind his enemies.

Such was the military dictator under whose administration Cicero dared to take his first public case. One of the men who had been proscribed was the father of Sextus Roscius, Cicero's client. Sextus had severely criticized an order of sale of his father's estate for a trifling sum to Lucius Chrysogonus, one of Sulla's freedmen. The dictator, enraged at such public censure, lent his influence to Chrysogonus, who instituted a prosecution of Sextus by accusing him of the murder of his own father. The dread of Sulla's cruelty was such that the older lawyers were afraid to appear for the defense. The friends of Sextus then sought out Cicero, whose skill in civil trials had been attracting favorable comment, and induced him to undertake the case. He was opposed in the trial by the crafty and malicious Erucius, the hired prosecutor. In Rome there was no officer corresponding to our public prosecutors. The president of each court (*judex quaestionis*) was charged with the administration of the law, but the preferring of accusations was left largely to citizens, who then, either personally or by counsel, assumed the prosecution of the cases thus instituted.

Cicero may have expected some indulgence because of his past service under Sulla's command. He may also have been encouraged by the fact that after the storm of Sulla's vengeance had spent its force, the dictator's avowed purpose was the reconstruction of the Republic. Still Cicero's mind was too alert and too sensitive not to appreciate all the dangers. His fate and his life depended on the outcome of the case. It was a test of his skill as a lawyer and his worth as a man. He knew the fickle character of the populace that would crowd the Forum. He knew their disposition to play for favor with the men then in power. He had already felt the jealousy of the older lawyers, and he knew the hatred of the patricians for one of his equestrian rank. If his bearing and words should not catch and hold the attention of the crowd, if his logic should not win the regard of the judge and the jury, he might quickly be laughed to scorn and booed from the Rostra.

The controlling motive in taking the case and the feeling that bore him forward in face of all danger, was the consciousness of the performance of his duty as a lawyer. His profession can still feel proud of his determination "that at least Sextus should not find himself without counsel." Stimulated by the thought of the dependence and gratitude of his client, strengthened by the thought that he was the defender of a just man, and fortified by his knowledge of the orderly processes of the law, he resolutely ascended the Rostra and boldly surveyed the sea of faces before him. He first modestly and gracefully foiled the charge of presumption which the appearance of one so inexperienced might create. He artfully proclaimed his inexperience as a shield against the jealousy of older lawyers and the severity of the dictator:

I imagine that you jurors are wondering why it is that when so many eminent orators and noble men are sitting still I should get up, I who neither for age nor for ability nor for influence am to be compared with those who are sitting still. All these men whom you see present at this trial know that a man ought to be defended against an injury contrived against him by evil design; but because of the sad state of the times they do not dare to defend him. Thus it comes to pass that they are present here because they are attending to their business but they are silent because they are afraid of harm. What then? Am I the bravest of all these men? By no means. Am I then so much more attentive to my duties than the rest? I am not so covetous of that praise as to wish to rob others of it. What is it then that has impelled me rather than the others to undertake the cause of Sextus Roscius? If any of those men, men of such influence and dignity, should speak and say one word about public affairs, as must be done in this cause, he would be thought to have said much more than he really had said. But if I say all the things which must be said with ever so much freedom, yet my speech will never go forth nor be interpreted by the people in the same manner. Anything said by the others cannot be obscure because of their position and standing, and cannot be excused as being spoken carelessly, because of their age and prudence; but if I say anything with too much freedom it may be either unnoticed altogether because I have not yet mixed in public affairs, or it may be pardoned on account of my youth—although not only the method of pardoning but even the habit of examining into the truth is now eradicated from the state. There is this further reason, perhaps; the request to undertake this cause was made of the others so that they were free to comply or refuse without prejudice to their duty. But those men applied to me who have the greatest weight with me by reason of their friendship, of the kindnesses they have shown me, and of their own influence—whose kindness to me I could not be ignorant of, whose authority I could not despise, whose desires I could not neglect. For these reasons I have come forward as the advocate in this cause, not as the one who could plead with the greatest ability but as the one left of the whole body who could do so with the least danger; and not in order that Sextus Roscius might be defended by a sufficiently able advocate, but that he might not be wholly abandoned.

The young orator then, with a courteous gesture to the dictator, laid the blame for the crime upon Chrysogonus who, he said, planned or condoned the murder of the senior Roscius in order to obtain his estate. Cicero did not directly attack the proscriptions or retributive measures of Sulla, but he accused Chrysogonus and certain evil neighbors of having the name of the senior Roscius placed upon the proscribed list in order that they might murder him and take his property with impunity. He charged that they had taken advantage of the unsettled civil conditions and the want of law enforcement to organize what in modern times would be termed a "racket." As a clever military strategist would do, he tried to divide the forces against him. He absolved Sulla from responsibility on account of his absorption in other important affairs of state. But he pictured the crimes of Chrysogonus so terrible that no one would dare openly to defend them:

What is that dread and what is that alarm which hinder so many and such eminent men from assuming to speak as they usually do in behalf of the life and fortunes of another? It is not strange that you are ignorant of this, because all mention of the matter which has given rise to this trial has been designedly omitted by the accusers. What are the facts? The property of the father of this Sextus Roscius, worth six million sesterces, Lucius Cornelius Chrysogonus, one of the most influential young men of our city at this time, says he bought for two thousand sesterces of that gallant and illustrious Lucius Sulla, whom I name only to do him honor. Chrysogonus demands of you jurors that since he has taken possession of the abundant and splendid property of another without any right and now finds that the life of Sextus Roscius the son stands in the way and hinders his possession of that property, you will efface from his mind every apprehension and remove all his fear. He does not feel while this man is free that he can keep possession of the ample and splendid patrimony of an innocent man; but if that man be convicted and got rid of then he hopes he may be able to waste and squander in luxury what he has acquired by wickedness. He asks that you take from his mind the uneasiness which day and night is goading and harassing him, and thus profess yourselves his assistants in the enjoyment of his nefariously acquired booty. If his demand seems to you just and honorable, O jurors, I for my part make this brief request, one, I persuade myself, somewhat more reasonable. First of all, I ask Chrysogonus to be content with our money and our fortune and not to seek our blood and our lives. In the second place, I beg you jurors to resist the wickedness of audacious men, to relieve the calamities of the innocent, and in the case of Sextus Roscius to repel the danger which is being aimed at every one. . . . Though many things be infamous, still is not this the most infamous of all things, that it should be thought fitting by these fellows to expect to obtain by means of your sentences and your oaths what they have been hitherto in the habit of obtaining by lawlessness and the sword; that though you have been chosen out of the state into the senate because of your dignity, and out of the senate into this body because of your inflexible love of justice—still assassins and gladiators ask of you not only to allow them to escape the punishment which they ought to fear and dread at your hands for their crimes, but also that they may depart from this court adorned and enlarged with the spoils of Sextus Roscius. Of such serious and such atrocious actions I am aware that I can neither speak with sufficient propriety, complain with sufficient dignity, nor cry out against with sufficient freedom; for my want of capacity is a hindrance to my speaking with propriety; my age, to my speaking with dignity; the times themselves are an obstacle to my speaking with freedom. To this is added great fear, caused by my innate modesty, your dignity, the violence of our adversaries, and the danger to Sextus Roscius. For this reason I beg and entreat you, O jurors, to hear what I have to say with attention and with your favorable construction. Relying on your integrity and wisdom I have undertaken a greater burden than, I am well aware, I am able to bear. If you in some degree lighten this burden, O jurors, I will bear it as well as I can with zeal and industry. But if, as I do not expect, I am abandoned by you, still I shall not fail in courage, and I shall bear what I have undertaken as well as I can. If I cannot support it, I had rather be overwhelmed by the weight of my duty, than either through treachery betray, or through weakness of mind desert, that which has been once honestly entrusted to me.

He then analyzed the facts as set forth in the accusation, and marshaled them not only to defend Roscius but to accuse the prosecuting witnesses. He balanced the history and the character of his client against the history and character of the accusers. Roscius was a simple, honest rustic devoted to agricultural pursuits, which Cicero referred to as "most honorable and most delightful." His accusers he referred to as dealers or brokers in men's lives and fortunes, racketeers. The murder was committed in Rome. The accusers were in Rome. His client was as usual on his farm. He then compared the motives of the one and of the others, and followed the example of that impartial and able judge who, he said, used constantly to ask at trials, "to whom it had been any advantage." He reviewed the conduct of the accusers before and after the murder and showed who had profited. From his analysis the design of the conspiracy became apparent. He said: "Since I have found out by whose design he was murdered, by whose hand he was murdered, I do not care."

He weighed all the probabilities. He portrayed the nature of the crime charged against his client as almost impossible of belief:

The power of human feeling is great; the connection of blood is of mighty power; nature herself cries out against suspicions of this sort; it is a most undeniable portent and prodigy for any one to exist in human shape who can take the life of one from whom he has received life.

He insisted that "unless a parricide is proved in a manner almost visible it is not credible."

In his own language he gives us an intimate view, a "close-up," of the scene of the trial. Addressing his opponent he asks:

What have you given me to defend my client against? And what ground have you given these jurors for any suspicion? . . . You would not in truth have said a word if you had thought that any one would answer you. It is worth while for you jurors to notice this man's carelessness in bringing forward his accusations. I imagine when he saw what men were sitting on those benches that he inquired whether this man or that man was going to defend; that he never even dreamed of me because I had never before presented a public case. After he had found that none of those men who have the ability and are in the habit of doing so was going to defend, he became so careless that when it suited his fancy he sat down. Then he walked about. Sometimes he even called his boy, I suppose to give him orders for supper, and utterly overlooked your assembly and all this court as if it had been a complete desert. At length he summed up. He sat down. I got up. He seemed to breathe again because no one else rose to speak other than I. I began to speak. I noticed that he was joking and doing other things up to the time when I named Chrysogonus; but as soon as I mentioned him the accuser sat up and took notice. He seemed to be astonished. I knew what had pinched him. I named him a second time and a third. After that men began to run hither and thither, I suppose to tell Chrysogonus that there was some one who dared to speak contrary to his will, that the case was going on differently from what he expected, that the purchase of the goods was being attacked; that the conspiracy was being severely handled; that his influence and power were being disregarded; that the judges were attending diligently; that the matter appeared scandalous to the people. And since you were deceived in all this, O Erucius, and since you see that everything is altered; that the cause on behalf of Sextus Roscius is argued, if not as it should be, at all events with daring, since you see that he is defended who you thought was abandoned, that those who you expected would deliver him up to you are judging impartially, give us now at last some of your old skill and candor; confess that you came here with the hope that there would be a robbery, not a trial.

He disavowed any intention to champion the cause of the equestrian order to which he belonged. On the contrary he affirmed that in the recent civil strife he had supported the cause of the nobles. He said he and other Romans had supported the nobles because they expected that through them safety at home and authority abroad would be preserved.

I consider that the struggle was to a great extent with this object, and I confess that I shared in that desire in the part I took. But if the object was, and if arms were taken with the view of causing the lowest of the people to be enriched with the property of others, and of enabling them to make attacks on the fortunes of every one, and if it is unlawful not only to hinder that by deed, but even to blame it in words, then the Roman people seem to me not to have been strengthened and restored by that war, but to have been subdued and crushed. But the case is totally different; nothing of this, O jurors, is the truth; the cause of the nobility will not only not be injured if you resist these men, but it will even be embellished.

He then uttered that apostrophe which one wishes might be emblazoned above the lintel of every public building: "Unless those who rule over us are vigilant and virtuous and brave and merciful, they must abandon their offices to those men in whom these qualities do exist."

His conclusion identified the fate of Sextus with the fate of the Republic and elevated the defense of an individual to the defense of the ancient rights and liberties of Romans:

If we cannot prevail upon Chrysogonus to be content with our money and not to take our life; if he cannot be induced when he has taken from us everything which was our private property, not to wish to take away this light of life also which we have in common with all the world; if he does not consider it sufficient to satisfy his avarice with money without being also dyed with blood cruelly shed, there is one refuge, O jurors; there is one hope left to Sextus Roscius, the same which is left to the Republic—your ancient kindness and mercy. If that remain we can even yet be saved. But if that cruelty which at present stalks abroad in the Republic has made your dispositions also more harsh and more cruel (but that can never be the case), then there is an end of everything, O jurors; it is better to live among savage beasts than in such a state of affairs. Are you reserved for this? Are you chosen for this? To condemn those whom cutthroats and assassins have not been able to murder? . . . God forbid, O jurors, that this which our ancestors thought fit to style the public council should now be considered a guard for racketeers. . . . Is there any doubt to whom the guilt belongs when you see on one side a racketeer, an enemy, an assassin, who is at the same time our accuser, and on the other side a needy man, the son of the murdered man, highly thought of by his friends, against whom not only no crime but no suspicion can be fixed? Do you see anything else whatever against Roscius except that his father's property has been sold? . . .

It behooves wise men, and men endowed with the authority and power with which you are endowed, to remedy especially those evils by which the Republic is especially injured. There is not one of you who does not understand that the Roman populace, which used formerly to be thought extremely merciful toward its enemies, is at present suffering from cruelty exercised toward its fellow citizens. Remove this disease out of the state, O jurors. Do not allow it to remain any longer in the Republic. It has had not only the evil effect of destroying many citizens in a most atrocious manner but through habituating citizens to sights of distress it has even taken away clemency from the hearts of most merciful men; for when every hour we see or hear of something very cruel being done, even we who are by nature most merciful, through the constant repetition of miseries, lose from our minds every feeling of humanity.

Sextus was acquitted. Cicero's oration was a striking success. Although Cicero himself afterward considered it somewhat youthful in style, it is still generally considered a polemic masterpiece.

The performance was a noble instance of that courage which has been one of the strong influences in man's social evolution. This was the prototype of that courage which Bonnet exhibited when, in order to defend General Moreau, he defied Napoleon, the military dictator of his day; of that courage which Malesherbes exhibited when, in order that King Louis XVI should not be tried without counsel, he defied the Revolutionary Convention of the mob, and followed his sovereign to the guillotine; of that courage which Coke exhibited when he told King James, who held power of appointment and power of removal, that the king was under God and the Law; and of that courage which Erskine exhibited when he defied the very judge on the bench in order to defend the professional and sacred right and duty of the lawyer to champion his client. Such conduct, exemplified in less conspicuous cases at every bar, is of the very highest order of moral courage and one of the chief virtues of the legal profession.

Visit to Greece

The successful defense of Roscius afforded Cicero one of the keenest delights of life—the first faint sense of fame. His daring and his accomplishment had placed his name before all. The display of his attainments had increased the admiration of men of culture, and without any loss of his own dignity he had won the plaudits of the mob. He was now one of the prominent citizens of Rome. He soon began to feel, however, that his rapid advancement was inciting some opposition. His performance had excited some jealousy among the young lawyers striving for place, and among the older ones who seemed forced into the shade by this newcomer's brilliance. He also felt the active hatred of Sulla's henchmen, and that entailed some danger. But inspired by praise, challenged by opposition, and exhilarated even by the danger, he undertook the defense of another victim of Sulla's disfavor. He became the champion of a woman of Arretium (modern Arezzo) whose rights of citizenship had been denied. Again he was successful. But after this second case Sulla's hatred became a positive threat to his life. Cicero's friends persuaded him that it would be best for him and best for the Republic if he left Rome for a while.

He accordingly made a visit to Greece. He said he did so in order to improve his health and perfect his style of oratory. The young lawyer was not robust. He himself said, "I was at that time thin and of poor physique." But always he was spurred by his ambition to be a great advocate, and neither his absence nor his illness gave him respite. We have his own words that: "When, therefore, my friends and physicians pressed me to abandon the law I replied that I would risk any kind of danger rather than renounce the hopes I entertained of glory from advocacy."

In Cicero's life, as in the life of every great lawyer, the human will carried on its tragic struggle to predominate over the weakness of the flesh. Only by the most rigid discipline of the human organism can the mental exactions of the lawyer's life be met. Seldom is the human system subjected to a severer nervous strain than that which the lawyer endures in his active life. He is constantly worn by two contrary exactions: he must practice the most complete concentration and at the same time be alertly responsive to his environment. While solemnly maintaining his mental confinement, he must be gracious about interruption. He must master his own intellectual repugnances. He must be able to apply his mind to the driest documents with sufficient tenacity to absorb their contents. He must devote himself through weary hours to study and practice. Cicero had not only a delicate constitution, but a stomach so weak that he had to practice a rigid diet and could eat a full meal only late in the day. But by rugged adherence to a careful regimen of temperance and diligence he, in spite of his poor physique, attained success in an arduous calling.

In Cicero's day the Romans maintained a military mastery over the Greeks, but the Greeks still maintained a cultural dominance over the Romans. While Rome had become the military and civil capital of the world, Athens was still the intellectual and artistic capital. Civilization had grown more vigorous in Italy, but it was never more brilliant than in Attica. The wave of man's advance is always attended by a cultural undercurrent in the opposite direction. Education consists largely of familiarity with the history, the customs and manners of older nations. Just as America, though materially successful and politically independent, has continued through the years to send many of its youths to Europe for higher education, so Rome sent its more fortunate young men to Greece to imbibe the established arts and sciences and manners. The very vitality and exuberance which creates a new nation seems to beget customs and practices that are shocking to disciplined taste. The Romans of Cicero's day, in spite of their elaborate dwellings and lavish ways, retained many of the coarser habits of the military camp. It therefore became the fashion for young men of means to spend some time in Athens in order to become familiar with the Greek language, study philosophy, and acquire some elegance of manner. Cicero naturally felt the need of this foreign influence.

He brought a mature, experienced, and very receptive mind to the capital of culture. In his youthful imagination he had pictured the scenes now actually about him. He was now walking in the footsteps of the great characters of his early studies. He visited the Bema, which was hewn from living rock and at one time may have been decorated with rostra. The young orator was inspired when permitted to stand in the place that had resounded in the most beautiful of languages with the voices of Themistocles, Pericles and Alcibiades. He could almost hear the terrible imprecations and sublime inspirations of his own great model, Demosthenes.

With a lawyerlike consciousness of every improvement for the administration of justice he noted that in Athens the forum was farther removed from the influence of politics and popular clamor than in Rome. The Roman Forum was the center of all political activity. Politicians were always present and too frequently influenced the administration of the law. Justice was often perverted to serve political designs. Cases were not always argued according to the austere principles of the law; they were presented not to an impartial and impersonal jury but too often were influenced by the emotions of the mob. Because of the close proximity of the different agencies of government, politics and the law were too intimately allied. But in Athens the Areopagus, "the guardian of the laws," sat on the hill of Ares, while the ecclesia, which corresponded to the comitia of the Roman people, met on a neighboring hill, the Pnyx; and the Agora, the public place and center of civic and commercial life, was equally distant in the other direction.

Cicero visited the places of historic interest, admired the sculpture and architecture, attended the theater, noted the character and customs of the people; he listened to the poets, studied with the philosophers, and practiced with the orators. He went into Asiatic Greece and at Rhodes studied under Posidonius, the philosopher, and practiced before Apollonius Molo, the rhetorician, whom he had formerly met in Rome, and who while in Rome had been accorded the signal honor of being permitted to address the Senate in his native tongue. Cicero declaimed in Greek before Molo, and wrung from that great orator the pathetic tribute: "Roman, I praise and admire you; but I pity the destiny of Greece when I reflect that the only glory still left to us, that of the arts and of eloquence, is about to become through you the conquest of Rome."

Cicero's visit to Greece is a fine example of a lawyer's devotion to culture—a broad culture, embracing historic information, observation of social custom, interest in science, understanding of the different systems of law, critical opinion of the different schools of philosophy, ardent enjoyment of all the arts, and culminating in a capacity for free and full expression under the refining discipline of an exacting diction. The manifestations of such culture were so enrapturing to Cicero that he considered whether he should not abandon the Roman Forum to live a tranquil life in Athens, devoted to philosophy, beauty and art. But it is a fortunate requirement for human happiness that we must work and feel we are being useful. The higher the type of man the more he is influenced by this impulse. And Cicero of all men could never have remained in Greece as a spectator and scholar. He had his own ends to achieve; he was devoted to the Roman Republic and would help to mold its destiny. He could not be content merely to study the deeds and thoughts of others, especially those of an alien and vanquished race. However Rome might treat him, still it was the hub of the universe to him, and even the dangers there appealed to him more than his exiled peace in Greece. He grew tired of contentment and longed to return and mingle again in the strife and conflict of his country.

Cicero had been absent from Rome about two years and, as historians significantly state, now that Sulla had died, he seized the chance for safe return. The corruption of Sulla's administration had so defiled his own life that he died of phthiriasis, an actual and terrible infestation of the flesh. After he had gratified his vengeance against his enemies he wished only to live in luxury and base indulgence, and soon that way of life took its toll. He had however restored the government to the senatorial nobility. His arbitrary rule was therefore followed by a settled calm that was very advantageous to the second advent of Cicero into the life of Rome.

He must have brought back with him something of the atmosphere of Athens, an aura of Attic culture, for he was referred to by some of the wags as "Greek" and "scholastic." But he paid no heed to such gibes of ignorant fellows, going his own way with a lawyerlike disdain or passive pity for the unreasoning jealousy of the uninformed. He realized that culture is not sectional or national but universal, that a man can do no better than to infuse into his own life the best training of other nations and then use it to the benefit of his own country.

II

EARLY DOMESTIC AND PUBLIC LIFE

Marriage and Home

Before becoming again absorbed in public affairs, Cicero gave thought to the proper establishment of his private affairs. He had arrived at that age when a desire for home and family usually asserts itself. Lawyers are generally conservative as to the conventions of society—especially as to those customs which succeeding generations have established for the welfare of the family, the basic unit of the social structure. Being devotees of the law, they naturally have respect for the law's first cousin, social custom. Cicero therefore followed the accepted practices of his day regarding betrothal and marriage.

Before he had gone to Greece his attention had been drawn to Terentia, the daughter of a rich patrician family, and upon his return to Rome they were betrothed. The betrothal of that day was more an agreement between the families than a courtship between the young people. Consorts were bargained for rather than won by sweet and tender emotions. Recognition of the finer sensibilities regarding the conjugal relationship came after several centuries of Christianity and the teaching of such men as Saint Jerome. The Romans of Cicero's time were quite businesslike about their marriages, and the bride's dowry was of prime consideration. In other words, the Romans were unromantic. "If only she has a dowry," said a character in one of the comedies of Plautus, "she has no vice." A girl without dowry, being as Plautus said "unmarketable," was doomed to maidenhood or concubinage.

Terentia's dowry consisted of 120,000 denarii, some houses in Rome, and a forest near Tusculum. The value of Roman money can be only approximated in contemporary dollars. A denarius at that time was a silver coin, the equivalent of twenty cents, which would make her cash fortune about $24,000. Cicero had inherited about 90,000 denarii from relatives and clients and had acquired a residence in Rome. Their betrothal was therefore upon a very fair property basis. But commercial considerations did not prompt Cicero. He seems to have been truly fond of Terentia in a loverlike way. He no doubt gave more heed to her social than to her financial status. Social classifications were well defined and of great importance. The three main classes were the nobles, who constituted the senatorial party; the equites, frequently referred to as the knights, who constituted originally the cavalry and now the tax gatherers and the well-to-do; and the plebs, generally referred to as the commons. It was Cicero's hope that a better understanding between the nobles and the members of the equestrian order would establish peace and maintain the Republic. His marriage to a daughter of the noble class would soften their objections to him as a parvenu. In return for her noble station, Cicero offered an established position in the forum and an influence in public affairs.

The betrothal, although it made no change in the personal relation of the young people and permitted no intimacy, was nevertheless an important engagement. It was celebrated with appropriate ceremonies in the presence of relatives and friends. Gifts were exchanged. Among others, according to Roman custom, the young man gave his fiancée an iron ring as pledge of his fidelity.

Terentia was fourteen years old and Cicero was thirty—a rather great disparity of ages, it seems; but the customary ages for Roman marriages. Girls were given in marriage very early in life, and frequently to men who were old enough to be their fathers. Terentia was not considered one of Rome's beauties, but she had a pleasing face and lively expression. She was described as a typical Roman girl, with low forehead sharply outlined by black hair, a small, slightly aquiline nose, and very bright black eyes. Such eyes might have been a warning of the temper which Cicero later deplored, but now they meant only the beauty of youth and the promise of life.

If the bride was lacking in beauty of person, the lack was not accentuated by the appearance of the bridegroom. He was not a handsome youth either. He was tall and thin and his neck was a bit too long and slender. His toga hid his ill-shaped legs. But his want of symmetry of figure was cloaked best by his charm of expression. He had a broad brow and beneath it very intelligent and sympathetic eyes. His smile was bright and responsive, exposing very excellent white teeth. A dignity of bearing and commanding presence gave him distinction. His air of thoughtfulness was gracefully complemented by Terentia's playful vivacity. The young couple commanded attention, not by beauty of person, but by charm of personality.

After the betrothal the marriage was not long delayed, only long enough to provide the trousseau. The wedding was celebrated with much pomp and ceremony. Cicero, having come to Rome as a provincial, was ambitious for social recognition. And Terentia, in addition to the usual interest of the bride in her wedding, was exhilarated by the thought of the prominence of her husband. All the relatives and friends were invited, and many very prominent people. Arrangements were made to have the ceremony performed by the Pontifex Maximus. He was the head of the college of priests, to whom were intrusted the regulation of the calendar, the feasts and the fasts, and the general conduct of the national religion and much of the formality of the law. He was to be assisted by the priest of Jupiter, the Flamen Dialis, whose official abode was the Capitoline temple, and whose duty it was to direct sacred rites and ceremonies, expiations, and other means of appeasing the gods. Civil authorities at that time took no part in the celebration of marriages.

On the wedding day the home of the bride and the home into which the couple expected to move were decorated with green branches and flowers and made festive by the display of lights and the best furnishings. Before the wedding, however, there was a quaint ceremony witnessed by the immediate relatives with mingled feelings of pleasure and sadness. The bride dedicated upon the family altar her doll and other toys to the divinities which had protected her childhood. This was the last act of the age of innocence and the severance of the tenderest family ties. It marked the beginning of a new life, filled with more glorious realities and graver responsibilities. It was one of those events of life which are anticipated with joy, but which cannot be realized without sorrow. Such events are mileposts along the way of life; in prospect they mark the way we desire to go, in retrospect they mark the way we regret to leave. Terentia's doll babies were soon to be replaced by real babies, just as her little girl and little boy would in time become woman and man. So the bright dreams of expectation must be sacrificed upon the altar of accomplishment. To do so occasions sweet sorrow; not to do so occasions bitter regret. When these transitions come the mind seems to hold to the rail of life's barque as if wishing not to go on so fast; but the barque of life is in the stream of time and cannot stay.

The marriage ceremony was performed in the atrium of the bride's home. This was the principal room of a Roman house. It contained the family hearth, the altar, and the treasure chest; and in the recesses of its walls were the images of the family ancestors. These portraits were usually plaques or busts made of wax, but were sometimes, in the better homes, carved marble or cast bronze. On a wedding day they would be fully displayed, with their inscriptions of titles and honors.

We can imagine Terentia in the customary bridal attire entering the atrium of her home, amid the assembled guests. A flame-colored veil, flowing at the back and sides, would be set apart from her blushing cheeks by a narrow fringe of her black hair. Clasps of precious jewels which held the veil in place would sparkle like her eyes. She would wear about her throat a necklace of gold, and pearls in her ears. A girdle with jasper buckle would encircle her waist.

The marriage contract having been signed by the required witnesses, the matron of honor would then lead the bride to the bridegroom and join their right hands. Sacrifices were then offered upon the family altar and the numerous deities propitiated. This ended the ceremonies at the bride's home. A procession was then formed to escort the couple to their new home, where the husband had had a feast prepared for the guests. The dowry, the trousseau, and the bride's personal servants were furnished by her father; the feast was at the expense of the bridegroom.

The procession to the new home was a gala and festive occasion. There were acrobats, jesters, and dancers in the throng and they proceeded with music of flutes and gay songs. The whole neighborhood turned out to see the young husband take his bride in his arms and carry her over the threshold of his house—thus symbolizing his right of possession. It was also a deference to the modesty of the bride who did not wish to appear to enter too willingly. At the conjugal dwelling the new husband and wife, side by side, presided over the feast. Italy had at that time acquired a renown for excellent food and wine. The music and entertainment continued between courses.

The merriment of the occasion was interrupted by one untoward event. As the feast and fun progressed some of the young men, probably flushed with wine, began to mingle with the dancing girls. One couple made bold to give a demonstration of the notorious cordax dance, just recently imported from Greece. It was a very lascivious performance, suggesting the marriage act, and was accompanied by the deft use of a cord or girdle which was made to pass to and from the hands of the dancers while it entwined their writhing forms. Cicero as master of the feast prohibited the indecent exhibition and forbade the young men to mingle with the dancing girls. He announced his opinion that a man to dance at all must be drunk or crazy.

This moral stricture revealed the young lawyer's dignity and high regard for the honor of his home. It might also have served as a premonition of a phase of his character which later contributed to the couple's infelicity. The estrangement which eventually came was no doubt due to differences of character which were apparent from the first. Although they had the good taste and moral purpose to avoid the low standards and evil practices of their time, Cicero and Terentia could not avoid, especially after their children were reared, their essential difference of temperaments and habits of thought.

Terentia was not an intellectual person. Like a child she

was absorbed in life as she found it. She did not disturb herself as to why it was that way or as to what else it might be. Inherited tendencies prompted her always to act for her own best interests. Although more selfish than her husband she appeared less so because less assertive. Cicero's pronounced personality made him appear self-centered even in his most altruistic endeavors. But he was no doubt attracted to Terentia by her lack of heavy mentality. He found refreshment in her simplicity. Her vanity seemed innocent and her naïve questions and primitive reactions to the affairs of his great world amused him. But when they grew older her simplicity took on the aspect of indifference, if not stupidity, and her vanity became selfish greed and material ambition. She in turn wearied of his seriousness, his introspection and philosophizing. She yearned for more natural emotions, the joy of living and a freer social intercourse. She saw no benefit from his high moral principles; and to him her anxiety about property seemed avarice. This want of sympathy led to doubts, and when Cicero concluded that he could not believe Terentia in regard to money matters he could no longer love her. Still we cannot but feel that their complete estrangement might have been prevented if Cicero had just cultivated a little freer and lighter contact—if he had not allowed his mentality to become so heavy, his personality so pompous. A man of greater social grace and more tact would have prevented the indecent dancing at his feast without making so pronounced a display of his virtue, without affronting his guests with a moral commandment.

The event passed by without much comment, however; and when the young couple were finally left alone in their new home, there were many years of happy wedded life ahead of them. First a daughter was born to Cicero and

Terentia, and later a son. No doubt Cicero's masculine ego was disappointed when his first-born was not a boy—more modest men than Cicero have been chagrined by the failure of fate to reproduce them. The position of women, moreover, was distinctly inferior. But as usual in such cases the cause of his early disappointment became the chief comfort of his later life. The son lacked the abilities of the father and died at an early age without any distinction other than the office of augur and an unexpired term as consul. He made an honorable military record but was not a source of pride or pleasure to his father. The daughter, Tullia, however, inherited enough of the mentality and taste of her father to supply the sympathy and inspiration which Cicero could not obtain from Terentia. Tullia was a constant solace and pleasure to him, except for the grief occasioned by her unfortunate marriage and early death. The friction and opposition in a prominent lawyer's life make him feel a deep need of some sympathetic understanding—a need which can be supplied with peculiar grace by a daughter. The daughter of Chief Justice Coke was his "only domestic solace" during his stormy life. Even the trying life of Aaron Burr was made sweet by the influence of his daughter. And Cicero, in his later and more troubled years, said of Tullia: "In her I find my characteristics, my words, my soul. Thus, in the ruin of the Republic she is my support, my consolation, and the charm of her conversation makes me forget all my troubles."

With the development of his family and the advancement of his position in public life Cicero came to feel the need of a more imposing residence. He purchased the home of Crassus, which stood on the Palatine hill. He moved to this more fashionable and prominent neighborhood in order, he said, that his clients and friends might more easily find him. But the facility with which they found him made it necessary before long that he have a retreat in the country.

Man strives for prominence until he gets it—then he yearns for retirement. A lawyer wishes the support of more and more clients—and then finds he is a slave to them, that they and their affairs occupy his every wakeful hour. He goes to the city in search of social contacts—but in the end returns to the country to find himself. The gregarious instinct is at odds with the self-preservation instinct. Life is itself gregarious; yet, in order to persist in one's own being, one must at times eschew company.

The home which Cicero bought must have been a place of considerable pretension. We know Crassus was a very wealthy and prominent man, and had excited some comment by the elaborateness of his homes and their furnishings. Cicero complained in one of his letters to Atticus about the debt which the home had imposed upon him. There was a remarkable development in the construction and furnishing of Roman homes during the life of Cicero. Prior to his day they were noted for their simplicity. The early Romans prided themselves upon the rigor and austerity of their life. But after the conquests of Pompey and Lucullus and other Roman generals in the east the character of life at Rome changed. Rome itself changed, according to an old saying, from a city of bricks to a city of marble. The tales and evidence of eastern splendor and magnificence incited the Italians to an ostentatious display of their rapidly accumulating wealth.

This development appealed to the pride of the Roman lawyer. He was not sensuous nor self-indulgent; but he was jealous of his place in the public eye. In Cicero the soul of a stoic was joined with the nature of a politician. Furthermore, while in thought he was a philosopher, he was in taste an artist. Intellectually he was indifferent to luxury; temperamentally it attracted him. He admired the plain virtue of Cato, but he was challenged by the splendid position of Crassus.

There is a trend in architecture today which should help us to visualize the home of a prosperous Roman. The Spanish style of building and furnishing, which comes to us largely through Mexico and the southwest, is no doubt descended directly from the Romans. The Spanish patio is the same as the Roman peristyle. The kind of suburban home so prevalent in our country today is very suggestive of an Italian villa of Cicero's time. It is low and plain; and, if a large home, is rambling. It lacks ornament and embellishment. The façade is unimposing. Unity and decoration are sacrificed to use. Doorways and windows are placed for convenience, even though irregularly arranged, and there is often a marked inequality of height between the different parts of the building. So the Romans seem to have been indifferent to exterior symmetry.

The growth and influence of Rome made great public works necessary—roads and sewers, viaducts and aqueducts, religious temples and civic buildings. This expansion in public construction caused a corresponding development in private architecture. The homes became more spacious and elaborate. Vitruvius Pollio, an architect of the time, said that the home of an important personage should have a vestibule of royal aspect, a large atrium (living room) and peristyle (colonnade), a library, gallery, and grand basilica (hall), and be set in a spacious park with imposing driveways for chariots and equestrians. Many of the homes had central heating systems, especially for use in connection with the baths. As a part of such establishments there had to be extensive quarters for slaves and domestic animals, for a Roman home was quite an independent unit of economy. So there is not much exaggeration in the statement of writers of the period who said that many of the villas had become villages.

As a part of this development of the abodes of wealth there was a tendency to embellish the interiors and beautify the furnishings. Marble was brought from Mount Hymettus in Greece and from Numidia in Africa to make the cornices and columns of many a Roman atrium. Floors were fine examples of mosaic art; walls were decorated with paintings, architectural designs, arabesques, and medallions, depicting feasts and sacrifices. The bright light from the opening in the ceiling of the atrium was softened by purple hangings. The seats and chairs and beds, though they lacked the softness of our modern upholstering, were often highly polished and decorated with ivory, silver and gold.

It was quite customary for a well-to-do Roman to have a number of homes. In addition to his city house, he would have a country estate and a villa by the sea. Many had summer homes in the mountains and wintering places in the south. The vicinity of Mount Alba was favored for country estates, and the bay of Naples was a fashionable winter resort. Baiae on the northern shore of the bay was the most notable, but excavations at Pompeii on the southern shore have revealed the general extent of the development in that territory.

The extent of early Roman dominion can be traced today very largely by the ruins and remains of such villas. Wherever the Roman governors went they established their country seats. They were the precursors of the manor estates of later centuries. The extent and character of Roman influence in Britain is being studied today through excavations of such villas. Our English ancestors brought the influence to this country, and our closest approach to the life represented by the Roman villa is gained by a visit to Mount Vernon or Monticello. The builders of such homes felt the dignity of human character and lived their lives on a grand scale. From such homes they saw the world in noble perspective.

Cicero during his active years owned a number of villas—at Pompeii, at Formiae, at Antium, and near Cumae or Puteoli, all on the western coast of Italy. His favorite home, however, was his country estate at Tusculum, about twelve miles to the southeast of Rome. He delighted in rare and costly furnishings for these homes. His letters to Atticus contain many requests for Greek statuary, manuscripts and other articles. He spent 125,000 denarii for one table—the top of which was a highly polished cross section of a cypress or citrus tree, a form very popular at that time with the fastidious. He burdened his life with the upkeep of these homes. He wrote to Atticus: "I am charmed with my places at Tusculum and Pompeii, except that I find how they swallow up loads of good metal, not so much in Corinthian bronze, as in the humbler medium of exchange."

He did not always find in these villas the retirement which he craved. He replied to his friend, who had exhorted him to further composition, that nothing could be done because he seemed to be living in a courthouse rather than a villa, owing to the throng that filled his home. "See," said he, "to what people my attention is given up. It would be a fine opportunity if anybody wished now to purchase my Formian estate, while these people are about me."

But at Tusculum he lived a simple and yet cultivated life, enjoying literary and philosophical discussions with Greek and Roman men of letters. The bookishness of lawyers has often been remarked. To be a lawyer at all, one must be literate; to be a lawyer at best, one must be literary. Facility of expression is a great advantage in the ordinary work of drafting contracts, pleadings and correspondence. An impressive courtroom manner is impossible without the grace of speech and ready reference which come only from familiarity with the literary masters. Studious habits were the foundation of Cicero's impressive personality. His life seems to justify the saying of Webster that the lawyer works hard, lives well and dies poor. No man should do less nor ask more. If the lives of all men were so ordered most of the world's economic and social ills would be cured.

First Public Office: Quaestor

With his private and domestic affairs established, Cicero entered upon the most propitious period of his public life. At the youngest age allowed by law he was chosen quaestor, and, with only such time intervening as the law required, he advanced successively to the offices of aedile, praetor, and consul. Here we see the lawyer in politics, striving to be effective with the people while maintaining his professional standards. At first he was backward and timorous in applying for public offices. He had asked the oracle at Delphi how he might rise to the greatest glory; and that priestess had told him, "Follow your own genius, and make not the opinion of the multitude the guide of your life." This he earnestly tried to do. He wrote to Atticus: "I do not curry favor with the populace nor relax any principle."

But an ardent ambition made him sensitive to public opinion and allowed him no peace at any point short of the highest place—nor even then; for, according to the Latin proverb, "Beyond the Capitol is the Tarpeian

Rock," signifying the fall that usually follows ascent. Cicero masked his personal ambition even to himself as a patriotic desire to serve the people and advance the glory of his country, as many public men have done before and after him. Yet who can know which among them has been most unselfish, and indeed is not some personal ambition a necessary ingredient of public service? Cicero's mind was torn by the world-old struggle which still goes on in every sentient mind—the struggle between the desire for unity in one's own life and the desire to be all things to all men; the wish to maintain oneself in integrity and the wish to express oneself in diversity; the urge to save oneself and the urge to spend oneself; the yearning for peace and the yearning for glory.

The glory in which Cicero esteemed the highest office was clearly indicated in his fourth Catilinarian oration, where, after stating that he had risked his life for his country, he said nevertheless that death could not be premature for one who had been consul. To realize the glory of his ambition he made every honorable effort. "I am one," he said to Atticus, "who makes it a principle to disregard nothing." So he studied all that took place about him. He knew men as a mechanic knows his tools, the name, the place, the use of each. He made himself accessible to all classes and types of men except fools and crooks. He heard their grievances and helped them with their problems and declined to accept fee or present for his services. In the performance of his public duties he displayed a faculty, prudence and diligence, and gave proof of an honesty and justness that were quite uncommon at the time. That his methods were successful is shown by the fact that he was repeatedly elected to office and was chosen consul by the highest vote of all the candidates. Because the control of the government was within the one city and the voting was usually by tribes or centuries, it was possible for him to know personally all the key men. He knew them and judged them as human beings and advised them according to just and honorable principles. He therefore never had to resort to bribery, and it became a current comment in Rome that for Cicero to present himself for office meant that he would be elected, and as a matter of fact he was never defeated in any election.

The quaestors were provincial treasurers and had charge of the collection of taxes. Cicero after his election was assigned to Sicily, one of the most important provinces because of its wealth and population. In spite of the fact that he had to enforce very severe exactions on account of the scarcity of food and supplies at Rome, he nevertheless performed his duties with such consideration for the feelings and welfare of the provincial inhabitants that he received from them not only assurances of their gratitude but also substantial gifts. He was not only an efficient public administrator, but here, as later in his government of Cilicia, he proved himself a gracious ambassador, tempering to the provinces the cruel omnipotence of Rome, and winning for his government some measure of admiration and even liking.

The holding of office did not prevent entirely the practice of his profession. He frequently appeared as lawyer before the praetor, and won the gratitude of some of the very influential families of Rome for legal services regarding certain interests which they had in Sicily. It was during his stay in Sicily that he distinguished himself in archaeological research by discovering the tomb of Archimedes, who, while tracing geometrical figures in the sand, had been killed by a Roman soldier more than a century before. The honor following this discovery made belated amends to the ancient scientist. The incident sets in striking contrast the benighted antipathy of the soldier who killed Archimedes and the benign sympathy of the lawyer who honored him. It typifies the destructive force of war as opposed to the constructive force of law. The violence of war begets bigotry and hatred, and sets nation against nation and man against man. But the influence of the law establishes peace and order and draws men and nations into sympathetic understanding.

It was in Sicily also that the inordinate pride and egotism which marred Cicero's later life began to show itself. Flushed with the honors he had received in Sicily, he imagined that all Italy was talking about the success of his quaestorship. On returning to Rome he met an important citizen of the capital, asked him what was being said in Rome about what he had done, and was stupefied by the reply: "Eh! Where have you been then, Cicero, all this time?" If he could only have learned from this incident how thoroughly people are engrossed in their own interests, how fickle they are in their affections, and how fleeting is public favor, he might have ordered his life so as to avoid the reproaches that later befell him. But the way of the lawyer is the public way, and he must suffer the hisses that follow the hurrahs. The changeableness of popular feeling is proverbial. The public mind is a fickle mind. A man of self-respect cannot be subservient to it forever. One who seeks public office should therefore be prepared for disfavor. But Cicero had no premonition of dark days to come. He was now in the midst of propitious times. He moved on to the office next in line of advancement.

Aedile

As aedile in 69 B.C. Cicero had charge of public works, public markets, the grain supply, the policing of Rome, and the public games. This office afforded an excellent opportunity for peculation and extortion. Many incumbents had amassed great fortunes, while they beguiled the people with lavish expenditures for cruel entertainments in the public circuses. But to Cicero's eternal credit—a credit of which his profession may be proud—he did not indulge in graft or cruelty. He tried to substitute theatrical representations for the barbaric games; but the Romans generally preferred the amusements of the amphitheater to those of the theater. Since he had beheld the beauty of the Greek festivals, the bloody games of the Circus Maximus or of the Circus Flaminius had no charm for him. "What pleasure," he wrote to his friend Marcus Marius, "can come to a refined and humanized mind from seeing a noble animal struck to the heart by its merciless hunter or one of our own weak species cruelly mangled by a beast of superior strength? The terrible slaughter of these poor animals (elephants) created general commiseration: as it is a prevailing notion that these creatures, in some degree, share our rational faculties." This chance comment to a friend, together with his often-quoted remark that no cruelty is useful, reveals Cicero as something more than a child of his age, as one able to withstand a predominant evil tendency and thus attest to future generations the inherent dignity of our nature. It reveals the mind and heart of the philosopher, shocked at acts which violate the universal harmony. It is a recognition of the ideals of natural law, a statement of the universal justice which characterized the Stoic philosophy—a philosophy that fascinated Cicero, and has influenced the thinking of the greatest jurists of all times.

In this the philosopher-aedile was a precursor of the philosopher-emperor, in whom the Stoic doctrine found its highest example. The immortal notebook of Marcus Aurelius—the very highest expression of pagan love of virtue—is a reiteration of the belief in a universal order founded upon the law of nature and in universal justice founded upon eternal unity: "For the world-order is one made out of all things, and god is one pervading all, and being is one, and law is one." Cicero not only exemplified this doctrine in his conduct of office, but later gave it beautiful exposition in his philosophic writings.

Cicero's forbearance from using the aedileship for corrupt purposes was not a mere gesture or game of expediency. His life was ordered according to higher principles. It is not mere idle phrasing when in *De Officiis* he says: "It ought, therefore, to be a main consideration with us to avoid the love of money; for nothing so truly characterizes a narrow, groveling disposition as avarice does; and nothing is more noble and more exalted than to despise riches, if you have them not, and if you have them, to employ them in virtuous and generous purposes."

Cicero's words constitute a fine expression of the general attitude of the legal profession. That there have been many individual exceptions—too many—one cannot deny; but the rule has been that true lawyers are not controlled by avarice, are quite free indeed from "a narrow, groveling disposition" toward riches. The lawyer's place in society imposes duties which must be performed regardless of personal considerations. The very nature of his work forces him to put emphasis upon fundamental principles and impersonal forces. His oath of office pledges his fealty to country, court and client. His own interests must ever be subordinate. Former President Hoover, at the peak of individualism, near the end of his term of office, recognized this; in addressing the American Bar Association he said: "You occupy a position unlike that of other men, who may honorably pursue only their private gain." It should be noted, however, that the number of these "other men" grows constantly less. The process of social evolution has tended to discredit the mere pursuit of private gain; it imposes the standards of professional ethics even upon business and trade. Thus the legal profession has led in the way of social evolution. The attitude of the true lawyer has always been so magnanimous that he could not be incited to avarice or envy of riches. Cicero gave us a very fine definition of this magnanimity, or elevation of spirit, as he called it. He said it was chiefly discernible by two requirements, the first of which was to despise the outside of things, to hold in contempt mere temporary considerations. And then he adds, "The other characteristic of magnanimity is, that possessed of such a spirit as I have pointed out, you enter upon some undertaking, not only of great importance in itself, and of great utility to the public, but extremely arduous, full of difficulties, and dangerous both to life and to many of its concomitants." Thus at the dawn of professional history Cicero placed the ideals of legal practice high above the materialistic, acquisitive, and selfish attitude which has characterized our age of industrial capitalism.

First Prosecution

In the year 70 B.C., Cicero conducted his first public prosecution. He took charge of the case which the Sicilians brought against Verres, in which the former praetor was accused of corruption and extortion. Some historians think he took the case to further his own political fortune—and no doubt the outcome had that effect. Other historians, however, cite his conduct as another instance of his professional courage and devotion to the Republic. Even if Cicero did anticipate political favor from the successful conduct of the case, he could not be certain of a successful outcome under conditions at that time. The provinces were controlled by the Senate. The favorites of the Senate were dispatched to wealthy provinces with the tacit understanding that they should fill their pockets there. A provincial magistrate could not be prosecuted while in office, and if charges were filed after expiration of his term, his case was submitted to a court controlled by senators, who, naturally, would be reluctant to impeach their own administration and thus undermine the system by which some of them had profited and others hoped to profit. But Cicero seized this occasion to make a truculent attack on the corruption of the senatorial juries and the consequent oppression of the provinces.

There is no doubt as to the guilt of Verres. He had lived in extravagant luxury since his return from Sicily. He was known as one of Rome's great voluptuaries. His extravagant way of life was a matter of general comment. That the Sicilians were deeply aggrieved is apparent from the fact that they would assume the trouble and risks of such a prosecution. If they failed, their fortunes and personal liberties would be in danger under the next governor. They knew the Roman court would be hostile to them, and the prosecution a great expense. Their witnesses had to come from great distances, making arduous journeys by boat and horseback. Due to these hardships the provincials would naturally suffer a great deal of injustice and persecution before they would bring a case to Rome. But in this instance these difficulties were all patiently borne. And the advocacy of Cicero so exposed the wrongs and so aroused the indignation of the people that the magistrates were afraid to give judgment in favor of Verres. The accused did not even wait for the decision, but fled into exile. Cicero proved to the Romans, and to his profession, that while mere oratory may not win a case, "eloquence founded on truth is invincible."

This case demonstrates that Cicero was a master of trial tactics as well as of oratory. Orators generally have been prone to rely upon their gift of speech to the neglect of facts and their proper presentation. But Cicero made no such mistake. He studied his case thoroughly, marshaled all the facts and supported all his charges with a wealth of evidence. He knew the political influence at work in the court and he completely overcame it by instance after instance of corruption and oppression, and buttressed his allegations with living witnesses and irrefutable records.

In his argument Cicero said:

When Verres had come to Catina, a wealthy, honorable, influential city, he ordered Dionysiarchus the proagorus, that is to say, the chief magistrate, to be summoned before him; he openly ordered him to take care that all the silver plate which could be found in the homes of Catina be collected and brought to him. Did you not hear Philarchus of Centuripa, a man of the highest position, noble birth, virtue, and riches, say the same thing on his oath; namely, that Verres had charged and commanded him to collect together and convey to him all the silver plate at Centuripa, by far the largest and wealthiest city in all Sicily? In the same manner at Agyrium, all the Corinthian vessels there, in accordance with his command, were transported to Syracuse by the agency of Apollodorus, whom you have heard as a witness.

Fearing the results of a tedious recitation of details Cicero said:

I shall not detain you to follow up this charge from door to door, and show you that he stole a goblet from Aeschylus the Tyndaritan; a dish from another citizen of Tyndaris named Thraso; a censer from Nymphodorus of Agrigentum. Having produced my witnesses from Sicily, he may select whom he pleases for me to examine about dishes, goblets and censers.

But he did not present his case as if he were merely championing some disgruntled provincials, he made it clear that he was concerned for the honor of Rome and for rights that were sacred to all mankind. He told how Verres had pillaged not only private homes, but the public buildings and also the temples of the gods. Even the statues which Romans had erected to commemorate Roman victories were not exempt from the rapacity of this "painstaking and industrious praetor," as Cicero cynically described him. Verres violated not only the hospitality of individuals who entertained him by taking their gold and silver plate and the statues of their household deities, he violated the confidence of King Antiochus, while a guest in Syracuse, by wresting from him a magnificent candelabrum which the king had dedicated to Jupiter and was then on his way to Rome to install in the temple. Cicero addressing the court then asked:

And to you, O judges, what can appear more scandalous or more intolerable than this? Shall Verres have at his own house a candelabrum, made of jewels and gold, belonging to the great and good Jupiter? Shall that ornament be set out in his house at banquets which will be one scene of adultery and debauchery, with the brilliancy of which the temple of the great and good Jupiter ought to glow and to be lighted up? . . . That temple which private men are decorating and are intending to decorate out of their own riches, Caius Verres would not suffer to be decorated by a king; and, accordingly, after he had once conceived this nefarious wickedness, he considered nothing in all Sicily afterward sacred or hallowed; and he behaved himself in his province for three years in such manner that war was thought to have been declared by him, not only against men, but also against the immortal gods.

Then turning to Verres he asked:

If at the time, by reason of your covetousness and audacity, you did not, while in command, fear the religious feelings of the population, do you not fear them now, at a time of such peril to yourself? What man, against the will of the immortal gods, or what god, when you so trample on all the religious reverence due to them, do you think will come to your assistance?

Roman procedure gave wide latitude for argument. When we consider the length of some of the orations, we marvel at the patience of the magistrates and jurors. Cicero composed seven orations for the trial of Verres but only two were actually delivered. This case proves that Cicero knew not only when and how to speak but also when to be silent. The case was heard toward the close of the term of the magistrates, some of whom were to be succeeded by close friends of Verres, and an attempt was made to carry the case over to a more favorable court. Through partiality to Verres the trial had been put off by several adjournments to nearly the last day of the term. Cicero, seeing the time was short, waived his right to argue further and insisted that the court should give its judgment immediately. This stroke won the day. The insistence upon prompt judgment following so closely the masterful presentation and array of facts left no doubt as to the outcome. Verres did not even await the announcement of the verdict.

Cicero was given an ovation. His successful prosecution of this important case and his fearless exposure of the gross corruption—too gross in this case for the Senate to condone—elevated him to a position of first rank. From this time he was generally recognized as the leading advocate of Rome. The Sicilians were deeply grateful for his services. As an expression of their gratitude they sent him a number of wild animals and a great supply of cattle—evidently the only medium of payment left them by Verres. As aedile he exhibited the wild animals to the populace in the circuses. The cattle were distributed among the people, thus affording the poorer classes some relief against the high price of provisions. This generosity assuaged the grudge which some bore because of Cicero's conservatism regarding the public games. Cicero missed no opportunity to court public favor, and even his adherence to principle had good political effect. In the year 66 B.C. he was raised to the praetorship.

III

JUDGE AND ORATOR

Praetor

Because the Romans did not separate the different functions of government, the magistrates had to perform legislative, administrative and judicial duties. A lawyer moreover could carry on his practice while in public office, so long as his duties as advocate did not interfere directly with his specific official duties. The refinement of professional obligations and relations had not yet been developed. Feelings were not yet sensitive as to inconsistent positions and divided loyalties, and there was no demand for a detached and independent judiciary. The office which was devoted most exclusively to judicial functions was the praetorship. Cicero recognized this with keen professional sensibility and acknowledged that a proper performance of that office required some detachment. During his incumbency he therefore abandoned advocacy in order to devote himself exclusively to his judicial duties. His high regard for the office and his impartiality won the esteem of his fellow citizens. He presided over the court with great integrity and honor, and kept strict watch against corruption or bias in the court.

A man imbued with the spirit of the law always holds the judicial office in high regard and believes in the universality of justice. Cicero's judgments were consonant with the theory advanced in his writings that "justice is due even to the lowest of mankind." He gave not only theoretical expression but practical application to the conception of the Greek philosophers that every human being embodies an element of value which the law is bound to respect, and to the ideal of universal justice which he said ought to be realized in the civil law of every community. His administration of the judicial office exemplified the principle announced so clearly in his speech against Q. Caecilius that the proper guardians of the law were the judges and that the welfare not only of Rome but of all the world required that the law should be kept inviolate and in uniform application. By word and by conduct he respected "the dignity of the judgment seat and of the law."

The profession of the law was not at that time highly developed as a separate and distinct calling, and the administration of justice could not offer a permanent judicial career. Law and politics were intimately allied and the incumbents of the principal judicial offices were constantly changing. The work of an advocate moreover was more congenial to Cicero's temperament than the work of a judge. He had an intense yearning for popular acclaim and an ardent ambition to hold the highest public office. No doubt it would have been better for him if he had adhered more strictly to a professional career, but by the bent of his own nature and the conditions of the time he was impelled toward a more spectacular role.

Broader Public Life

While praetor, Cicero made his first purely political speech. He addressed the assembly of the people (concilium plebis) in favor of the Manilian Law. By that measure Pompey was invested with complete military command on land and sea, with authority to raise necessary men and money, to make war, peace, and alliances as he pleased, and with civil control over the wealthiest provinces. Cicero's support of this proposal has brought upon him much adverse criticism and the epithets "political trimmer," "self-seeker," "flatterer." The enactment was a great stride toward dictatorship. It is therefore difficult to explain the advocacy of such a law by one so devoted to the constitution of the Republic. We of this day have witnessed great countries succumb to the argument that national and economic gains can be made more quickly and effectually under a single leader than through the more ponderous movements of a parliamentary machine. We have learned from current history that the country which hands all power to a military leader in order to increase its wealth and national prestige soon finds that it has sold to that leader or his successor its own soul and the personal freedom of its people. It is therefore hard for us to understand why the Manilian Law did not betray itself to Cicero's keen perception as the dangerous palliative which it was.

In order, however, to understand the problem, we must transpose ourselves to Cicero's time and try to see the conditions as he saw them. The Manilian Law was a development and an extension of the Gabinian Law. Under that measure Pompey had been given complete command of all naval forces with power to do whatever was necessary to suppress the piracy which dominated the Mediterranean Sea. The factious and corrupt Senate had proved absolutely incompetent to control the situation. It was so immersed in its own political machinations, and its leaders were devoted so much more to their own personal concerns than to the welfare of the state, that no effective force could be delivered against the national menace. The pirates had almost destroyed Rome's commerce. The boats that carried grain from the provinces to the Roman populace had been swept from the sea. No shipper would risk the hazards of transport unless under military protection. Grain had become so scarce that the people of Rome were in actual want. When the people were hungry they were not concerned with theories of government. They wrested from the Senate a great part of its power and placed it temporarily in the hands of a military commander. The end soon justified the means. The triumphant success of Pompey in clearing the seas of pirates made living in Rome much easier.

But now a new danger threatened the Roman supremacy. Its wealthy eastern provinces were in insurrection. The taxes and commerce from that source had so declined that there was a general economic depression in Rome. A succession of military expeditions had failed to bring Mithridates and Tigranes into subjection. Although the Roman generals had been reporting great gains and great victories, still those leaders of the revolt were at large and their military expeditions continued to disrupt Roman rule. The Roman forces were rendered ineffectual because they were treated as mere chessmen in the political game played by the Senate. Military command was a matter of political bickering, and military leaders were subjected to the sabotage of jealous rivals. When the people came to understand that the colonial prestige of Rome was being assailed by foreign armies, and that the failure of their trade and prosperity at home was due to the inefficiency of the Senate and the generals, it was quite natural for them to turn again to that popular military commander who had delivered them from the clutch of the pirates. The tribune of the people, C. Manilius, sensing the popular emotion and being anxious for popular favor, proposed a new law by which Pompey would be given supreme command over all military forces and complete dominion in the affected provinces, with authority unfettered by old constitutional procedure.

The senatorial party, containing some of Rome's ablest statesmen, fought hard against the law, but they offered no effective alternative. They pointed out the law's incompatibility with the ancient constitution of the Republic. They said it was extremely dangerous to place so much power under the control of a military leader. But their opposition was unavailing. Their theories of government were of no effect with a people in want and deeply disgusted by the inefficiency of senatorial administration. The passage of the law seemed certain. Cicero was nominally a member of the senatorial party, but he had attained that position by popular vote. The aristocrats, though at times quite glad to have him with them, had never made him one of them. He cast his vote and voice with the people and spoke in extravagant praise of Pompey. His views and his arguments assume fresh interest today.

In a pleasant introduction he acknowledged the honor of being permitted to speak to the Roman people from "this most exalted place"; he expressed his gratitude for their having made him their first choice for praetor; and he accepted the obligation to devote to them both the authority which they had vested in him and such facilities of speech as daily forensic practice had developed in him. He rejoiced that he had as subject a cause which could fail no one as inspiration for an oration. "For," said he, "when the singular and eminent virtue of Pompey is to be discussed, it is more difficult to find a termination than a beginning." He then continued:

In order that my oration may proceed from the very beginning of the cause of this discussion, let me say that a grave and dangerous war is being waged against your revenues and your allies by two most powerful kings, Mithridates and Tigranes. Because one of them has been neglected and the other provoked, they think an occasion is offered them to possess Asia. Letters are continually coming from Asia to the Roman knights, most honorable men, advising that their vast investment in the collection of your revenues is at stake. Because of my intimate connection with the order of knights, they have brought to me the cause of the Republic and the threat to their fortunes.

In Bithynia, which is now your province, many villages have been burnt; the kingdom of Ariobarzanes, which is at the edge of your tributaries, is completely under the power of the enemy; Lucullus, who has accomplished great things, is retiring from the war; and he who is likely to succeed Lucullus has not been adequately prepared for the administration of so great a war. One person is required and demanded both by our allies and by our citizens as the commander for that war. That one person is feared by the enemy, who fear no one else.

You see now the cause, consider next what is to be done. It seems to me that we ought to discuss first the nature of the war, next, its magnitude, and then the commander to be chosen. The nature of the war is such as ought to excite and inflame your minds with a determination to carry it to a successful conclusion, for the glory of the Roman people is at stake, a glory which has come down to you from your ancestors who, while great in all things, were greatest in military accomplishments. The safety of our allies and friends is at stake, a cause for which your ancestors waged many great and grave wars. The most reliable and greatest source of revenue to the Roman people is at stake, and through its loss you will be deprived of both the ornaments of peace and the subsidies of war. The property of many citizens is at stake, for which you should be deeply concerned both for the sake of those interested and for the sake of the Republic.

Cicero then made a further appeal to national pride. He mentioned the glory of the Roman name, and reminded his hearers that the stain cast upon it by Mithridates, who by one order and in one day had caused the slaughter of many Roman citizens in all the cities of Asia, had remained unavenged for twenty-three years. He reminded his hearers that the perpetrator of that great insult to the Roman people was not in hiding but was still carrying on his warlike operations among their tributaries. "For," said Cicero, "your generals have so contended with that king that they have carried off from him the tokens of victory but not victory itself. Sulla triumphed over Mithridates, Murena also triumphed over him, two most valiant men and the greatest commanders, but they triumphed in such manner that Mithridates, repulsed and defeated, still reigns. But in truth praise is to be given to those generals for what they did; pardon is to be granted for what they left undone; because the Republic recalled Sulla from the war to Italy, and Sulla recalled Murena."

Further to inflame the national feeling, he reminded his hearers that their ancestors had determined that Corinth, the light of all Greece, should be extinguished merely because Roman ambassadors had been addressed too haughtily, while they had allowed that king to go unpunished who had murdered an ambassador of the Roman people, of consular dignity, after having him placed in chains and tortured by scourgings.

Next the orator enlarged upon the plans and operations of Mithridates, telling of his assembly of great fleets and armies, of his dispatch of emissaries to Spain in order to compel the Romans to carry on a war "by land and by sea in two widely separated and very dissimilar places."

He stated that while the revenues of other provinces were hardly sufficient for the defense of those provinces, Asia on the other hand was so fertile and productive that it readily excelled all other countries in richness of soil, in variety of produce, in the extent of its pastures, and in the diversity of its exports. "Therefore," he insisted, "this province, if you wish to sustain it for usefulness in time of war and dignity in time of peace, is to be defended not only against calamity, but also against the fear of calamity. In other things, when a calamity arrives the damage is done; but in the matter of revenue not only the arrival of calamity but also the fear of it brings disaster."

He reminded his hearers of the economic interdependence of Rome and her provinces. Former disasters had taught them that when many large fortunes had been lost in Asia, all credit had failed in Rome through the general default in obligations. "For," said he, "it is impossible for numerous men of one city to lose their property and fortunes without drawing many others into the same general collapse. The financial structure of Asia cannot fall without by the same motion shaking the credit of Rome. Therefore ought you not to apply yourselves with all zeal to the prosecution of that war by which the glory of your name, the safety of your allies, your greatest revenues, the fortunes of many citizens, are defended along with the Republic?"

Attention was then drawn to the commander who should be selected: "I wish, O Romans, that you had so many brave and illustrious men that it would be difficult for you to determine which one was most especially suited to command such a war. But now when there is Gnaeus Pompey alone who has exceeded in valor not only the men of our time but also all recollections of antiquity, what is there in the mind of anyone that can raise a doubt?"

No language, he said, was adequate to describe the virtues of Pompey.

The virtues of a general were diligence in administration, fortitude amid dangers, energy in action, rapidity of execution, foresight in planning; and then he added that all these existed in as great perfection in Pompey as in all other generals put together whom his hearers had ever seen or of whom they had ever heard. In support of his statement he cited Pompey's campaigns in Italy, in Sicily, in Africa, in Gaul, in Spain, and finally his campaign against the pirates. "Who," he asked, "would ever have supposed that a war of such extent, so exasperating, so long continued, a war so extensive in its operation, so widely scattered, could have been terminated by all our generals together in one year or by one general in all the years of his life?"

He recited the ravages and humiliations which the pirates had inflicted upon Romans, and reminded them that almost under their very eyes (at the mouth of the Tiber) a fleet under the command of a Roman consul had been destroyed by the pirates. "But," said he, "all the pirates who were anywhere to be found were now either taken prisoner and put to death or else had surrendered themselves voluntarily to the power and authority of this one man. And thus Pompey at the end of winter prepared, at the beginning of spring undertook, and by the middle of summer terminated this most serious war, which had lasted so long, which was scattered in such distant and such various places, and by which every nation and country had been incessantly distressed."

He then reminded his hearers that the perfect general should be possessed not only of skill in war, but of many other qualities and virtues: "And first of all, how great should be the incorruptibility of generals! How great should be their moderation in everything! How perfect their good faith! How universal should be their affability! How brilliant their genius! How tender their humanity!"

He extolled Pompey for these virtues and contrasted the conduct of other Roman generals who had sold the minor offices in their armies and who had used the funds appropriated for their campaigns to buy the favor of civil officers and to make profitable investments. He said the billeting of the troops of such generals in the cities of their allies had proved as devastating as a capture by the enemy. "Do you think," he asked, "that of late years more cities of the enemy have been destroyed by the arms of your soldiers or more cities of your own allies by the winter quartering of your armies?" He then portrayed the moderation, restraint and forbearance of Pompey, not only toward their allies but toward their enemies. "Therefore," he concluded, "everyone in those countries looks upon Pompey as someone descended from heaven, not as someone sent out from this city. Now they begin to believe that formerly there really were Romans of the same moderation, a fact which foreign nations had come to believe incredible, a false and ridiculous tradition. Now the splendor of your dominion is really brilliant in the eyes of those nations. Now they understand it was not without reason, when magistrates of such moderation were given them, that their ancestors preferred being subject to the Roman people rather than being themselves lords of their own nations."

Cicero's argument became most lawyerlike when he directed his remarks to the opponents of the proposed law. He said:

That most illustrious man, Quintus Catulus, a man most sincerely devoted to the Republic, as evidenced by your kindness and many honors to him; and also Quintus Hortensius, a man endowed with the highest qualities of honor and fortune and virtue and genius, disapprove of this proposal; and I admit that their authority has in many instances had the greatest weight with you, and that it ought to have the greatest weight; but in this case, although you are aware that the opinions of many brave and illustrious men are at variance, still it is possible for us, disregarding those authorities, to arrive at the truth by the circumstances of the case and by reason; and this is made easy because those very men admit that everything which has been said by me up to this time is true—that the war is necessary, that it is an important war, and that all the requisite qualifications are in the highest perfection found in Pompey. What then does Hortensius say? He says, "If all power must be given to one man, Pompey alone is most worthy to have it; but nevertheless, such power ought not to be intrusted to one individual." That argument, however, has now become obsolete, having been refuted much more by facts than by words. Quintus Hortensius said many things in the Senate with great force and fluency against that brave man Aulus Gabinius when he had proposed the law which made Pompey commander in chief against the pirates. And also from this place where I now stand he made a long speech against that law. What then? By the immortal gods, if his authority had had greater weight with the Roman people than the real safety of the Roman people itself, would we this day be in possession of our present glory and of the empire of the whole earth? . . . When you opposed that law, Hortensius, the Roman people thought that you and the others who held the same opinion with you delivered your sentiments in a bold and gallant spirit. But still in a matter affecting the safety of the commonwealth, the Roman people preferred their own feelings of indignation to your authority. Accordingly one law, one man, and one year delivered us not only from that misery and disgrace, but also caused us again at length to appear really to be the masters of all nations and countries, by land and sea. . . .

It remains for me to speak of the authority and opinion of Quintus Catulus. He asked you, since you now seemed to place all your dependence in Pompey, in whom you would have any hope if anything were to happen to that man, and he received a splendid reward for his own virtue and worth when you all, with almost one voice, cried out that you would in that case put all your trust in him.

In truth he is such a man that no affair can be so important, or so difficult, that he could not manage it with his wisdom, defend it with his integrity, terminate it by his valor. But in this case I entirely differ from him; because, the less certain and the less lasting the life of man is, the more ought the Republic to avail itself of the life and valor of any admirable man, as long as the immortal gods allow it to do so.

Cicero asserted that if the people, at the time they chose Pompey to direct the war against the pirates, showed more foresight in the affairs of state than the objectors, and if in spite of resistance the people conferred dignity on the empire and safety on the whole world, then at this time those noble objectors should confess that both they and all other men ought to obey the authority of the Roman people.

He then counterbalanced against the men opposing the law the many worthy men who had spoken in its favor, and concluded: "Consider therefore whether we do not seem by the authority of these men to give a sufficient answer to the speeches of those men who differ from us."

His confidence in the people is displayed by the remark that "When we see such a multitude present, displaying such zeal in our cause as we now see displayed, when for a second time the same man is appointed to the supreme command, how can we doubt or question our power to achieve our end?"

He closed his oration thus:

Whatever I have undertaken in this cause, O Romans, I assure you has been undertaken wholly for the sake of the Republic. And I am far from thinking that I have gained by it the favor of any influential man, because I know on the other hand that I have brought on myself many enmities, some secret, some undisguised, which I need never have incurred. But I have considered that I, invested with my present honors and obligated by many kindnesses from you, ought to prefer your inclination, the dignity of the Republic, and the safety of your provinces and allies to all considerations of my own private interest.

Statesman and Politician

Now we see that Cicero was in business a statesman, in statecraft a business man, in politics a humanist. He began his discussion with the plain statement that a dangerous war was being waged against Roman revenues. His very point of departure was a concern for the national income, taxes, credit, world trade, and the fortunes of Roman citizens. But he saw all these things in relation to and as dependent on state policy, Roman dominion, and established civil order. His recommendations of government were based upon their contribution to the faith and confidence essential to good business.

In spite of all his efforts, we have a rather unpleasant consciousness that he spoke as a politician. His unctuous praise of all whom he named, his reluctance to offend, are quite at variance with the modern requirement of plain and forthright speech. Regardless of the self-denial and consecration contained in his closing remarks, and in spite of the fact that he believed what he said, still the oration as a whole reveals self-consciousness, a deep concern for his own popularity. But his bid for popularity was based on a sincere regard for the welfare of the people, all the people, even the people of the countries at war with Rome. His description of a great general made him a philanthropist and benefactor. Even in war Cicero was devoted to abiding humanitarian principles. Although he was a nationalist, and swelled with Roman pride, still he was a universalist, devoted to permanent world values, in other words a humanist.

True, he spoke in favor of war. But it is to be noted

that to him war was a means to an end. It was not a good in and of itself. He did not make a cult of force as did the modern dictators. Cicero was imbued with the Roman ambition "to enlarge the boundaries of peace, order and justice." Force and war were transitional steps in the achievement of a peaceful humanity, a unified world empire of equal races and men. He did not believe as the modern Fascists that "War alone brings up to its highest tension all human energy and puts a stamp of nobility upon the peoples." On the other hand, he avoided the extreme pacifism of the modern liberals who fail to accept the realities of social conflict. He looked upon conflict as a disease of social life, but recognized that some of the best medicines are poisons taken in moderation. He accepted the necessity of coercion for the sake of securing social co-operation and the necessity of resistance to power for the sake of securing justice.

It is nevertheless true that the law which Cicero sponsored tended toward dictatorship. It interrupted the authority of the Senate, the life-center of the Republic to which he was devoted. But he knew the Senate had failed. His conduct of the case against Verres had revealed the selfishness and corruption of most of the senators. He looked upon the Manilian Law as a drastic but necessary measure to maintain the efficiency of government. The law was to be passed by the Comitia and would therefore be the grant of the people, and Pompey would be beholden to them. He was not superimposing an arbitrary ruler from above. He was recommending an increase of executive authority by free choice of the people. He recognized that a representative republic could not maintain itself in the world unless it could deliver a united and aggressive force against those who would destroy it. Mithridates was a conqueror and subjugator of nations. He had conducted ruthless campaigns against the allies of the Romans. Tigranes had conquered Cappadocia and had carried back to his kingdom of Armenia three hundred thousand prisoners as slaves. The law was not the kind of measure which Cicero's philosophy would formulate, but it was an expedient for the actual conditions of life at that time.

Pompey moreover was not a dictator or despot. While we frankly acknowledge that Cicero's praise of him was too fulsome, yet we cannot say that Cicero's confidence in him was unwarranted. The republican institutions of Rome subsequently failed because of their own weakness and corruption. Pompey did not destroy them. There was nothing in his nature and nothing in Cicero's support of him that cannot be distinguished from the coercive and deceptive methods of the dictators of our own day. The old city government was insufficient for the needs of an empire, and a new frame of government had not yet been constructed. Cicero was not willfully false to his own ideals because he recommended a present practical expedient. His conduct of government was not on the same ideal plane as his philosophy of government but that was due to the conditions of the world, not to any weakness of his own nature—as subsequent events proved. The people of the world have not yet attained a development which will support world order based upon law.

As to the charge that Cicero was prompted by personal ambition and desire for advancement in office, there can be no categorical answer. Here again Cicero's attitude may be somewhat short of his philosophy. But we should note that the Stoic philosophy, which at first discountenanced ambition, by Cicero's time had been so weakened under Panaetius that the desire for honor and reputation if properly guarded was justifiable. Moreover since Cicero was primarily a lawyer and not a philosopher, it was necessary for him to take a part in public affairs. Great lawyers have always been great citizens. Their interest has necessarily extended beyond their professional activities. They have always taken a full share in the life of their day and have assumed the responsibility of leadership. But what are the limits of self-interest?

Ambition has never been considered altogether an evil. Man requires some egoism; he must have a little to maintain himself, and a little more to assert himself. To have just the right amount is, of course, a delicate task. The golden mean between self-assertion and self-effacement is most difficult to maintain. The rule should be neither to seek nor to shirk. One's ambition should be to give and not to get. To seek office merely for personal gain or to gratify personal vanity is in fact a form of graft; but to champion high principles and practices and to pursue them if need be into public office is very commendable. It prompts the most glorious kind of service. That many men mistake the form for the substance, there can be little doubt. They think high office will make them great and a title will afford them honor. There is, however, no short cut to moral worth. A man cannot lift himself by his own bootstraps, nor elevate himself by selfishness. If a fool sits on the throne he does not thereby become a king; he merely displays his foolishness. True and lasting honor cannot be forced. If it be not freely given it cannot be had. The only way to get it is to deserve it. Cicero should not be blamed for striving to deserve it.

While we cannot say that Cicero did not deserve honor, yet we must admit that he was too anxious about it. It seems that he was vainglorious. That weakness dimmed and still dims his fame. He himself said quite distinctly that an inordinate passion for glory was to be guarded against; but he also admitted that "scarcely can there be found a man who, after enduring toils and encountering dangers, does not pant for popularity as the reward of his exploits"—a direct admission as forthright as Bacon's confession of "an overweening love of fine feathers." The tragedy of life is that man knows his own fate and is powerless to prevent it. Conscious of his own frailties, Cicero faced an inexorable destiny.

If he had adhered to his own profession he might have lived an easier life and escaped much trouble. But the man of Rome had learned from Greece the importance of a public career. The highest ethical good which the Athenian could conceive was the distinguished performance of public service, and that idea imbued the life of Cicero. While it can be said in all verity that Cicero was never reprobate, vicious or corrupt, yet we must admit that his public conduct while praetor seemed more that of a business man concerned with practical ends than of a statesman concerned with theories of government; more that of a politician on his way to the consulship, than that of a jurist concerned with the administration of law.

Advocate

After his praetorship Cicero could have had, according to custom, a lucrative propraetorship in one of the provinces. But he preferred to return to the practice of his profession. His oratory and legal services had carried him to his present position, and he was content to rely upon them to advance him to the consulship. Two years had to intervene between the praetorship and the consulship, and during this period Cicero seems to have been well employed. He was now an ex-praetor and an advocate of great experience. He had represented many prominent persons, and had taken part—mainly as counsel for defense—in many notable trials. He had defended clients accused of fraud, extortion, conspiracy, murder, and high treason against the Republic. The term of his praetorship, and the two years following, were probably the happiest period of his life. They were years devoted to the work which was most congenial to his nature. Greater glory awaited him—and great humiliation. But now he felt the gratification of some accomplishment, while ambition still fired his zeal, and the way before him was bright with hope. These were years of comparative tranquility, family joys, interesting labor, and success in advocacy. This was the zenith of the lawyer.

The principal requirement of a lawyer in Cicero's time was oratory. Lawyers in that day did not constitute a licensed professional class. They were volunteers and free-lances, without organization among themselves or control by the state. For more than a hundred years men of experience in public affairs had been assuming to give legal advice and oratorical service; but not until the time of Augustus did the government recognize them as a profession, and not until the time of Diocletian, several hundred years later, was the administration of law confided to professional lawyers. During the Republic anyone who had confidence in his own legal knowledge gave legal advice to others who had confidence enough to accept it. Because the praetors and judices were usually men of little or no training in law, they welcomed the advice of lawyers of experience, and the jurisconsults grew into a position of power. The study of law then became common in Rome. Ambitious men who were ill fitted for military life courted popularity by giving legal advice to numerous clients and by acting as spokesmen for such as were slow of speech or too timid to plead their own causes in the public forum. Because of the character of the Roman government, the nature of its legal administration, and the temper of the Roman people, the effective orator became a man of great influence. Forensic oratory was highly developed as an art. The principal schooling of Roman youth was under the rhetorical master. Oratory was indeed the popular literature of Rome, just as truly as journalism has been the popular literature of our time, and just as the radio is returning the spoken word to popular favor.

It is easy to understand why oratory played a very influential part in a Roman trial—especially in a criminal trial (*judicia publica*). While there was a well established system of procedure, some rules of evidence and legal technicalities, yet a trial was not a strict logical proceeding without emotional appeal; public sentiment was an important element. It still is, but its influence is much more indirect. Although legal administration in Cicero's time had been extensively delegated through the Senate to certain courts (*quaestiones*), presided over usually by the praetors, still in theory the supreme jurisdiction in criminal cases always rested with the people in their assemblies. Even in cases tried by courts the magistrates and jurors (judices) acted, at least in theory, as agents of the people. The praetors merely directed the proceedings; the verdict of the jury, determined by majority vote, was the judgment of the court. And some accusations, such as charges of high treason, were always tried directly before the Comitia, unless special commissioners were delegated by the people to hear them. Even then there was the right of appeal to the people; only a *judicium publicum* was final. It was an adage that the head (caput) of a Roman citizen could not be touched without the sanction of the people.

Moreover the law did not set forth or define all the

cognizable offenses; they were chiefly determined by custom, or by public sentiment of the time, regardless of its *ex post facto* effect. The advocates, therefore, regardless of their ostensible auditors, were always addressing themselves, directly or indirectly, to the people. One cannot read the history of those times without reading between lines a terrible apprehension on the part of all public persons concerning the populace. Not only lawyers and statesmen, but even the great military commanders, were continually playing for and placating popular opinion. In fact, the events of the time seem like a tragedy enacted in volcanic country—always we hear the subterranean mutterings of the mob. In the mind of every actor is a presentiment of his doom, and there is something propitiatory in his every act and word.

But Cicero was well accoutered for his time. Oratory was his sword and his buckler. In psalter phrase, his teeth were spears and arrows and his tongue a sharp sword; his words were softer than oil, yet were they drawn swords. Not only was he endowed with the gift of speech, he had the instinct and temperament of an orator. He was a master of that medium by which the mind is formed. He could command the word. Only on two occasions did this ability fail him. In the defense of Licinius Murena he was so anxious to outdo Hortensius, who had won great applause, that he sat up all night to prepare, and then on the morrow lacked the strength and grace to carry out his preparation. And at the trial of Milo for the murder of Clodius, Cicero was so overcome by the adverse attitude and hostile cries of the people and the formidable presence of Pompey, who had prompted the prosecution, that he was confounded and could scarcely begin his oration in defense. He was so distracted by the glittering weapons of Pompey's soldiers that his tongue faltered, his delivery was cold and uncertain. He failed to gain the mastery of himself or the favor of his audience. His speech at best was nothing more than a string of long and violent invectives against Clodius, and failed to gain Milo an acquittal.

But these cases were rare exceptions and did not long depress him. In spite of the fact that he always approached the Rostra with fear and trembling, he usually gained a quick composure and acquired the ascendancy of his audience. Quintilian referred to Cicero as "that artist in swaying minds."

The style of Cicero's oratory is familiar. While it is superior, still it has the characteristics of other oratory of the period. All public speaking was influenced and colored by the conditions of the day, and particularly by the ardent character of the Roman people. But in spite of our consciousness of its popular appeal, it strikes us now as rather labored, ponderous and florid. The comparisons and similes seem too elaborate. The oratory contrasts strangely with the writing of the same period. Cicero's orations are verbose and prolix, compared to the terse, vivid Commentaries of Caesar. And the public speeches of our day seem quite conversational, compared to the extended figures and involved sentences of Cicero's formal delivery.

But we are here not so much concerned with his literary style as with his forensic skill, for his orations were meant to be spoken, not read. It was his custom to begin an address with some pleasantry, a jest, a play upon some word, a pun, which strikes us today as insipid and quite out of place in discourse so serious. But a cultivated taste had not yet been formed in Rome. Popular standards were those of a pioneer period. Cicero himself knew better; he referred to these sallies of wit as effervescences of the imagination. Yet he had a penchant for them, and a great susceptibility to the applause which they produced. Having won the favor of his audience, he would advance his arguments with logical progression—which is the very essence of convincing discourse. His thoughts were dignified, at times majestic; his expressions were forceful, full of contrast; and his posture and gestures well suited to the thoughts. He had studied and practiced with the best actors and they in turn came to hear and watch him. Borrowing some of the phrases which he himself used to describe the functions of a good orator, we can say: he knew how to entangle his opponent in a web of close and rapid argumentation; he could relax the severity of judges by an agreeable digression; turn by turn, he could rouse the indignation of his auditors or make their tears flow; and finally, he possessed the capital perfection of an orator—the ability to communicate to the mind of the judge every favorable aspect of the suit. He could please, persuade, impassion and prevail.

It would be interesting to know just how Cicero determined who should, and who should not, have the benefit of his services. He was not uniformly available. We know that he declined to represent some litigants, and that he represented others whose cases were quite questionable. It was his habit in early years to decline all fees and presents offered for professional service; but in later years he fell in line with the growing custom of acceptance; in certain cases he received considerable sums. That he was ever influenced by the prospect of financial gain there is no proof. There is convincing evidence, however, that he was influenced by the hope of political favor. But whatever the incentive, when he once took a case he tried hard to win, no matter what the merits of his client.

It is to the credit of the legal profession generally that

it is more frequently blamed for overzealous loyalty to undeserving clients than for faithlessness or treachery to clients. There is something in the very nature of the relationship that begets sympathy and loyalty in the lawyer. To be appealed to for help makes one a champion. And the plight of even the worst offender, when haled before the bar of justice with the world against him, inspires pity. The story he confides to his lawyer dissolves all censure. "To know all is to forgive all." As a result of this, lawyers must bear some blame for having helped so many culprits to escape. But on the other hand they are entitled to praise for their unfailing devotion to causes espoused. It is indeed to the credit of humankind generally that in the long history of the legal profession, through cases as numerous as the sands of the sea, in all kinds of circumstances, and under the greatest opportunities and temptations, the actual instances of perfidy are rare indeed. But, of course, every lawyer should remember that loyalty to a client can never require or condone dishonesty to the court. And above all, the lawyer must be true to himself. The law is technical and occasions technical defenses. But a lie can no more be condoned in court than in conscience. An upright man is an upright lawyer. No principle of legal ethics or professional charity has ever approved dishonesty.

Cicero's defense of certain clients afterwards caused him regret—and he made the mistake of publicly expressing it. When Numatius, whom Cicero had successfully defended, afterwards prosecuted one of Cicero's friends, Cicero said to him: "Do you think it was the merit of your cause that saved you, and not rather the cloud which I threw over your crimes, and which kept them from the sight of the court?" When Cicero denounced Crassus, upon whom but a few days before he had publicly pronounced a glowing encomium, Crassus asked: "Did you not lately praise me in the place where you now stand?" And Cicero replied, "True but I did it by way of experiment, to see what I could make of a bad subject." That may be good repartee, but it is poor professional conduct. Such expressions slander the client and undermine confidence in the lawyer. Such want of decorum brings the whole administration of law into contempt. But alas, lawyers are too often more concerned about their personal reputation than about the reputation of their calling! The adversary nature of their employment develops a contentious disposition, and the acclaim which they receive from a contest-loving populace develops a high conceit of their own wit, and then they are frequently tempted, and too frequently ready, to sacrifice their standing professionally in order to prevail personally.

Cicero took a very broad view of such conduct. In his opinion, and in the general opinion of the times, the lawyer had great latitude as to the men and measures he would support or oppose and as to the methods he would employ. In his oration for Cluentius he said: "It is a great mistake to consider the speeches we deliver before the courts as a faithful depository of our personal opinions. All these speeches emanate from the cause and the circumstances rather than the man and the orator, for if the cause could speak for itself there would be no need of counsel. We are therefore called upon not to utter our own maxims, but to bring out everything of significance that the cause can furnish. A man of superior intelligence, Antony [grandfather of Mark Antony], used to say that he made it a rule never to write any of his speeches, so that if he ever happened to say too much he could disavow it." Cato, however, set a better standard. He defined a lawyer as *Vir bonus, dicendi peritus,* an honest man learned in the art of speech.

But in practice that ideal was and still is too often lost. The lawyer too frequently becomes a consummate sophist. The learned speaker speaks; while the honest man becomes submerged in specious professional reasoning.

The fact is that oratory as an agency in the administration of the law has had little merit. Its influence has been more often against than for the discovery of truth. Its emotionalism and personal appeal militate against exact and even-handed justice. And in Cicero's time the evolution of legal administration had not progressed far. The concept of truth and the idea of justice were matters for philosophers. They were talked about by orators, but they did not constitute the conscious object of a trial. A trial, even a criminal trial, was not so much an affair of the state as a contest between individuals, the prosecuting witness on one side and the defendant on the other. The contest was presided over and directed by a public officer as a kind of referee, who had been established for the purpose of preventing private wars. Trial at law had supplanted trial by battle and orators had superseded fighters; but still the proceeding retained many primitive characteristics, mental cunning and coercion having been substituted for physical feint and force.

The general trend of legal evolution has proceeded away from trial by battle, whether battle of brawn or battle of brain. Such contests can hardly discover truth or establish justice. According to two ancient maxims, "Truth is lost in the midst of disputes," and "Justice dwells only with lovers of peace." In the progress of time the scientific spirit has tended to prevail over the adversary attitude, and our courts have lost the characteristics of the arena and taken on the character of the laboratory. Lawyers and judges have come to recognize with Aristotle that "The only true eloquence is the expression of the beautiful," and they find a very practical significance in the saying of Keats that "Beauty is truth, truth beauty."

But we do not deny to a great general our commendation of his military talents because we question the ways of war. In Cicero's time forensic oratory was next in importance to military genius. At one of the periods when the art of speech was at its highest, Cicero was a master of that art.

IV

CONSUL—AND SAVIOR OF ROME

Political and Moral Conditions

WHATEVER its merits in law, in politics Cicero's oratory served a very good purpose. He employed it to expose the machinations of evil conspirators and to bring public sentiment to bear against unwholesome measures. Frequently when his actions were challenged and his opponents appealed to the people, he accepted the challenge with alacrity and won the people's support. A few days before his term as praetor expired an information had been filed against Manilius for embezzlement of public funds. When Cicero, as president of the courts, was asked to assign a time for the trial, he appointed the next day, although it had been customary to allow at least ten days. This offended the people, because Manilius was a favorite with them and they believed he was being persecuted by the enemies of Pompey. The tribunes therefore cited Cicero to appear before the people and give an account of his conduct. He complied promptly and spoke in his own defense. He reminded his hearers of his established policy of moderation and justice toward persons accused, but said that to leave the trial to some other magistrate seemed to him not the course of one inclined to serve Manilius. This changed the minds of the people and they were lavish in their praise.

He did not hesitate to counter the commons, for his oratorical talents gave him courage. He knew he could sway them, and enjoyed testing his power in justifiable causes. While consul he even reproved the people at a time when their emotions were greatly disturbed. Lucius Otho as tribune had separated the knights from the plebeians and reserved seats in the theater for the members of the equestrian order. The people took offense at this and hissed and insulted Otho. The knights, on the other hand, greatly applauded him. Applause was answered by reproaches, and the theater was thrown into the greatest disorder. The disturbance became so great that Cicero was appealed to as consul. In accordance with the authority of his office he called the people into assembly in the Temple Bellona, a building erected in honor of the goddess of war, where the Senate entertained foreign ambassadors and received generals returned from war. There he reproved the violence of the people, and changed their attitude by lenient and good-natured explanations. So complete was his success that the people returned to the theater, expressed their approval of Otho's order and vied with the knights in doing him honor.

While this incident demonstrates Cicero's persuasive oratory, it also shows that the government of Rome was still principally a city government. It seems strange indeed that the chief executive of the vast Roman dominion should be called into a disturbance which today would be cared for by the police.

When Cicero's orations against the agrarian bill defeated that measure in the Senate, the proposers of the law appealed to the people. The proposal purported to extend the land-reform policy originated by the Gracchi, but it exceeded the requirements of land settlement. It created a board of ten commissioners with power to buy lands with public funds and assume control of public domains in Italy and the provinces. It was a piece of political jobbery; but nevertheless it appealed to a large section of the land-hungry populace. Cicero readily accepted the challenge of the advocates of the law and commanded the Senate to appear with him before the people. He so exposed the sinister effects of the law that it was completely discredited and withdrawn. He spoke with such power that the tribunes gave up other measures which they had intended to present in order to force Cicero either to support evil legislation or to oppose proposals which appealed to the cupidity of many.

Cicero's greatest achievement while consul was of course his frustration of Catiline's conspiracy. Catiline and Cicero were first brought into direct antagonism at the time of the consular election. In addition to these two men, Gaius Antonius was also a candidate. He was a pliable character without any strong characteristics for good or evil. Catiline had no doubt of his own election and expected that Antonius would be the other successful candidate because they were patricians and Cicero was not of their social caste. Catiline's ancestry, however, was all there was to recommend him. He had been a member of the profligate set in Rome which advocated violent changes and cancellation of debts. He had been accused of seditious conspiracy. It has been reported that Cicero at one time defended him, but best historic opinion now discredits that report. Cicero in an address to the Senate just prior to the election did not hesitate to expose Catiline's record.

Although Cicero's political influence had hitherto been largely opposed to the senatorial party, the leaders of that party preferred to support him whom they disliked rather than Catiline whom they feared. The aristocrats could have no confidence in Catiline, and people of property were suspicious of his revolutionary inclinations. Cicero, with the support of these elements together with his customary support from the people, was given a complete victory. Antonius took second place and Catiline went down in defeat—although he had almost as many votes as Antonius. His defeat by Cicero, whom he had referred to as an immigrant, fired him with intense hatred.

Infuriated by humiliation and harassed by debts, Catiline lost all regard for Rome and adopted the most desperate course. He decided to force himself into a position of power. The unemployed veterans of Sulla's army and the gladiators afforded him the nucleus of a military force. The quickly acquired wealth of Sulla's soldiers had as quickly disappeared, and they were now anxious for another chance to plunder. Moreover the sons of those men whom Sulla had proscribed afforded Catiline the nucleus of a political party. Their requests for reinstatement to citizenship, with the right to hold office, had been denied by the Senate, and he made the most of their resentment against the government. To these forces Catiline added the victims of economic and financial conditions who had been dispossessed of their property and the disgruntled selfseekers who had entered politics for personal profit and had been disappointed. His plans encompassed all who had shared his profligacy; the frivolous, the voluptuous, the corrupt; all who wanted luxury without effort; the degenerates and criminals; and all who like himself were dissatisfied with their lot in life, had nothing to lose, and hoped to gain from a general upheaval. With the assistance of many treacherous matrons of Rome, the other conspirators hoped to take advantage of the Saturnalia, slaves' holiday, and planned to arm the slaves and add them to the revolution.

There is a tendency to underestimate Cicero's accomplishment regarding this conspiracy. A cursory reading of the history of the period does not give a proper impression of the seriousness of the danger. It hardly seems possible that great Rome should be made to tremble by the machinations of such renegades as Catiline, Lentulus and their associates. A reading of Cicero's Catilinarian orations is apt to create the impression that he overestimated the danger and magnified his own accomplishment. In order to gain a sympathetic understanding of the problem that confronted Cicero and a correct estimate of his skill in solving it, we must understand the conditions in Rome at that time. The facility with which factions have overthrown great governments in recent years and the sinister influence of gangsters and racketeers in many of our great modern cities should help us to a realization of the circumstances in Rome.

Conditions then were worse than any we have yet known. The Roman military had become a menace. The great victories of the Romans had been achieved under the Republic, when the army was made up of citizens who had a country to love, property of their own, and an interest and share in the government. But as Gibbon has said, war had been gradually improved into an art, and then degraded into a trade. The purpose of the militarism of that age, like the purpose of the imperialism of our age, was to make the rest of the world tributary. By Cicero's time the army was made up largely of mercenary troops, the common soldiers being drawn frequently from the meanest and most profligate of mankind. And these soldiers were under the control, not of the state, but of the great military commanders. They were looked upon as the personal possessions of the generals who had raised them, just as the great economic power of our day has been considered the possession of the captains of industry. The influence and force of these soldiers were used to promote personal ambitions and selfish ends. Rivalries were intense and quarrels frequent. Parties contended for the influence of offices and the wealth of provinces. There was general disrespect for law, and constant cabals. The public peace and general well-being were sacrificed to private interest. There were insurrections and civil wars. The Roman army, whose legions, like the coils of a mighty serpent, had entwined the world, was now recoiling and sinking its deadly fangs into its own flesh.

The conquest of foreign lands had brought untold wealth and countless slaves to Rome, but the more the Romans had, the more they wanted. And both wealth and slaves had a dire effect upon the morals of the people. Every form of discipline was repudiated; most men sought nothing but the satisfaction of their avarice and lust; the getting of money was the preoccupation of all. Not only the men, but the women too, feverishly courted easy wealth by speculation and political connivance. These activities weakened the very heart of Roman order and culture, and spread corruption throughout the empire. As public security disappeared Romans thought of nothing but the enjoyment of the moment and went to any length to realize their aims. The inordinate desire for wealth, and the consequent prominence and advantage given to wealth, undermined the ancient devotion to the Republic and brought about a most destructive practice—the buying and selling of votes. When votes were bought, they were paid for out of the perquisites of office, and the whole public service became corrupt.

With the influx of people from all lands Rome had become thoroughly cosmopolitan. The pristine character of the people and the fundamental institutions of the Republic had been affected by this strong foreign influence. Not only were the morals, manners and speech corrupted, but the ancient Roman religion was lost in a motley of strange rites and ceremonies. Rome became the common temple of her subjects and, as Gibbon has said, the freedom of the city was granted to all the gods of mankind. When allegiance was divided devotion was destroyed.

Without personal and social discipline, the sanctity of the home and the purity of domestic relations could not be maintained. The vigor and virtue of a people are dependent on these things. It may be said of a nation as has been said of a family that its honor depends upon the virtue of its women. Except for the code of honor still maintained by a few old aristocratic families and the simple decent practices of families recently from the rural sections, there were no social or domestic standards in Rome. Laws were lax and conduct loose. Religious sentiment had ceased to hallow marriage, and divorce became so free it made marriage a mockery.

As a result of the excessive licentiousness and sensuality, courtesans gained a powerful influence in the affairs of state. Many of them were women of remarkable accomplishments as well as personal charm. They could dance, play the lute, lead a chorus, and recite poetry. Some were as well educated as the men and could discuss philosophy and policies of state. But they were luxury-loving, ambitious and jealous. They would ingratiate themselves into the favor of prominent men by marriage, concubinage, stupration, and participation in all kinds of crime. They were called "catinae" and "amicae." We can imagine that the former appellation originated with the jealous matrons of Rome, while the latter word found favor with the dissembling men.

The conditions caused by the courtesans were bad enough, but public morals became much worse when Roman matrons put themselves into competition with Roman mistresses. During the earlier days of the Republic the wife of a Roman was protected from the world and given an inviolable position of honor and dignity. To her was intrusted the care of the home, the supervision of servants, and the education of children. And the good women of Rome preserved for a long time the purity of speech, manners, customs and ideals of the past. But it was not to be expected that they would confine their attention to domestic duties forever while their husbands were the sport and pawns of women of the world. An interest in their own fate dictated that they take a hand in the game of life. The men in their egotistic stupidity attempted to maintain the double standard, and the women in their stupid jealousy retaliated by adopting the standards of men. So the Roman matrons discarded their veils, entered public life, and soon were enmeshed in political imbroglios and scandals; they put aside their modesty, entered public places, and soon were absorbed in the pleasures and vices of voluptuous dissipation. Thus the stream of Roman life became poisoned at its source. While at first the courtesans were more experienced in the seductive arts, the ladies of the nobility had an advantage in their rank and social distinction. But the ladies were not content with that advantage. In an effort to retain their influence over the men, they employed every subtlety and abandoned all reserve. They surpassed the courtesans in immodesty. Many of them came to lead lives of scandalous debauchery and indulged in the most unnatural practices.

Conspiracy

The inciting mind of the Catilinarian conspiracy was that of Aurelia Orestilla, whom Sallust characterized as "a woman in whom honest people found nothing to praise but her beauty." It is reported that her influence over

Catiline was so strong that when she hesitated to become his wife because of the child of his former wife, he had his stepson murdered. Not only was Aurelia anxious to gain the advantage which would come to her if her lover held a position of power, she was also moved by a jealous hatred of Cicero. She was envious of the influence which Cicero's talents and virtue had given him. Her mind was thoroughly inoculated with a double resentment—the resentment which her social set felt toward this *novus homo,* this on-comer, and the resentment which the licentious always feel toward the champion of public morals. Virtue, however humble, always gives affront to immorality, and Cicero did not even try to mollify this effect. His temperament accentuated it. He seemed to delight in employing his most scathing sarcasm against Aurelia's associates. He took every occasion in his public speeches to use it. Aurelia was stung by his epithets, and the recklessness of a woman's scorn is proverbial.

Catiline was of course commander in chief of the conspiracy. Under his generalship Lentulus was to direct affairs in Rome, while Manlius took charge of the army outside Rome. Lentulus had been consul, but had been ejected from the Senate for corruption. Manlius had been an officer in Sulla's army and was therefore very helpful in assembling the veterans from all over Italy; but he was now a dissolute soldier of fortune. Cethegus, a dissatisfied and ferocious senator, and Vargunteius, a disgruntled and impetuous knight, were honored by being assigned to murder Cicero. The plan was to fire the city in twelve places and post conspirators at the fountains and water pipes in order to massacre all those who sought means to quench the flames. At the first signal of the fire Manlius was to march against the city with his army. And in the midst of the confusion, not only the consuls but many senators were to be murdered, that there might be no one left to question the control of the conspirators. The time set was just before the new consuls, elected to succeed Cicero and Antonius, were to take office.

But of course a plan so extensive could not be kept secret. Rumor and gossip were rife. A very general fear soon pervaded the people. Not only public officials, nobles and capitalists, but all who had any possessions, the merchants, shopkeepers and farmers, were filled with a dread apprehension. Yet there was nothing definite—no overt acts, no tangible proof. The danger was imminent, but what could be done about it?

Betrayal

Fulvia helped to solve the difficulty. Two Fulvias played prominent parts in Cicero's career. Fulvia of the nobility contributed meanly to his elevation, and Fulvia the plebeian contributed meanly to his humiliation. The latter does not enter until the last scene; this was the time of the upper-class lady. She had been the mistress of Quintus Curius, one of the conspirators. He also was a noble, but because of his dissolute character had been barred from the Senate. He had wasted his fortune and now had nothing to give his mistress but reports of his desperate plans. Having been unable to keep his position or his possessions, he now proved unable to keep even the confidence of his confederates. Fulvia had grown indifferent toward him, and did not hesitate to use his disclosures as freely as she had used his wealth. She soon became acquainted with all details of the conspiracy. And through her hope of reward from the Senate, the whole plan was imparted to Cicero. Her disclosures were supported by premonitory letters delivered to Crassus and by him taken to the home of Cicero.

Thus fortified with facts, Cicero was encouraged to take steps against the conspiracy. But he was a lawyer and therefore knew that he did not have sufficient proof to sustain a legal prosecution. His judgment of the case against Catiline was better than Jefferson's judgment of the case against Burr—it required no opinion of court to inform him that in order to sustain an arrest there must be some evidence of an overt act. Intentions, while usually an essential ingredient of crime, are not in themselves sufficient to sustain conviction, even if they can be proved. Men are not punished for thoughts. Moreover Cicero dared not expose Fulvia by making her a witness. He was therefore forced to resort to a very old specific for the prevention of sedition—publicity. Public exposure, while insufficient in itself to convict a conspirator, has nevertheless served many times to foil a conspiracy.

Cicero summoned the Senate to the Temple of Jupiter Stator, where meetings were held in times of public alarm, and disclosed all the plans of the conspirators. Catiline, not knowing of the betrayal of Quintus Curius by Fulvia, attended this meeting. Cicero, shocked at his audacious presence, turned to him and opened his first Catilinarian oration with the apostrophe: "How long, O Catiline, will you continue to abuse our patience?" Then followed a flood of denunciation that constitutes the high-water mark of oratorical invective.

How different in that setting were all those plans which Catiline had outlined with enthusiasm to the conspirators! What he had announced with pride he now heard with shame. The senators withdrew from him and vacated the seats around him. Even his accomplices dared not recognize him. But he had the temerity to attempt a reply. "Is it possible," he inquired, "that a patrician walking in the footsteps of his fathers, and having like them rendered great services to the Republic, should be interested in overthrowing it, while a Marcus Tullius, a newcomer to Rome, should be its savior?" Thus did Cicero's enemy acclaim him, and predict his future recognition as Savior of Rome. Catiline would have proceeded further, but his voice was drowned by indignant murmurs and threatening cries. Then Cicero ordered him to leave Rome.

That night he left Rome unostentatiously, and with a few followers made his way to the camp of Manlius. On the following morning Cicero assembled the people in the Forum and in his second oration told them of the flight of Catiline, and expressed the hope that all his associates would follow him. If they should not depart, said he, they must take the consequences—as consul he would protect the city.

But they did not depart. Although Catiline had quit the city, he had not quit the conspiracy. Vanity grows even from injury, and Catiline, stung by defeat and enraged by denunciation, became more zealous than ever in his efforts to overthrow the government. The Senate passed a decree proclaiming Catiline a public enemy; directing the Consul Antonius to take an army against Catiline and Manlius; and entrusting to Cicero the care of the city.

Detection

The conspirators in their desperation had opened negotiations with the Allobroges, a warlike Gallic tribe, in the hope of stirring them to insurrection against Rome. A delegation from this tribe was in Rome to complain of exactions imposed by Roman generals and to solicit cancellation or modification of debts owing to Roman financiers and the Roman treasury. The Senate had heard them coldly, and the conspirators tried to take advantage of their dissatisfaction. At first the Allobroges looked with favor upon the suggestions of the conspirators, but later decided it was best to disclose all to Q. Fabius Sanga, their Roman representative. He in turn reported this activity of the conspirators to Cicero. This afforded Cicero the anxiously awaited chance to obtain convincing evidence, and he took complete advantage of the opportunity. By his directions the Allobrogian delegates continued the intrigue until they had obtained written orders signed by the conspirators and letters from Lentulus to Catiline. When they departed from Rome at night with these credentials, he had them intercepted at the Mulvian bridge, arrested, and returned to Rome with all their papers.

Next morning he summoned the chief conspirators before the Senate, which he had assembled in the Temple of Concord. Ignorant of what had happened during the night, the conspirators were confounded by the evidence which the consul presented against them. In the presence of the Allobrogian captives they could not deny their complicity. They confessed their signatures to the treasonable documents. The Senate decreed that they should be held as prisoners until their fate should be determined. Cicero then went into the Forum and in his third Catilinarian speech detailed to the assembled populace how the conspiracy had been discovered and how it had been thwarted.

The people were delighted. Their fear was dispelled. All Rome had been pale with terror. But with the arrest of the leaders of the conspiracy, the city breathed a sigh of relief. It was saved from anarchy and devastation. The praetors ordered solemn prayers to be offered in all the temples. The Senate passed a vote of thanks to Cicero. He was acclaimed "Savior of the Republic." He was on the crest of the wave of popular approval and it carried him in triumphal ascent.

SENTENCE

But the fate of the conspirators was yet to be determined. And when Cicero took his stand on this matter, his feet were on the edge of the Tarpeian rock! The manner in which Cicero played his part as consul has generally been praised by historians. Plutarch says he took all necessary steps with extreme caution, consummate prudence and sound judgment. As far as the immediate welfare of the city is concerned, that praise is just. Cicero foiled the conspirators and saved the Republic. But in his achievement as consul lay his failure as counsel; when he succeeded as public officer he failed as lawyer. As is so often the case, immediate acclaim was purchased at the price of ultimate accomplishment. In the circumstances of his success lurked the seed of his decline.

Two days after the arrest the Senate was convened for the purpose of determining what should be done with the captive conspirators. A rumor was current that a forcible liberation might be attempted. It was a serious situation. They were confessed traitors. But what authority had the Senate to inflict punishment? We have seen the sacred regard for Roman citizenship. It was a firm principle of constitutional law, as ancient as the time of the kings, that the life of a citizen could not be taken without the sanction of the people. Cicero knew this full well. He had defended Rabirius, who had been accused of slaying one of the followers of the insurrectionist, Saturninus. And the fact that the slain man was bearing arms in a seditious uprising did not prevent the condemnation of Rabirius for taking a Roman life without sanction of court. And the trial of Rabirius was during Cicero's consulship—too recent to have been forgotten. But Cicero's zeal misled him; his responsibility for the safety of the city and his desire for immediate and complete victory over the conspirators prevented a more lawyerlike, more statesmanlike view of their case.

When the question came up for discussion the consul-elect, Silanus, was asked first for his opinion, according to the procedure of the Roman Senate. He said the conspirators should be put to death without more ado. Other senators spoke in favor of the extreme penalty. Tiberius Nero, grandfather of the future emperor, moved adjournment—the old ruse of the evasive legislator. But he was less evasive, though also less discreet—than Crassus, Metellus Nepos and Hortensius, who absented themselves entirely in order to avoid responsibility. The prevailing sentiment was for death—until Julius Caesar spoke. His incisive statements turned the tide—at least temporarily. Many senators, including Cicero's brother, changed their opinion as a result of Caesar's speech. Certainly there was more of sound legal logic and statesmanship in Caesar's cryptic remarks than in all the other orations: "Laws," said he, "are made to be men's defenses not only against others but against their own emotions. They are man's safeguards against man's passions. The proposal before the house is to put citizens to death. It is illegal. Whenever in the past the great bulwark of the law has been weakened, the consequences have invariably been calamitous. If by any act it should now be seriously impaired, the danger is that it may be ultimately completely overthrown, to the disaster of all within the state." Caesar, however, did not quite follow his own legal logic to its natural conclusion. He did not emphasize the need of trial but recommended imprisonment and confiscation of property.

If Cicero had been counsel instead of consul he might have spoken for judicial process. But the lawyer was submerged in the immediate affairs of office. Again his statecraft was too businesslike, too matter-of-fact. He thought the safety of the Republic depended upon the immediate exemplary death of the conspirators rather than upon the maintenance of the established law. In his fourth Catilinarian oration he urged the Senate to order the conspirators put to death. The oration is deliberative and while somewhat specious, is very generally considered Cicero's masterpiece. Cicero urged that by instigating men to take up arms against the Republic, the conspirators had become enemies of the Republic, had forfeited their citizenship, and that by their arrest and confession they seemed already condemned.

His argument sounds like the false premises of the police prosecutors of our day who defend "third-degree" methods of crime detection by assumption of guilt. We are disappointed that Cicero, whose legal instinct was usually shocked at any divergence from the regular process of law, should in this instance be a champion of peremptory action and summary remedies. In his deep consciousness he must have known that the proposed action of the Senate would be nothing more than a moral sanction, not a legal sentence. The law of Porcius Laeca and Gaius Gracchus prohibited expressly the taking of life without formal hearing before the people. He himself, on other occasions, pointed out that freedom, of which he was always an oracle, is but the absence of arbitrary control; that the control of the law, being rational in essence and uniform in operation, is not arbitrary. If the rights of citizenship could be declared forfeited otherwise than by judicial process as prescribed by law, what would become of man's freedom and who would be safe?

While lacking in sound legal principle, the oration is nevertheless charged with exalted sentiments. While Cicero exalted himself, yet he offered himself to his country. He asked the Senate not to be concerned for his safety but to think only of the welfare of the state. He affirmed that he would support everything with courage and even joy if it were for the glory and well-being of the Roman people; that death would not be feared by a brave man, would not be premature for one who had been consul, nor grievous to a man of wisdom. He was undismayed—whatever might happen to him, his fame was secure. He urged the Senate to act rigorously—severity to the conspirators being mercy to the city. Death was none too severe.

Cicero was ardently supported by Cato. In an oration directed mainly against Caesar (who had made Cato's sister his paramour and otherwise outraged Cato's sensibilities), Cato, who was an idol of the senatorial class, demanded the infliction of capital punishment. With this support Cicero's recommendation carried. The death sentence was voted almost unanimously.

We should of course be on guard against a tendency to judge Cicero solely by the standards of today. The division of legislative and judicial functions, as we have seen, was not then so nicely made. The Roman Senate exercised a much wider jurisdiction, more of all the functions of government, than does any legislative body today. Cicero addressed the Senate as a court or tribunal and referred to its orders as judgments. It is apparent that some court other than the popular assembly should have been invested with summary authority to dispose of such a case. But in the absence of amendment of the old city-state law the Senate should not have usurped such authority. After making all due allowances, and even after being moved by the fine rhetoric and exalted emotions of his oratory, still we are not convinced that the Republic could have been greatly endangered by requiring that the conspirators be sentenced in due course of judicial procedure. The people, incensed as they then were, would, it seems now, have condemned them, and the only difference would have been a little more time and a far more just and orderly procedure, for which Rome, when the red clouds of its anger had cleared, would have thanked Cicero. The state should set the highest example of respect for the orderly process of law. If any branch of government takes life by peremptory action, it thereby encourages like conduct in other branches, and as a result there is a corresponding disrespect for law in all the individual units of society. Cicero, who was so devoted to the Republic, should have remembered that the Republic rested upon the fundamental principles of the constitution.

It was not long before Cicero had cause to rue his overzealous haste. But at the time popular sentiment ratified the action of the Senate. Cicero, having done all that he could to fix the fate of the conspirators, was evidently desirous of softening the effect of his excessive zeal; he declared publicly that he saw no reason to interfere with destiny. He himself conducted the condemned conspirators to the Tullianum and turned them over to the executioner, whom he ordered to do his duty. They were lowered into the dungeon and strangled. After the execution, Cicero was met at the prison by the senators and knights and escorted to his home. It was nearly night, but lamps were set at every door and lights placed upon the roofs of the houses. A great procession of people followed, bearing torches, shouting and clapping, and acclaiming him "The Savior and New Founder of Rome." When the procession reached his home, Cicero was proclaimed "Father of his Country" by the venerable Catulus—the first time that Rome had given that title to one of her citizens. And the next day the title was confirmed by the Senate.

That was the heyday of Cicero's life—the zenith of his public career. For once his avid ambition was satisfied. And Terentia, who had recommended severity and firmness in dealing with the conspirators, shared his elation. What he himself thought of that day is shown by a statement he makes in his essay on *Friendship:* "This we may assert with truth, that of the many glorious and joyous days which P. Scipio witnessed in the course of his life, that day was the most glorious when, on the breaking up of the Senate, he was escorted home in the evening by the conscript fathers, by the allies of the Roman people, and the Latins, the day before he died; so that from so high a position of dignity he may seem to have passed to the gods above rather than to those below."

But poor Cicero could not maintain so high a position of dignity. His fate brought him down to those below.

V

DISFAVOR AND EXILE

General Conditions

Some historians attribute Cicero's loss of favor to the machinations of certain men, and no doubt Pompey, Caesar and Clodius played their part to that end. Other historians lay the blame on Cicero's own foibles, his sarcasm, his vanity, self-praise, and egocentric ambition, and no doubt they played their part. For the most part, however, he was the victim of his times. The great republican went down with the Republic, because the spirit of the times had grown adverse to its constitution. The people abandoned the law—and deserted the lawyer.

Before considering these three factors that contributed to Cicero's loss of favor, let us consider briefly the conditions of the time. After the suppression of Catiline's conspiracy Italy forgot for a while the disorders of the social and civil wars; debtors paid the debts which they had hoped to have canceled by legislation; factionalism abated and senators, equites, and plebeians seemed drawn together in support of sound government. Cicero hoped that this interlude of tranquility might be developed into a permanent "Concord of Good Men."

His panacea, however, was not an adequate remedy for the ills of the Republic. The senatorial aristocracy required an infusion of new blood to bring it nearer the common interests; the city of Rome needed adequate and permanent protection against rioters and assassins; and the graft of the senators, the commercialism of the tax gatherers, the parasitism of the urban proletariat required eradication. Cicero moreover knew, in spite of his extravagant laudation of the accomplishments of his consulship, that the worst danger to the Republic lay not so much in mob leaders and rebels of Catiline's type, as in military commanders who might attempt a repetition of the usurpations of Marius and Sulla. The need of a strong central government was so great that every military commander was tempted to supply it. Not only were the senators jealous of the power of the great generals, but such generals were jealous of one another. Each feared the other might take the supreme command. Pompey conspired with the senators to deprive Marcius Rex, Metellus Creticus and L. Lucullus of their requested triumphs. He then employed Metellus Nepos to devise means by which he himself might predominate in Rome.

The manner of Pompey's return from the east had been an object of fear to the senators from the time of his departure, and his victories and his attitude toward affairs at Rome now made his return a positive threat. It was Cicero's plan to draw Pompey into support of constitutional government. Before that could be accomplished, however, Caesar had distinguished himself both by his civil administration and his military campaigns in Spain, and he was at the gates of the city demanding both a triumph and an election as consul. Before the storm over Pompey had abated, the wind, as Cicero said, was blowing full into Caesar's sails. The desperate intrigues to which these leaders resorted afforded employment and position to men of degenerate principles like Clodius and Nepos, and all these conditions worked against the champion of law and order.

Individuals Against Him

There is no doubt that Cicero had many very strong men against him. His enemies naturally increased with his fame. Pompey and Caesar were not only jealous of each other, they were both jealous of Cicero. The stratagem to undermine his growing influence with the people was one of the very few plans in which the two great generals could co-operate. Cicero's dealings with them give a sharp portrayal of the difference between the man of principle and the man of action—between the man of law and the man of force. We have seen during our own industrial era the lawyer discounted by the captain of finance. The man of the world, the man who seeks immediate and material accomplishments, imposes upon himself none of the handicaps which the man must bear who champions justice and orderly processes. The very principles which the just man espouses make him an easy opponent, because his action can be foretold. His disadvantage indeed seems so great that he is generally referred to as an impractical idealist, while the man of force and deceit is acclaimed as a realist. The world has also been painfully conscious recently of the disadvantage of the champions of liberalism and constitutionalism in their negotiations with dictators. The champions of peace have no weapons which despots fear. Yet the reason that all humanism has not perished from the earth under the rivalry of dictators and the consequent acceleration of despotism, is that there have been Ciceros and Catos and Churchills who, in spite of immediate odds and immediate failure, have had enough confidence in the ultimate success of just principles to oppose the Pompeys and Caesars and Hitlers.

The personal relationship between the great lawyer and the great militarists of Rome should be understood.

Cicero, it seems, was always preferring Pompey, in spite of the fact that Caesar was much more generous to him. There are several reasons for this: Pompey was a man of Cicero's own age. Caesar was somewhat younger. Pompey had distinguished himself by remarkable military accomplishments, while Caesar was at first thought by Cicero to be merely an instigator, a politician of questionable purposes. Pompey, the military dictator, became—more by force of circumstance than by choice—the leader of the senatorial party, the champion of the Republic; while Caesar, the avowed "defender of the democracy," became—also very much by force of circumstance—dictator and "almost king."

Pompey, always arrogant, looked upon Cicero with cold disdain. To him the only honorable calling was the military life. (How like the arrogance of more recent militarists!) He considered Cicero an ordinary fellow, a common politician. Their relation is revealed by a letter which Cicero wrote to Pompey: "Let me assure you that what I have done for the preservation of my country has earned the applause of the whole world, and when you return to Rome you will find that I behaved with so much prudence and greatness of spirit that you will consider me not too undeserving of your friendship." The tendency of Cicero to place his accomplishments at Rome upon a plane with the military accomplishments of Pompey abroad, created in Pompey a cynical disgust. The comparison was to him so ridiculous that he accepted it humorously. The letter reveals that Cicero could be at once both supercilious and obsequious—traits which, though apparently paradoxical, are merely opposite sides of one weakness of character. Cicero's self-praise might have been indulged if that had been all, but in foiling Catiline's conspiracy he had robbed Pompey of a rare opportunity to take command at home. This Pompey could not He neglected Cicero's letters, and refused to s when he called at his house. These slights and tesies Cicero seems to have accepted philosophically. Pompey, however, never accepted Cicero until he needed him.

Caesar looked upon Cicero somewhat as a preceptor. This feeling had been engendered when as a young man he had been invited to Cicero's conversations in the Forum. Cicero by his kind attentions to young men helped to establish that admirable custom by which older members of the profession act as sponsors and tutors to their successors at the bar—a custom that has done much to create and maintain an excellent professional feeling. It is quite likely that young Julius obtained his taste for letters from Cicero; certain it is that, prompted by what he had heard Cicero say of Greek culture, he had left Rome for a time in order to study the art of eloquence under the Greek critics and under Molo of Rhodes. Caesar's later leniency toward Cicero, in spite of Cicero's adherence to Pompey, is accounted for largely by Caesar's admiration for Cicero's literary accomplishments. He not only indulged, he enjoyed the old lawyer's cynical wit. He made a collection of his jokes.

At the beginning of their acquaintance Cicero was Caesar's patron. At the end Caesar was Cicero's patron. Only during Caesar's absence during the Gallic war did they maintain a friendship upon free, equal and cordial relations. Their letters then portray the best of their natures. Between the time of Caesar's studies and his campaign in Gaul, the two were suspicious of each other, and each did much to thwart the other's purposes. Cicero said of Caesar's courteous and affable manner that it was "like the smiling but delusive calm of the sea." In the public cases of the Forum and the discussions in the Senate, they usually found themselves arguing on opposite sides, and of course these verbal tilts could add nothing to their friendship. They were on opposite sides of the proposal to restore to citizenship the descendants of persons who had been proscribed by Sulla; Caesar favored, Cicero opposed the agrarian law of Rullus; Caesar prosecuted, Cicero defended Rabirius. In these, and in other controversies, Cicero at the outset had the unpopular side. But he was right, and he had the courage and persuasive force to convince the people that he labored in the cause of justice.

In the controversy over the execution of the conspirators, however, Cicero at first had the popular side; but he was not right, and was therefore not so well fortified against the subsequent attack which his enemies set against him. While the fear of the conspiracy was upon the people, Cicero was a hero. But after the execution of the conspirators and the defeat and death of Catiline at Pistoria, the people soon forgot their fear. In the calm that followed, the very ghosts of Lentulus and Cethegus seemed to stalk the streets of Rome and incite the popular mind against Cicero for having put to death Roman citizens—yes, Roman senators—without trial. His enemies opened a campaign of popular oratory against his illegal conduct.

When, at the close of his term of office, Cicero according to custom went into the Forum to give an account of his consulship, he found the space back of the Rostra occupied by the seats of the tribunes. It was customary for consuls to take two oaths; when they assumed office they swore that they would act according to law and when they retired from office they swore that they had not acted contrary to law. Metellus Nepos, exercising the prohibitive power of a tribune, denied Cicero the right to address the assembly, saying that men should be judged by their actions, not by their words, and that he would not permit a man who had put Roman citizens to death to swear that he had not acted contrary to law. Cicero, however, arose amid the clamor and swore that he had saved Rome and preserved his country.

Nepos next presented a bill before the concilium plebis, inviting Pompey to rescue the constitution from autocracy. The real purpose of the bill was to obtain for Pompey a commission which would have the appearance of saving Rome from enemies at home. Caesar, seeing the temporary advantage of an alliance with Pompey, supported the bill and made a show of indignation against Cicero. Only dour old Cato stood by Cicero, but he was not very effective against Caesar and Pompey. They were unhampered by the mores that restricted Cato. They followed only the light of their own ambitions. They were therefore willing to fan the flame of popular indignation that consumed Cicero's influence.

The lawyer was now past the meridian of life. He began to feel old, tired, saddened, deeply aware for the first time of mortality. Everywhere he went he felt the undercurrent of hostility, where only admiration had been before. At first his mind and heart refused to credit what his eyes saw. It seemed incredible to him that the people for whom he had given his best efforts could now desert him, yet as he went about the Forum he became increasingly conscious of antagonistic murmurs. Men would stop talking as he approached. He would catch them eyeing him suspiciously along the streets. Men would look solemnly away from him when he approached. He became painfully aware of the discrepancy between his ideal man and the real man of the street. Even if he had made a mistake it was induced by his excessive ardor for the welfare of Rome and the safety of the people; but they did not recognize that. He was wounded in his most vulnerable spot—his vanity. He was no longer the self-confident Cicero, the master of the mob and companion of leaders. His efforts in his own behalf were futile. When he arose to speak he lacked assurance. His genius was suppressed by fear and anger and wounded sensibilities. It was bitter experience to find that even his own talents depended partly on popular response. That part of his profession which was an art was nevertheless subject to that dependence which all the arts of direct communication must feel. At the time of his greatest need his talents therefore seemed to desert him.

Still another agent deserves consideration if we are to understand the destruction of Cicero's popular favor. Clodius was one of those striking young men of history whose prominence exceeds their merits, whose greatness is thrust upon them. The scion of a patrician family, the Claudii, he was a young man of attractive appearance and extraordinary audacity, a ready tool in the hands of ambitious men. And he had a facility for making the plans of others serve his own advancement.

At first he had been an ardent admirer of Cicero. His declarations of friendship were profuse. But he had been estranged, just as Catiline had been embittered, by the part Cicero had taken in his prosecution. Each of these young rakes had been accused of an offense that shocked the religious sensibilities of the Romans. Catiline had been charged with the seduction of a vestal virgin. Clodius was prosecuted for desecrating the sacred ceremonies of the Good Goddess. He had attempted to gain admission to the apartment of Caesar's wife, Pompeia, during the celebration of the mysteries of that deity. The celebration was held at the residence of Caesar, who was Pontifex

Maximus. During such rites the building was held sacred to female creatures, not even a male animal being admitted within the confines. Taking advantage of Caesar's absence, Clodius had hoped to gratify his lust for Pompeia by gaining access to her home while disguised as an attending woman. He was betrayed by his voice. He escaped, but news of the sacrilege was spread abroad. Caesar, being unable to disregard so great an offense, acted in a very characteristic manner. He demanded the prosecution of Clodius, and, while asserting the innocence of his wife, nevertheless divorced her, with the now famous remark that Caesar's wife must be above suspicion.

Cicero had taken charge of the prosecution of Catiline, but he acted only as witness against Clodius. Nevertheless the same enmity resulted. Clodius relied for his defense upon an alibi, declaring that he was at Baiae, the fashionable watering place, during the observance of the mysteries of the Good Goddess. But Cicero swore that he had spoken to him that day in Rome.

Caesar, having requested the pontifices to institute proceedings against Clodius, refused to support the prosecution with his evidence. Crassus supported the defendant with his wealth. Clodius was acquitted. Cicero, shocked at the result, issued a scathing denunciation of the judges, saying that they had sold themselves and that the Republic had been disgraced by a verdict dictated by avarice and prostitution. He charged Clodius with bribery, not only by use of money, but by procuring for some of his supporters the illicit favors of women. That the verdict was corrupt is supported by the fact that the venerable Catulus openly told one of the jurors that the reason he and his fellows had demanded a bodyguard was that they were afraid of being robbed of their bribes.

With reference to these charges it is well to recall how such a Roman court was constituted. The judices—sometimes referred to as jurors, sometimes as judges—were arbiters of both law and the facts. Their large number—usually fifty or more—diminished the sense of individual responsibility. There was no strict law of evidence to protect the jurors against what we would term improper testimony, and, although presided over by the praetor, or other magistrate, they were not assisted by a judicial summing-up. A majority determined the verdict, the vote being taken by each judex depositing in an urn one of three tablets, furnished by the praetor and marked respectively, A, for acquittal; C, for condemnation; and N.L. (*non liquet*) for "case not clear." In earlier years jury service (office of judex) had been restricted to the senatorial class. At this time it had been extended to the equestrian order. Although the parties, by a system of challenges, were given some part in the selection of a jury, the selection was still so limited to a known class that jurors could easily be reached in advance by sinister influence. As heretofore pointed out, the administration of justice was inextricably entangled with politics. When, therefore, politics was corrupt, corruption was in the courts.

From a personal point of view it was, no doubt, indiscreet for Cicero to testify against a young man as popular, as unscrupulous and as vindictive as Clodius. It was moreover very impolitic for him to accuse the judges publicly of fraud. But his act showed admirable courage and a lawyerlike contempt for corruption in judicial administration. Plutarch, it is true, does not give Cicero much credit for testifying against Clodius. While admitting the facts as stated by Cicero, he nevertheless adds that it was not so much the influence of truth, as the necessity of satisfying his wife Terentia that induced him to act as he did. Plutarch states that Terentia was a woman of imperious temper and had insisted that Cicero testify against Clodius because she hated his sister Clodia. He says Terentia believed that Clodia wanted Cicero for her husband. Delayen admits that Cicero had aroused Terentia's suspicious jealousy by his visits to the patrician lady's home, which was in their neighborhood, but says her jealousy was groundless because the union of Cicero and his wife was a happy exception to the existing disorder and prevailing laxity.

Even if there existed a reason for Terentia to prompt Cicero to testify, there was no reason for her to prompt him to denounce the judges. This conduct must be accounted for by his love of truth and justice. He knew that the life of the Republic, to which he was devoted, depended upon an honest administration of the law. It is true, as we have seen, that Cicero practiced the artifices, tricks and stratagems of his profession, but he admitted that he did. It is therefore also true that he was intellectually honest. He wrote to his friend Atticus about his oratorical effects with delightful humor: "All that purple I so often use to decorate my speeches—the passage about fire and sword—you know the paints I have on my pallet. You know how I can thunder!" But all that was mere stage play and not to be confused with dishonesty. With a true lawyer's sensibility, he hated perjury and loathed corruption in office. It is not to be marveled at that he would defend the temple of justice against an assault so direct, when we consider how unerringly his legal instinct detected more insidious injustice. Did he not criticize the proposal to purchase land for Pompey's veterans and cause it to be redrafted so as not to threaten existing tenures? While Cicero continually changed his mind in judging persons and situations, he stood consistently by the principle of parliamentary government, and seldom wavered in his attachment to existing constitutional usage. He loved justice and knew that it could be maintained only by clean administration of the law. His nature therefore revolted at conduct which would corrupt the legal process at its source.

But the nobility of Cicero's feelings did not meliorate in any way the passionate desire of Clodius for revenge. Clodius's first attempt to gratify this desire, however, served only to increase it. He made the mistake of engaging Cicero in a tilt of repartee before the Senate, and drew forth some telling thrusts of sarcasm—Cicero's ever ready weapon. When Clodius said, referring to Cicero, that a clown from Arpinum would be out of place at such a fashionable watering place as Baiae, Cicero replied that he would not be so ridiculous there as Clodius in the role of a female musician at the rites of the Good Goddess. And when Clodius criticized Cicero's extravagance in buying a home on the Palatine, Cicero suggested that such a purchase was better than buying a jury. But these acrimonious witticisms only intensified the zeal of Clodius for vengeance, and thus sharpened the edge of the instrument which Caesar, Pompey and Crassus were to use to undermine Cicero's position.

Idiosyncrasies Against Him

Clodius was not the only Roman who had felt the smart of Cicero's caustic remarks. Cicero prided himself on his wit. Like many other lawyers then and since, his pride induced him to use it too recklessly. There are many instances of his cutting personal gibes. He so much affected the wit that he sometimes became a buffoon and by affecting gaiety in serious things he on several occasions offended against the rules of propriety and decorum. It was such excessive and ill-timed facetiousness at the impeachment of Murena that induced Cato to remark, "What a pleasant consul we have!"

It would not have been so bad for Cicero if he had only been funny, even though excessively so. But his facetiousness frequently gave way to asperity. He plied his wit and sarcasm against persons who continued to feel the sting of his words long after the occasion had been forgotten by the orator. Not only Clodius, but Crassus, Vatinius, Metellus Nepos, and many others who became active against him, had felt the effect of his acrimonious jests. When Crassus, who had acquired his great wealth by methods that were questionable, professed one day a fondness for the Stoic maxim: "The good man is always rich," Cicero retorted, "There is another probably more agreeable to you: 'All things belong to the prudent.'" Vatinius, who had scrofulous tumors on his neck, had been referred to by Cicero as "the tumid orator." When Nepos accused him of having ruined more with his evidence than he had saved with his advocacy, Cicero said, "I grant it, for I have more truth than eloquence." And his hearers were no doubt prompted to add: "And more vanity than discretion." Cicero had occasion to examine as a witness one of the members of his own profession who was known for his lack of legal learning, and when the witness replied that he knew nothing about the matter, Cicero remarked: "Perhaps you think I am asking you a question of law."

Cicero, like others of his profession, learned too late that irony is a weapon that is jagged and double-edged. It is difficult to handle it even to one's own satisfaction. It frequently wounds most him by whom it is employed. The truth is, wit is not wisdom. Irony and sarcasm are to the mind what jewels are to the body—they embellish but they afford no warmth or nourishment. They bespeak vanity and beget rivalry and ill will. At best wit and sarcasm are only partial truths. Being but partial truths they are often the meanest lies. Lacking sincerity they are therefore dissemblers. Like condiments they can well be used as a relish, they add spice and zest; but a continued use causes virulent irritation. And this Cicero learned to his sorrow.

Not only did Cicero's pride and vanity cause an excessive display of sarcastic wit, it led Cicero into the error of self-laudation. When he felt his influence waning and heard himself being defamed, he could not forget, nor allow others to forget, his services to the Republic. In the Senate, before the popular assemblies, even in court, his defeat of Catiline and Lentulus was the burden of his song. With annoying persistence he would sing his own praise because in the face of danger he had not thrown off the toga of civil life to assume the sagum of military life. His suppression of the conspiracy without resort to arms he thought so wonderful that he was moved to poetic expression. A line of one of his verses he dinned into the ears of his hearers: *"Cedant arma togae, concedat laurea linguae."* (Let arms yield to the toga, let the victor's crown yield to eloquence.)

All Cicero's biographers and students of his time are shocked at his want of modesty. Plutarch says that the excessive praise that he bestowed on himself, his constant boasting, wounded those who heard him and caused many to hate him. And a modern biographer inquires: "Was Cicero, that everlasting word-monger, letter-writer, and self-praiser, ever natural save in his megalomania and his whining?"

But such criticism is too harsh. Cicero had the alert, responsive, imaginative mind of the artist, rather than the indifferent, self-centered mind of the man of affairs. His letters give us the key to his success and failure as a political leader. They reveal that it was his sensitive understanding of distant consequences that made him alert in defense of the Republic. His oversensitiveness to his own fate, however, is mistaken for egotism. Generously appreciative of all good qualities in others, he was so susceptible to adverse criticism of himself that he was tempted into the error of self-praise by way of defensive apology. But self-praise, as always, defeated its object. No one can give praise to one who praises himself. It is indeed impossible to commend one who asks for or even expects commendation. And self-praise when repeated creates disgust. This little weakness in Cicero cost him dearly, while other men of his time, in spite of more serious vices, went uncondemned.

But it was this very sensitiveness which made Cicero an effective orator. It was this quality that gave him the ability to perceive the attitudes and feelings of his hearers. It was his insight that gave him power to ingratiate himself with all kinds of people. By penetrating into the minds of his audience, he could talk to them on their own plane and show them his visions, whether that audience were the populace of Rome, the dignified senators, or the judges. Cicero's keen mind, however, must have realized the futility of his self-defensive efforts; yet he was powerless to discontinue them. That sensitive perception which enabled him to read and play upon the feelings and secret emotions of others would not allow him to be indifferent to the hatred of his enemies, the growing coolness of friends, the boredom of strangers. It made him cry out for understanding.

There is moreover something in the very function of the lawyer that tends to make him conceited and contentious. Being called upon so frequently to instruct the ignorant and direct the doubtful, he comes in time to be wise in his own conceit and takes on the airs of Sir Oracle. He becomes didactic; he declaims. Being so often the champion of the accused and the advocate of mooted measures, he develops an adversary attitude. Beginning with pride in his profession, he develops pride in his position, and stands like a zealous sentry at the gate of his life's citadel, quick in its praise and determined in its defense. Above all a good sentry must be alert and responsive, and always sensitive to the danger of attack. This sensitiveness made for much of Cicero's success. But these very embellishments of armory, when viewed from the reverse side, appear as blemishes. We cannot deny, nor should we condone, Cicero's faults; but when we understand that they are only overaccentuated phases of the lawyer's essential traits of character, we can view them charitably.

It is difficult to see the man and see his faults and estimate them separately. Usually we fall into one of two errors: we see the faults and condemn the man, or we idolize the man and then blink his faults. It is not easy to maintain a balanced judgment. It is easier to go to extremes. The human judgment is prone to condemn and then justify its condemnation by pointing to a man's mistakes; or, when it champions a man, it at once indulges in hero-worship, it glosses, it even emulates his faults. "Nothing extenuate, nor aught set down in malice," is an admonition more easily given than followed.

But the purpose of history is to show us men as they were, their hopes, their plans, their efforts, and wherein they failed and why. And it is tragic to contemplate what petty foibles have wrecked magnificent careers. The noble effort of a lifetime is marred by some idiosyncrasy. A foible entails a penalty quite out of proportion to its importance. Measures and movements depend on men, and the fate of nations and the happiness of generations are affected by our poor personalities. What might not Wilson have accomplished for the peace of the world, but for his imperiousness? What might not George III have accomplished for the British Empire, but for his obstinacy? And what might not Cicero have accomplished for the Roman Republic but for his vanity? A man's personality is his fate. Too often it affects the fate of the most commendable causes of his life.

And yet, while these personalities move like boats upon the surface of the water and seem to control the trend of the world's affairs, the deep broad stream of life moves on relentlessly in the course prepared for it by cosmic forces. And so Cicero was swept along by the current of events to the destiny of his beloved Republic.

Events Against Him

The boasted—too much boasted!—accomplishment of Cicero's consulship was a demonstration that the law could be made to prevail over revolution, that the Senate under proper leadership could hold its own against physical force. The need of united effort against the Catilinarian conspiracy had brought into alliance all the respectable elements in the commonwealth that stood to lose by revolution. And as has been stated, when he retired from office it was Cicero's most earnest concern to preserve this Concord of Good Men (*Concordia Ordinum*) as a means of preserving the Republic and realizing the ideal of every patriotic republican for peace with honor (*otium cum dignitate*).

But there were two destructive forces which Cicero could not control—military individualism and economic parasitism. Under such military arrangement, armies were directed by their generals instead of by the government, and senators and prominent citizens freely maintained armed bands. As a result the Senate was intimidated and Rome was exposed to riots and assassinations. Under such economic arrangement, the senators, as provincial governors, and the knights, as tax gatherers, impoverished the Roman provinces while the urban proletariat, by ever increasing dependence upon public bounty, impoverished the Roman treasury.

Pompey had returned from his eastern conquests and had disbanded his army upon landing at Brundusium, retaining only an escort for his triumph. Upon his arrival at Rome he submitted to the Senate two demands: confirmation of his administrative settlement of affairs in the east, and a grant of lands for the soldiers whom he had dismissed. Both requests were reasonable. For the sake of peace and order his military decrees should have been approved and made permanent. And the practice of awarding land for military service was well established, and Pompey's conquests had greatly increased the revenues of Rome.

Pompey's attitude toward the Senate was respectful, and if the Senate had shown a willingness to meet his reasonable expectations his military strength might have been brought to the support of the senatorial party and the institutions of the Republic maintained. But Pompey's enemies—Metellus and Lucullus, whose military ambitions he had rudely opposed, and Cato, who honestly suspected him as a usurper—led the Senate in a campaign of obstruction. Cicero saw the importance of a friendly alignment and tried to effect a conciliation. He discerned that Pompey, having realized his ambition as conqueror and having reached years of maturity and conservatism, would be willing to play the part of champion of the established order. But Cicero's efforts as mediator were in vain, and the Concordia came to an end. The opposition and ill will of the Senate produced a definite estrangement. Pompey could no doubt have forced action by recalling his troops; but this he declined to do. Whether his inaction was due to a growing respect for constitutional forms or to irresolution which had been advancing upon him with advancing years, we cannot be certain. But we suspect that irresolution was the controlling factor, because he allowed Caesar to do what he had not done.

Caesar's glory, if not his life, certainly began at forty. In 61–60 B.C., while propraetor in Spain, he distinguished himself both as public administrator and as military commander. So inspired was he by his remarkable accomplishments that he turned toward Rome with three definite ambitions: a triumph, a consulship, and then a proconsulship, in order to prove his military abilities in a broader field. But the Senate made the same mistake it had made with Pompey—it opposed him in all his plans. Caesar, however, did not take the same course as Pompey—he did not submit.

Arriving at the gates of Rome on the eve of the consular election, he asked leave of the Senate to enter his name as a candidate while absent, because if he had set foot in Rome he would have forfeited his claim to a triumph. This request Cato persuaded the Senate to decline. With characteristic decision Caesar then passed up the triumph and entered Rome to declare his candidacy in person. His past efforts for popular favor, and particularly his generosity, made him a certain winner. But the senatorial party managed to elect a bitter opponent as co-

consul. Then taking up the assignment of provinces the Senate, in a further effort to block Caesar's career, gave him a commission something like that of a forest ranger. To a military commander it was a position of disgraceful insignificance. Their efforts served only to antagonize Caesar and remove their last chance for a military champion.

Caesar took prompt advantage of the estrangement between the senators and Pompey, and soon made an informal alliance with Pompey. This was readily accomplished because of Caesar's past conduct toward Pompey and because he had supported legislation favorable to him. And after the alliance was made it was strengthened by the marriage of Caesar's daughter Julia to Pompey. Such an arrangement between the two great commanders, while it lasted, was in itself sufficient to control affairs at Rome. But Caesar further strengthened it by drawing Crassus and the sinister influence of his wealth into the coalition.

Caesar made an offer to include Cicero in the arrangement. It was a tempting offer, and Cicero seems to have given it some consideration. Since the Senate had rejected his advice and Pompey's friendship, an alliance with Caesar held out to him a bright prospect of personal influence. It seemed to him moreover that there might be some possibility of drawing Caesar to the support of the Republic. One can hardly suppress the wish that he had tried. Caesar was always magnanimous, he probably would have accepted the challenge. If only Cicero could have given Caesar his confidence and support, the course of history might have been changed. At any rate the feeling persists that the abilities of the commander, blended with the abilities of the lawyer, might have reconstructed the government, and Caesar's genius might have been used to create an efficient republic instead of a despotic empire.

While Cicero recognized that Caesar was a man who "managed affairs with greatest address," and while he was careful not to affront him even when he opposed him, yet he could never cease to mistrust him. He therefore denied him his co-operation. In spite of rebuffs from Pompey, Cicero had labored for an alliance between Pompey and the Senate because Pompey seemed to respect constitutional authority. In spite of overtures from Caesar, he opposed the coalition because Caesar seemed to disregard constitutional authority.

The coalition formed by Caesar, Pompey and Crassus is generally referred to as The First Triumvirate. It really marked the passing of the Republic. The Senate as the heart of the Republic still throbbed, but only convulsively; its life-giving force was spent. We have seen our modern cities outgrow their council form of government and take on city managers. So Rome outgrew its Senate; but failing to establish a new order for efficient government, it became absolutely subject to the Triumvirs. Constitutional formalities continued to be used, but only as a cloak for arbitrary power.

Thereafter Caesar brought forward the legislation favored by Pompey and Crassus and himself, and had it passed by intimidation and force. Pompey's veterans had been drifting in to Rome to swell the hordes of unemployed. Having spent the bounty which had been paid to them on dismissal, they were now living on the doles. They were a ready lot of rioters. Though Pompey had refused to use force on his own account, he did not hesitate to fulfill his compact with Caesar by placing his soldiers at Caesar's command. Caesar proposed his agrarian bill for the purpose of rewarding Pompey's soldiers and relieving the congestion of population in Rome. And when Cato obstructed its passage, he was hauled away and threatened with imprisonment. The tribunes and Bibulus, the other consul, who also opposed the bill, were swept from the Forum by force of arms. The measure was submitted to the Comitia and passed by popular vote, with the added provision that all senators should take an oath of non-resistance or be subject to exile. This action taught the Senate the futility of further resistance. It thereupon gave up its policy of obstruction and decided to keep at least the appearance of authority by passing the measures which Caesar desired, knowing that if it did not do so, Caesar would carry them to the people's assembly and have them enacted there.

The legislation which Caesar wanted was initiated by his agent, the tribune Vatinius. A short act confirmed entirely Pompey's settlement of Eastern affairs. Vatinius then had repealed the Senate's assignment of consular provinces by which the Senate had attempted to confine Caesar's future activities to the forests and cattle ranges (*silvae callesque*) of Italy. And thereafter Caesar secured the governorship of all Gaul for a period of five years.

Before leaving for Gaul, however, it was expedient for Caesar to consolidate all his gains in Rome and provide against future attack. His enemies had declared that the laws of his consulship were unconstitutional and void, and they threatened to impeach him and all his official acts. It was largely the fear of such nullification that kept the Triumvirate together. In order to hold his ground it became necessary for Caesar to have a new electoral agent, one not so closely identified with him as Vatinius, one unscrupulous and audacious enough to control the mob. To this end he established a liaison with Clodius.

This was an unfortunate arrangement for Cicero. But no doubt the thing that prompted the choice of Clodius was his well known hatred for Cicero. Caesar knew that the two men best qualified and most likely to consolidate and lead the forces of opposition were Cato and Cicero. Cato was devoted to the Republic, a leader of the senatorial party, and Caesar's most implacable personal enemy. Cicero was also devoted to the Republic, an orator of convincing force, still a man of influence in the Senate, with the knights, and with some elements of the Italian people. Caesar needed an agent who could be relied on to take whatever action might be necessary against Cicero, since his own efforts to placate the orator had failed.

Having found Cicero unresponsive to his suggestion of alliance with Pompey, Crassus, and himself, Caesar next offered to make him a land commissioner under his agrarian law, or legate on his proconsular staff in Gaul, and finally he offered him a foreign mission on Cicero's own terms. It was by the last method that the Triumvirate got rid of Cato. They deposed the king of Cyprus and sent Cato to take over the government of the province. But Cicero declined all such offers. He was devoted to parliamentary rule. He owed it to himself and his profession not to join in the new government. His profession was the law of the Republic. And his performance equaled his profession.

With reference to Cato's dismissal to foreign shores Cicero said that because his hands could not be stained his tongue was plucked out. But Cato's fate did not teach Cicero to hold his own tongue. He continued to make disparaging public statements about the condition of the Republic. Under the Triumvirate such conduct could not be continued with impunity. Caesar determined that the orator should be silenced. And the means to that end were soon provided.

Clodius had shown an ambition to exercise the powers of a tribune of the people; but his patrician birth disqualified him. He had attempted to remove this disqualification by being adopted into a plebeian family; but this proceeding proved futile because it had not been confirmed by the Comitia Curiata. But now that the Triumvirate could be served by Clodius as tribune, the Comitia Curiata was assembled, Pompey as an augur pronounced the omens propitious, Caesar as Pontifex Maximus assured the appropriate ritual, and the *traductio ad plebem* was completed. Clodius was duly invested with plebeian status, and it made no difference that the adoptive parent was younger than he was. The tribunate, the office of the plebs, was thus made available to a patrician. And thus another provision for the protection of the people was subverted by the "defender of the democracy." Democracy is always led into despotism by a demagogue.

As soon as Clodius assumed the tribuneship he began to fortify the position of the Triumvirs against attack and began to develop his own position into a dictatorship. He first brought forth laws that extended the powers of the tribunes and restricted the authority of the magistrates, who were still under the influence of the senatorial party. His next move was a bid for the support of the urban populace. To that end he secured the passage of two laws that were demagogic in nature and pernicious in effect.

The first provided free wheat for the people of Rome. Several years before honest Cato, who was at the time tribune, had made a bid for popular favor by furnishing wheat to the people (five pecks a month each to about 320,000) at less than half the market price. He thought the provision necessary for the Republic and did not see or did not heed the evil it would lead to. He sacrificed principle to expediency and gave a hostage to calamity. The history of governments is largely the record of a game of expediency. Seldom does it reveal a statesman with sufficient perspicacity to apprehend the consequences of expedients, and rarely indeed does it show us a ruler like Louis XIV, both frank and flippant enough to say, *Après moi, le déluge!* Cato the patriot bid for popular support. But now Cato was outbid by Clodius the demagogue. Wheat was furnished free of charge. It mattered nothing to Clodius that such bounty consumed more than half the revenue from Pompey's conquests. Thus Rome impoverished her provinces and pauperized her people.

The second law sponsored by Clodius abolished all restrictions on association in Rome. After the Catilinarian conspiracy, plots and rumors of plots had followed thick and fast; and riots were always impending. The Senate, in order to get rid of certain aggregations of lawless men who were ever ready to lead political agitations, had restricted the right of assembly and issued a ban against all *collegia.* These restrictions Clodius now repealed. He wished to systematize these clubs and associations in order to have a body of personal supporters subject to call. And so he opened the floodgates to mob violence. It afterward cost him his life; he was killed by the armed followers of his enemy Milo. But the surf-rider has little choice of direction; one that rides the flood must land where the flood takes him. The Roman populace was a terrible force to leave unrestrained. It was made up of disgruntled veterans, expatriated freedmen, soldiers of fortune, fugitive slaves, and gladiators—gamblers all, gamblers most of them with life and death, ready for riot or revolution at the very challenge of a fight and the chance of plunder. Rome had grown glorious by conquest; how could her people love peace?

While all this was being done, Cicero, seeing the futility of opposition, had gone into partial retirement. Not only was the Senate as a body intimidated, but Cicero had been singled out for abuse and subjected to severest criticism, accusation, and slander. To those who urged him to retaliate with violent measures, he had replied, "Enough of surgery, now for dieting." He withdrew to his Tusculan country home near Alba, and went to Rome only to look after his private practice. He avoided bitter controversies in the Senate and spent most of his time in literary labor. He indulged himself in writing the memoirs of his consulship. But more important, he began the studies which led to *De Re Publica,* a political treatise proposing a balance of political forces and general theory of government, which he hoped Caesar and Pompey would adopt and support. The value of this treatise lies not so much in its suggestion for a form of government as in its application of ethical ideals to politics, its emphasis on man's duty to interest himself in questions of government, and in its presentation of political life as the highest form of human achievement.

Although this work has been highly valued by succeeding generations, Cicero's own generation gave it slight consideration. His noble efforts were futile against the tide of mob fury that was rising against him. Clodius still burned with a desire for revenge; and when he felt that his dominion in Rome was fixed and that the Triumvirs would support him, he launched his long-delayed attack. He brought forward a statute of banishment which "debarred from fire and water anyone who had condemned a Roman citizen without trial."

Although the statute was drawn in general terms, Cicero of course knew it was directed against him, and made a desperate effort to prevent its enactment. He sent entreaties to Caesar and most humbly implored Pompey; they were the only men with sufficient power to save him, and he knew it. But they were now indifferent to his distress. Mob violence was in the ascendant. The Republic had sought a champion in vain, the great republican now begged for help in vain. The Law had been abandoned, and the Lawyer was defenseless.

The new consuls were appealed to, but one was a lieutenant of Pompey, the other a relative of Caesar. The weight of their influence and their official acts were against Cicero. The Senate gave recognition of its obligations to Cicero and its consciousness of the calamity which had befallen him and the city. It adopted a resolution of mourning requesting all citizens to show their grief in the customary way by allowing their beards and hair to grow untrimmed. But one of the consuls issued an order forbidding compliance with the request. And deputations from suburban Italy that came to plead for the orator were not favorably received. Cicero in his desperation extended his supplications to passers-by in the streets, but he received only hisses and insults. When he attempted to remind them of his services, they threw stones at him. He himself said they spat on him.

Clodius assembled the people in the Circus Flaminius and asked their approval of his order of banishment. He issued a call to the nobles and knights, with whom Cicero's influence was still strong, to attend and give an account of their connections with the former consul. He ordered a brazier of live coals to be set before the assembly and upon it he poured a libation; and while he invoked the aid of all formidable divinities, he pronounced the most terrible imprecations against Cicero and his friends. The tribune of the people incited the populace against their only true defender. The instigator of lawlessness condemned Cicero for violating the law. The desecrator of the ceremonies of the Good Goddess implored the aid of the Roman gods. Clodius was a good actor and a master of stage properties. He knew how to inflame the mob mind. At a signal given by him the partisans of Cicero were set upon and badly beaten. Those who were unsuccessful in flight were severely injured. Hortensius was almost killed and Vibienus died later of his wounds.

A report of this outbreak was brought to Cicero by some of his close friends. They advised him to leave the country in order to save Rome from civil strife. The only alternative was to gather an armed force and oppose the forces now set against him. His friends urged that by his departure he could save Rome a second time from internal warfare and spare his friends and relatives great suffering. The thought of becoming a factionist and resorting to force and arms filled him with repugnance. To take up arms seemed to him an abandonment of everything he championed. There was nothing else for him to do but to leave. He hastily gave what directions he could regarding his affairs. He permitted his unhappy wife to stay in Rome in order, as he advised his brother Quintus by letter, to take care of the children and the remains of their fortune. Then secretly he departed from the city at night.

There is a legend that as he made his way from the city the first gray light of dawn revealed to him a crowd of people approaching the temple of Juno Moneta. There was great clatter and outcry. The people were bearing with them geese, bedecked with purple and gold, and dogs which had been nailed to crosses. The geese were sacred to Juno and were being venerated as the descendants of those fowls whose cackling had saved the capital from the attack of the Gauls, and the dogs were suffering vicarious punishment because their forbears had been asleep on that occasion. Cicero as he beheld this ceremony wondered how Rome, when she thus remembered the contributions of animals, could be so ungrateful to him whom she had proclaimed father of his country.

Pater Patriae! Quantum mutatus ab illo!

What a change, indeed! The father of his country an outcast from his country!

But Cicero's experience was but another instance of the proverbial ingratitude of people. Though history has made the changeableness of public opinion a byword, still that does not alleviate the suffering which the public benefactor must endure when he finds himself abandoned and denounced.

Again Cicero made his way to Greece. At this time, however, he was in no frame of mind to enjoy its philosophy and art. He was disappointed, dejected, disconsolate. At the time of his former visit he had been a student, culling the gems of Greek culture in order to reset them in Rome. But now he had no hope of further service to his country. He was an exile and, no matter how clearly his reason told him that he was a victim of injustice, still he knew that in the public mind he was disgraced. Although he saw himself as the victim of circumstances, the victim of a destiny much greater than its figureheads, Caesar, Pompey, and Clodius, still resentment festered within him, making him querulous and bitter. His letters at this time are a succession of complaints. He questioned his friends' loyalty. He berated his enemies and deprecated himself. He spent his days in deepest depression, lamenting that he had lived too long, although he was at this time not yet quite fifty.

Neither nature nor meditation gave him respite. He could not be resigned to inactivity. He yearned for participation in the movement of the great world; he wanted his usual place in its political life. He had been the most important man in Rome; for nearly twenty years had been in the forefront of its affairs; a great figure thundering denunciation against frauds, pleading passionately for justice, encouraging a factious Senate to stand by the Republic. He could not endure his solitude. The lawyer's mind functions in human relationships. He cannot with equanimity be isolated from his fellows as can the pure philosopher. To the philosopher, thought and theories are themselves sufficient; to the lawyer and statesman they are arid without vital application in the affairs of men. Cicero's heartstrings were no Aeolian harp to be played by the lonely wind—they were attuned to the grand Roman symphony and harmonized only with its human counterpoint.

VI

RECALL AND LATE ACCOMPLISHMENTS

ONLY PARTIALLY RESTORED

CICERO was in exile less than two years. With Cicero gone Pompey had grown increasingly dissatisfied over his relations with Caesar and Crassus. Clodius, Caesar's watchdog, was more than Pompey could endure. During Caesar's absence in Gaul Clodius had assumed the powers of a dictator. He trafficked in honors and perquisites and practiced extortion against the monarchies, cities and colonial possessions. With an army of trained rioters at his back he defied Pompey, whose veterans had been drafted away from Rome. He stationed an armed slave in the Senate, ostensibly for the purpose of murdering Pompey, and thereby created such fear in Pompey's mind that the general for a while kept to his private house. He went so far, however, that Pompey was forced to devise means of counterattack. One of the tribunes, T. Annius Milo, was an enemy of Clodius, and Pompey assisted him in collecting a body of retainers. The general paid a visit to his veterans at Capua, and as a result of his quiet efforts an armed force was gathered in Rome to offset the followers of Clodius. Pompey then made an appeal to the suburban Italians, with whom his influence had always been strong, to pass resolutions in their municipal assemblies requesting Cicero's recall. He felt the need of a vocal champion in the Forum—someone who would have the courage to proclaim the law in the presence of the forces of lawlessness.

Cicero had never lost the good will of the rural Italians, and when their efforts were organized their influence was effective in the Senate. Morever some of the magistrates in office at that time were men who had been active with Cicero in suppressing the Catilinarian conspiracy. They too had found Clodius's methods irksome and dangerous. They held Cicero in high regard and were now beginning to feel the need of his leadership in the Senate and with the people in order to present a united front against the arbitrary forces of violence. After one or two futile attempts, a sufficient power was finally developed to effect Cicero's recall to Rome and his place in the Senate. When the senators learned that they could oppose Clodius with safety they asserted their influence very effectively. The resolution was passed by 416 votes against the solitary dissent of Clodius, and promptly thereafter the recall was approved by the Comitia.

Cicero started for Rome as soon as he received the news. The people were enthusiastic, and his journey was one continuous welcome. Deputations were sent from Rome and from other cities to meet him. His countrymen pressed about him along the way and gave him most hearty acclaim. "It seemed," said he, "as though Rome itself had left its foundations to greet its benefactor." At Rome the people again carried him to the Capitol and again proclaimed him savior of his country. He was overjoyed at these expressions of regard, coming as they did so soon after the misery of his banishment. "I think that I am not only returning from exile," he said, "but it seems to me that I am borne up to the skies." Such a feeling should have been a premonition of another fall. It seems he had not learned yet the instability of popular favor.

If Cicero's peculiar susceptibility to popular acclaim had but allowed him sufficient detachment to read the resolution of his recall, he might have been saved from any overexaltation. The enactment of the Senate and the Comitia did not simply repeal the previous enactments against Cicero, but rather it declared them ineffective on the ground that no banishment could be valid unless it followed a proper judicial trial. Thus in the law of his recall was a pronouncement against his own condemnation of the Catilinarian conspirators.

Cicero's triumphal return afforded but a brief chance to enjoy such glory. He was only fifty years old, but as far as the active affairs of Rome were concerned he was over the crest. Much of his best literary work was yet to be done, but his influence as lawyer and statesman had passed its prime. Thirteen more years of life were before him, but they were years of compromise, concession, disillusionment and disappointment.

Cicero was now playing the part of the old lawyer upon the stage of life. The characteristics of the role are very similar in different ages, but Cicero's character and circumstances gave it a striking delineation. In him the part was accentuated. He had had great honors and therefore assumed an air of importance. But the other performers in the Roman scene were unwilling to recognize his worth. They looked, they listened, but they would not follow. They marveled, but they were not moved. Events had pressed him from the center of the stage and he was unable to regain it. And yet his speech was too sonorous, his manner too pompous for a minor part. His position was tragic, yet comic. He made the most of it by affecting the wit. But finally he was so conscious of the errors of those playing the leading roles that he became a caustic critic. When he obstructed their play they removed him from the scene.

When an antlered monarch of the forest has been deposed by younger blood, he can no longer lead, yet he will not follow; he will not be one of the herd, yet he will not give up the herd. Cicero's position in the life at Rome was much like that—he was still with it, but no longer of it. He was there, but a thing apart. Because he was not submerged in the life about him he however could better observe it. In his position of partial retirement it was natural for him to become critic and commentator. And the loss of his own generation became the gain of future generations.

Under First Triumvirate

Cicero was not permitted to return to Rome unconditionally. The Triumvirs imposed terms. If they were gracious they were nevertheless cautious and firm. Caesar knew that Cato was his most implacable enemy, but he also knew that Cicero was the most likely, most potential, leader of an adverse movement. Pompey was not yet willing to break with Caesar, and when he consulted him about Cicero's return Caesar imposed conditions. He provided a guaranty of Cicero's future behavior by a pledge from his brother Quintus, and then accepted Quintus as liaison officer to his own staff in Gaul. A loan to Cicero was a further restraint and obligation. In response to a courteous but insistent request, Cicero consented to serve as spokesman for the Triumvirate.

He no doubt appeased his feelings with the hope that while the Triumvirate maintained a semblance of constitutional government and offered protection against the lawlessness of Clodius and his ruffians, something might yet be done to restore the Republic. But that hope gradually waned. When the joy over his return subsided he settled down to a mood of cynicism and sullen caution, avoided acrimonious debate in the Senate, and made it his guiding principle in politics to offend no one.

Three days after his re-entry into Rome, Cicero helped to rescue the city from another famine. The condition was the same as at the time of the pirate wars. But this time the pirates were in Rome. Commercial speculators had succeeded in cornering the grain supply and were using the artificial scarcity to exact extortionate prices. The crisis was so intense that a hungry mob had stormed the Senate and threatened a general massacre. Cicero introduced a resolution that Pompey be appointed food dictator, and upon approval of the Senate, the Comitia conferred upon Pompey the power to purchase grain and to charter transport for a term of five years. With a display of his oldtime vigor Pompey, in spite of winter, sent ships to Sicily, Sardinia and Africa, and promptly replenished Rome's granaries. Thus the inordinate greed of the speculators gave a setting for the inordinate ambition of the general, and Cicero was afforded an opportunity to discharge, at least in part, his obligation to Pompey.

He ingratiated himself with Caesar by supporting his Gallic campaign. At a time when the senators were suspicious of Caesar's intentions in Gaul, Cicero carried through the Senate measures appropriating money for the payment of his legions, increasing his forces, and extending his term, so that the conquest could be completed. This conduct of Cicero was also prompted by farseeing statesmanship. It is generally conceded that the victories of Caesar extended the power of Rome for hundreds of years. Cicero, while taking advantage of an opportunity to conciliate Caesar, was not unmindful of the danger to Rome from another invasion from the north. It was at this time that relations between Cicero and Caesar were most cordial. Their correspondence scintillates with gracious expressions of praise and good will. Cicero also established friendly relations with Crassus, his old enemy, whom he had formerly referred to as "old baldpate." Thus the former enemy of the Triumvirate became the leader of the friends of the Triumvirs. He helped to organize the senatorial majority necessary to give legal sanction to the power which they arbitrarily exercised.

For this support he gained not only the thanks of the Triumvirs but the congratulations of his friend Atticus, whose business sense naturally approved such conduct. Cicero now held an envied position, influence, and security from attack. He was made a member of the board of augurs. It was an office of great dignity, and Cicero was proud of his election. The function of the augurs was to read the sky for omens and to report whether the gods were propitious for some proposed action. It was to him merely religious formality, but the office was enjoyed for the political power which it conferred. Clodius and his other enemies feared him. But his position could not save him from the severe criticism of those senators who still opposed the Triumvirate. For his conduct at that time he still is blamed by many critics. That is not the worst of it—he blamed himself. He suffered keen remorse for serving men whose ambitious designs he felt were contrary to the constitution of the Republic and subversive of the liberty of his countrymen.

But what could he do? The common people could not be relied on; they were as changeable as the wind. The very character of the citizenry of Rome had changed. They had to be ruled by force; they seemed not only to require it, but to wish it. The Senate inspired no confidence; it was factious and corrupt. The nobles never had accepted him wholeheartedly; to them he was always the parvenu. They liked him only when they needed him. Their envy revived with his return. Many of them were free associates of Clodius. Their selfish aims were not consonant with Cicero's theory of government. And as he said, they hated to see his clipped wings grow again.

The Senate would not give him the support it had given against Catiline, nor could he gain the support of the people at a general election. Free elections belonged to the past. Leaders no longer took the trouble to buy votes, they seized them by force. The city on election day was the scene of a succession of battles and sieges, and the election was carried by that party or force which retained possession of the place at the close of the day. No election, no popular assembly occurred without bloodshed. Cicero himself gives us the results of one of these contests; he says the Tiber was full of corpses, the public sewers were choked with bodies and the blood had to be mopped from the Forum. Such violent convulsions were indicative of the ebbing life and imminent death of the Republic. About the last display of wholesome life in the Republic was during Cicero's consulship. When the *Concordia Ordinum* could not be maintained, it was futile to expect that it might be regained.

Cicero's severer critics compare him with Caesar and Pompey and then condemn him for want of vigor, decision, and executive power. They say he was weak, that he temporized and vacillated. But they forget that he was a man of law, not of force. To criticize him for not wresting the power from the Triumvirs is merely to criticize him for not being himself a dictator. He declined to resort to the tactics that he condemned in others. His aim was not to rule Rome, but to establish order and freedom and justice. His aim was expressed in his motto: *Otium cum dignitate.* He should not be accounted unsuccessful because he failed to arrive at a goal which he did not seek, nor because he did not attain a position which had no honorable place in his philosophy of life. The eternal glory of some lives lies in the fact that they dare to fail in a worldly sense. If the measure of a man's success is his contribution to the social evolution of mankind, then Cicero's success is greater than Pompey's and greater than Caesar's.

Cicero held the scales of justice, Caesar held the sword. Out of the ashes of the Republic grew the Empire, and Caesar was its inspiration. His shining sword was its emblem of authority. His name became the title of its ruler—a synonym of autocratic power. Cicero's ideas and ideals became the light of republics that in time grew up out of the ashes and broken fragments of the empire. His scales of justice were raised again by republican hands. His philosophy of government revived and sustained a faith in concerted reason and parliamentary rule. He became and still is an inspiration to the champions of freedom and humanism.

But so far as the fate of the Roman Republic is concerned, it would be quite wrong to place the blame on any one man. Neither Caesar's aggression nor Cicero's deference had much to do with it. Rome had sown the wind and had to reap the whirlwind. The character of her population had changed. It was made up of the most disparate elements and for that reason lacked all unity of purpose. The ancient Roman character was dissolved in the anarchy of the mob. Every public assembly was fraught with danger. Public opinion was for the most part formed and expressed at the gladiatorial games. As Cicero said, applause was immortality, a hiss was death. The strongest characters truckled to the crowd. Rome that ruled the world was overrun by vagabond strangers, freedmen demoralized by slavery, gladiators whom Rome had trained to fight man or beast, fugitive slaves who were the most relentless enemies of society, hordes of soldiers of fortune who owned nothing, respected nothing, had nothing to lose and nothing to fear. These elements of society were the natural reactions to the unnatural activities of Rome. They were produced by Rome's resort to force and exploitation. They formed the undertow that pulled the ship of state from its moorings. And the men that should have manned the ship and controlled its course, the senators and the knights, were vying with one another in the gratification of their avarice, greed and lust. They lacked the power of self-discipline and therefore could not rule. But the Empire was not born until the Republic had died—it did not cause the death.

To try to interpret the great national and world movements of that time in terms of individual lives is to lose the vision of the forest in an inspection of the trees; it is not only a failure to catch the spirit of the times, a failure to comprehend the underlying process of cause and effect that moves from generation to generation, but it also involves a failure to see the real glory of those individual lives. We must hold in view the whole forest to see how majestically some trees rise above their kind.

The marvel is that in such times and under such conditions men like Cicero and Caesar should exist. In spite of the general decadence, these men drew to themselves the refinement of Attic culture and the force of Roman character and developed two of the most remarkable minds in history. They exhibited the highest ability both in constructive public leadership and in artistic literary achievement. In statesmanship they should not be compared; they operated in different spheres; one was a man of principle, one a man of action. Caesar was a master of men, magnetic, magnanimous, magnificent; he contemned Rome, campaigned afar and conquered Rome; in the end he was a victim of his own genius. Cicero was a champion of the constitution, conscientious, conceited, constrained; he loved

Rome, lingered at Rome, lost Rome; in the end he was a martyr to his principles. In their literary accomplishments, though, the two men may well be compared—such comparison adds to the glory of each. Cicero published his treatise on the Republic and Caesar his commentaries on Gaul at about the same time. Such works reveal clearly the difference between the two men, but both are works of the highest literary merit. Their devotion to literary pursuits, even while weighed down with heaviest responsibilities and torn by most exacting duties, is almost pathetic. That such discipline and character should arise out of general subsidence of discipline and character is but another instance of the miracle of the renewal of life.

We should not marvel today that Rome lacked the self-discipline necessary to maintain the Republic. The marvel is that so few nations have been able to profit by the experiences of Rome. Much of the world today has had to be redeemed from absolutism. Men again and again abandon ideals for compulsion and forsake reason for force. They prefer the ruthless will to power rather than the stabilizing discipline of law. Blinded by their greed for immediate gain and their lust for self-assertion, they lose all vision of the ultimate beneficence of justice. They forget that the Roman Republic failed because Romans failed generally to comprehend the moral order of social life and the universality of law. And the liberal governments that still exist show startling tendencies toward uncontrolled democracy. Their republican institutions are continuously and insidiously wasted by pandering politicians. In their justifiable efforts to bring the selfish interests of industrialism into social control they act with such class indulgence that they run the risk of upsetting the balance of power and stability of law which provide a firm rule. It is a serious question today whether the so-called democracies can be liberal enough to be fair to all classes and still be strong enough to maintain social discipline. It is not enough to deliver a united offense against dictators abroad. They must be firm against demagogues at home.

But the purpose here is not so much to comment upon the fall of the Roman Republic and the trend of our times as to observe the bearing and behavior of Cicero as he faced that fall. This literary artist, this philosopher, this champion of reason and justice and order, was compelled by caprice of fortune to participate in one of the great transitions of history. This man of study and reflection, who had no arms but his words, who claimed the laurel for eloquence, what could he do in a struggle with forces so deep and so powerful?

That Cicero himself realized the impossibility of his position is made clear by his letters. He pours out his heart to his friend Atticus in these words: "Is anything sadder than our life, mine above all? If I speak according to my convictions, I am considered a mad man; if I heed my own interests, I am accused of being a slave; if I remain silent, they say I am afraid."

To his brother Quintus he said: "I suffer from the bottom of my heart when I see us without the Republic, without justice, and when I find myself reduced to practice at the bar." It is sad to contemplate how many lawyers have been reduced from high positions in the councils of their states to the irksomeness and tedium of private practice. The petty concerns of individuals and individual cases can no longer challenge their expanded minds. Few indeed are the men who can return to the bar with the zeal of youth. Every profession has certain aspects which grow wearisome in the course of time, and such weariness is accentuated when, after absence in broader pursuits, one must return. Cicero wrote to his friend Marius:

Believe me, I would willingly renounce my profession to spend my days with you and some others of a like turn of mind. I had already grown weary of this employment when youth and ambition prompted my perseverance and I was still free to refuse the cases of those whom I did not wish to defend. But in the present conditions it is insupportable. On the one hand, I can never hope to reap any reward from my labors; on the other hand, I am sometimes obliged at the request of those to whom I am under obligation to defend men who ill deserve that favor from me. For these reasons I seek every pretext for living according to my own tastes and inclination.

But such professional obligations as were assumed were discharged with remarkable ability.

Past Master of His Profession

In spite of his general feelings of disappointment, Cicero delivered at this time many very able orations and conducted many cases with admirable ability. Not only were his powers increased by his broad experience and mature judgment, but a certain skill resulted from his very feelings of dissatisfaction. His discontent afforded him a kind of detachment. It made him more daring. He had the assurance of the older lawyer; he was not intimidated; his zeal did not blind him. He was not immersed in the immediate and personal. His position was more frequently on the sideline, and that position enabled him to observe more keenly and his wit and humor were given freer play.

A case that reveals not only Cicero's skill but his times is the prosecution of Caelius Rufus. Cicero was asked to defend Caelius. And this is one case that we can imagine he accepted with alacrity. He was moved to do so in the first instance by a kindly feeling toward the defendant. Caelius had been his pupil, and no doubt a feeling of regard had been created in Cicero's mind by the clever though cynical letters he had received from Caelius. A second though more moving consideration was the fact that Clodia was the prosecuting witness. Although the prosecution was being conducted in the name of Lucius Atratinus, Cicero was convinced it was inspired by Clodia, sister of Clodius, the man most directly responsible for his recent misfortunes. Clodia herself had been intensely bitter toward Cicero and his family while he was in exile. She had been zealous in support of her brother and arrogant toward Cicero's wife and children. Cicero's professional abilities were moreover challenged by all the possibilities of the case. He saw in it a chance for his peculiar talents—a rare chance to inveigh not only against Clodia but against the degradation she typified.

Caelius was accused of having paid men to assassinate Dio, an envoy from Egypt, with money stolen from Clodia, and with having attempted to poison Clodia. Not only the nature of the indictment but the social standing of the defendant and the prosecuting witness insured a wide interest in the case and a good attendance at the trial. Cicero was challenged by the scene and was practical enough to know that a mastery of the situation would do his own position no harm.

Caelius was one of the social elite, a shining member of the fast set of Rome. Above the average of that class in intellect, he was a young man of considerable charm of personality—he must have been to have made so favorable an impression upon one as experienced as Clodia. He had not had the good fortune to inherit wealth, nor had he taken the time to accumulate any; but Clodia out of her family abundance had relieved this deficiency. Caelius had lived in her house on the Palatine Hill. Their names had been joined in ribald jest. He had given her the nickname, then current in Rome, of "Quadrantaria" (easy money!).

Clodia's life had run the gamut of the social register. Born in the highest social stratum, she descended to the lowest. A daughter of one of Rome's noblest families, a patrician of patricians, she became a woman of the street, the consort of commons. Having been the inspiration of Catullus, the Lesbia of his ardent love poems, her name became a byword and a jest. Born with beauty, wealth and social distinction, her life finally touched the low-water mark of Rome's degradation.

At the time of the prosecution of Caelius she had evidently passed her prime. She who had been able to pick her lovers freely and dismiss them ruthlessly, had found herself unable to hold Caelius, the most elegant of Rome's belli. He had left her home without repaying the money she had given him. And Cicero in his defense of Caelius made this "migration from the Palatine Hill" the whole cause of the prosecution. The rapier thrusts in Cicero's speech were prompted by the knowledge that Clodius, at the time of his prosecution for violating the rites of the Good Goddess, had been accused of incest with his sister. Such scandal had not been forgotten. And moreover it was now common gossip that Clodia had caused the death of her husband, the excellent and respected Metellus, who had died suddenly and violently of poison.

Clodia was a prominent spectator at the trial. Cicero so indicates in his oration. No feelings of delicacy restrained her from a display of her interest in the prosecution. She was naturally a conspicuous person, the daughter of a prominent family, a woman of great personal charm and pleasing appearance. Moreover she took a prominent seat —arresting the attention of all by her striking and sensuous adornment. She was a dangerous element in the case. Most trial lawyers would as far as possible have ignored her presence and interest. They would have considered it sound strategy to draw attention away from her. Cicero, however, made her the pivotal person in the case and had the temerity to violate one of the fundamental rules of trial practice by openly attacking the character of the woman. Such procedure is dangerous, even if the woman is known to bear a sullied reputation. But Cicero accepted the challenge and avoided the dangers of such a course. It required a complete mastery of the facts, a keen analysis of human nature, and a supreme delicacy of presentation.

Cicero first pointed out the responsibility of others for the murder of Dio. He made it appear that only a strained interpretation of the facts could involve Caelius in that crime. He then directed attention to the fact that his client was being prosecuted by the son of Lucius Atratinus whom Caelius had prosecuted for bribery. He charged, however, that the weapons which were shot openly at the defendant had been supplied secretly through the influence of an evil woman. He then mentioned the intimate relationship between Caelius and Clodia. They had lived in the same neighborhood and a questionable association had developed. If such relations had led to scandalous charges against his client, he asked with deadly sarcasm, how could a neighbor expect to escape when even Clodia's brother could not? At another time in the course of his argument, he referred to Clodius as the husband of Clodia, and then promptly corrected himself by saying he had meant her brother, with an ironical comment about such a mistake.

Cicero, uttering these caustic remarks, was the master of his stage, the acknowledged leader of the Forum. He enjoyed the display of his prowess and skill. With his hand on his chin, a pose which the elderly lawyer now affected, and with apparent detachment if not disdain, he made remarks in mock seriousness and enjoyed the laughter which they provoked. He was the veteran basking in his professional experience and skill.

He made an artful defense of his client's misdeeds, by pleading for charity toward the indiscretions of youth generally. The argument is indeed so broad that it has been censured because it seems to approve an indulgence of such indiscretions. It was well known that Clodia was older than Caelius, and Cicero stressed the point that the charges of licentiousness against Caelius reflected more directly against her.

With such preliminary and general arguments he led up to what he called the essence of the case. There were two special counts in the indictment, he said with analytical skill: a charge respecting gold taken from Clodia, and a charge respecting poison sought for Clodia. All other allegations he dismissed as mere vituperation prompted by a petulant quarrel. He then proceeded to analyze the charges respecting the gold and the poison. He dismissed the testimony of witnesses with a statement that is an indictment of the times in which he lived. He said their testimony was something which might be easily purchased for any purpose. The ramifications of his discourse are startling to readers familiar with the modern rule that comments must be confined to facts supported by the evidence. It is quite shocking to our notions of legal procedure to hear him say he would conduct his case entirely by arguments. He proceeded to do so, nevertheless, and with withering effect upon the prosecution.

First, regarding the charge of gold, he developed a most ingenious method of exposing Clodia, without incurring the usual resentment that is engendered by an attack upon a woman's private character. After reiterating that the whole case rested upon Clodia, he apologized for seeming to quarrel with a woman, especially with one who not only was no man's adversary but, on the contrary, was considered to be the intimate of all. He said he did not wish to offend her and he asked her how she would prefer to be addressed—in the grave and serious fashion of the former day, or in the lighter vein of their own time. He then proceeded to speak to her in both ways. Having reminded his hearers that not only her grandfather, but her great-grandfather and her great-great-grandfather had been consuls of Rome, he said he would summon that one from the dead who had been blind, because being unable to see her he would be caused the least grief. He then assumed that it was her noble ancestor addressing her, and he had that ancient benefactor of Rome ask the questions which insinuated the charges Cicero dared not make directly:

"Clodia, what had been your relations with Caelius? Why is it that you were either so intimate with him as to give him money, or so hostile to him as to fear that you were to be poisoned by him? You, the descendant of generations of Rome's consuls, the wife of a man whom Rome delighted to honor, why did you allow such intimacy with Caelius? Was he your husband's friend? Was he related to you? Can it be that you are the daughter of those women who equaled their husbands in upright living? Did I terminate the peace with Rome's bitter foe that you might enter into an alliance of shameful love? Did I at so great effort bring the water to Rome merely to wash away your stain? Did I build the great highway that you might traffic thereon with strange men?"

Cicero then dismissed the formal and austere figure of her forebear, and assumed that Clodia would probably prefer to be spoken to by a man of the world, that perfect man of the world, her younger brother (and again with chin in hand) "who loves you so very much." He then put the questions that Clodius would presumably ask:

"What is all this fuss about? 'Why thus with outcry loud do you exalt such trifles into things of consequence?' Are you out of your head, sister, making so much of what really is nothing? You had a fancy for the young man next door. You liked his handsome face and figure. His father had left him no money. You tried to draw him to you with some of yours. But he found that he had to pay too high for your gifts and he has quit. What of it? Are there no others? Can you not choose other young men from those gardens of yours by the Tiber when they come there to swim? Why quarrel over a man who does not want you?"

Cicero then reverted to the charge of poison. Removing his hand from his chin, he changed the mocking tones for the resonant tones of righteous indignation.

He described the death of Clodia's husband. Cicero portrayed Metellus as a man in vigorous health and in honorable position, suddenly stricken down by poison administered by an unknown hand, but certainly from some hand employed in the house of Clodia. He detailed the struggles of the stricken man, his voice choked with agony, his paroxysms of pain; and he pictured the poor man pounding the wall as he struggled to assert with his last breath his concern not for himself but for the Roman Republic. Was it any wonder that such a woman as Clodia would fear poison?

While as stated we are shocked today at the latitude allowed to the Roman orator in such a trial, yet we should not let that interfere with our enjoyment of the skill with which Cicero handled the facts which he assumed in the case.

Cicero soon sensed that he was master of his audience. He could feel the resentment which his remarks had engendered against Clodia. He had convinced his hearers that the prosecution had been instigated by her, and he had aroused against her all the envy which her beauty and wealth had begotten, all the resentment which her haughty arrogance had caused, and all the bitterness and disgust which her crimes had created. There she sat in all her lust and luster—an object of contempt. Caelius was acquitted. The verdict, however, was not so much a vindication of Caelius as a condemnation of Clodia. The orator's object was attained, and he received the plaudits of the populace. Cicero was avenged against the Clodii.

Clodia's position was destroyed. As long as what had been said against her was only gossip, her arrogant manners discountenanced it. But now that such gossip was established fact, she herself was publicly discountenanced. Her brother Clodius was afterward killed in a battle between his armed followers and the followers of Milo when they met on the Appian way. But one of the family of the Clodii, the plebeian Fulvia, widow of Clodius, wife of Antony, was yet to give expression to the vengeance of the Clodii against Cicero.

Cicero took part in a number of other important trials at this time. He pursued his resentment of the Clodii too far, however, when he attempted to defend Milo for the murder of Clodius by disparaging the victim of the fray. Clodius and Clodia, no matter how bold they may have been in their immorality, had yet their friends in Rome. Rome was not a city of tender sensibilities, and a large part of the population were attracted by the very daring of the Clodii. When Clodius was killed the sympathy and resentment of the crowd asserted itself in mob violence, and Cicero was unable to save Milo from condemnation and banishment. He had, however, the courage and the loyalty to try.

Proconsul

Cicero was at this time given another opportunity to demonstrate his theories of government and his abilities as a conscientious public administrator. Pompey, in order to curtail the senatorial traffic in provincial government, had passed a law by which ex-consuls were forbidden to assume provincial rule until five years after their consulship. The enactment of such law made a temporary dearth of available provincial governors, and it was provided in the law that during such interim the provinces should be administered by those ex-consuls who had not held such office. This made it necessary for Cicero to serve. He and Bibulus cast lots for their assignments and Cicero drew Cilicia and its dependencies. Again he greatly deplored the prospect of absence from the capital of the world. He began at once to entreat his friends to see that his term should not be extended beyond the legal requirement of one year.

It is well for Cicero's reputation, however, and well not only for Cilicia but for the world, that he was compelled to act as provincial governor. His administration is one of the bright pages of the history of that period. His rule was a refreshing exception to the general extortion which provincial governors practiced. Command of a province was generally conceded to be an opportunity to recoup the costs of political campaigns at Rome, and proconsuls and propraetors set out for their respective provinces with predacious intent. The grant of authority was accepted as a kind of political indulgence, and it was used for the gratification of inordinate avarice and lust. Cilicia had been sorely oppressed by Cicero's predecessors, but his administration was honest, just and fair. If all Roman governors had been like Cicero and Cato, Rome might have continued to be the undisputed capital of the world. That there was something eternal in their precepts is shown by the fact that later ages have found in their practices a model of justice, morality and statesmanship. It is truly marvelous that any men could so elevate themselves above the passions, prejudices and customs of that pagan age as to become models of detachment and self-discipline even to later and more enlightened times. Cicero had written to Atticus that his duties as proconsul would put to test his philosophy. He accepted the challenge resolutely. By his own equanimity and goodness he proved to the world that his philosophy of law and government was practicable.

Instead of imposing the Roman law upon the provincial people he allowed them to try their causes in their own courts according to their own legal customs and before juries of their own countrymen. This gave the provincials a feeling of independence and enabled them to maintain their self-respect and dignity. When he himself was called upon to act as judge he again demonstrated his very high conception of the judicial function. He considered himself the impersonal voice of the law, and his judgments, therefore, expressed no personal feelings. He avoided opprobrious language and never added insult to the imposition of sentence. Justice was his aim, and he knew that a detached attitude was the best means to that end. Not only by his administration of the law but by his affability and courtesy, he ingratiated himself with all who came within his influence. He dispensed with the pomp and ceremony with which Roman governors usually surrounded themselves. No barrier of secretaries, chamberlains, and guards made him unapproachable to those desiring interviews. Acts of cruelty and oppression by subordinates were thus prevented by the knowledge that the governor was ever ready to hear the complaints of his subjects. His proconsulate, though brief, served to correct the evils of former governors and established wholesome relationships between the district and Rome. As he had remarked, a just administrator was Rome's best ambassador to her colonies. Although never happy when absent from Rome, Cicero was nevertheless gratified by his accomplishments in Cilicia.

But again, as at the time of his ascendancy in Rome, Cicero's record is somewhat marred by his vanity. This fault, especially in this instance, was quite harmless and, when compared with the arrogance and cruelty of other Romans of his time, quite insignificant. Nevertheless, we are surprised, amused, and disappointed to find such a trait in this great Roman lawyer. Soon after he took command of his province, he was called upon to conduct a military campaign, and his egotism and conceit magnified it beyond its true proportion.

The disturbances might have been more serious if they had not been promptly suppressed. The Parthians had crossed the Euphrates in force under the command of Pacorus, and a number of marauding bands were at work in Cilicia itself. Cicero promptly organized a military force and set out against the Parthians. Apparently he could on such occasion show dispatch and decision. His conduct belies the general criticism that he was weak and irresolute. His military maneuvers surprised the enemy and his campaign was quite successful. The result was of small import compared to other great Roman victories, but his soldiers acclaimed him Imperator. Cicero's letters to his friends referred to the fact that the scene of his victory had been the scene of Alexander's victory over Darius, and he suggested that the Senate should declare a public thanksgiving, saying that such a proclamation would be some reparation for the wrong done him by banishment. He even requested that the Senate grant him a triumph upon his return to Rome. But, alas, his return to Rome was to be far from a triumph.

VII

LAST YEARS AND DEATH

Civil War and Domestic Strife

Cicero left Cilicia in August, 50 B.C., but three years elapsed before he entered Rome. His son and his nephew had been with him in Cilicia, in order that he might direct their education, and before their return Cicero took them to Rhodes, Ephesus, and Athens. When Cicero finally reached the shores of Italy, he found the country in the throes of the struggle between Pompey and Caesar. At first he made overtures of peace with the hope of sparing his country the agony of another civil war. After the failure of such efforts he aligned himself with Pompey and the senatorial party. But those forces abandoned Rome at the approach of Caesar with his Gallic soldiers, and Cicero dared not go to Rome—not until after Caesar's victory. He then entered as a suppliant of the victor's favor, not as a triumphant proconsul.

These intervening years brought Cicero a succession of bitter experiences. In that interval he lost the love of his wife, the affection of his brother, the regard of many friends, and, worst of all, his last hope for the Republic. During that period also his beloved daughter Tullia lost her health, was divorced from her husband, and soon after died.

The estrangement which occurred between Cicero and Terentia is a psychological puzzle. History does not supply facts sufficient to afford a satisfactory explanation. It was Cicero's custom to leave Terentia in charge of their property whenever he was absent from Rome. Such separation afforded room for misunderstandings. Terentia had great capacity in handling accounts. She was a managing person in many ways. It seems she may have become too zealous in her own interests. Cicero complained that she had become more interested in business affairs than in her domestic duties. He developed a suspicion of her integrity in financial matters. Atticus had written that a certain amount of money was due from property belonging to Cicero. Terentia, however, sent her husband less than the amount which Atticus had named. He concluded that she was defrauding him, and told Atticus that this discrepancy was not the only cause of complaint he had against her. We know that by temperament and habit of mind she displayed exasperating qualities at times, but there was no sudden realization of incompatibility. A gulf had widened between them gradually. When he first arrived at Brundusium, Terentia wrote to express her joy over his return and offered to meet him there. Although his letters to her up to this time had been tender and expressive of a concern for her health and welfare, they now became firm and cold. He dissuaded her from the journey. He said the way was long and unsafe, and then added that he did not see what good she could do if she did come. This attitude on his part and her petulant disposition eventually led to their divorce, apparently without regret. Each soon remarried. Rome had grown coarse, and the Roman mind was not sensitive to the finer domestic relationships. Cicero and Terentia were unable to withstand altogether the current tendencies.

At the same time other attachments became strained. During his absence from Rome, letters were brought to Cicero from his brother Quintus which were full of bitter reproaches. Quintus blamed Cicero for his own misfortunes. He said it was due to Cicero's insistence that he had aligned himself with Pompey. He was then afraid of Caesar's success and power. He thought it might lead to the confiscation of all his property. With their usual magnanimity, however, both Cicero and Caesar discounted the misapprehensions of Quintus. They knew that misfortune had made him suspicious. And Cicero, in spite of this petulance, was generous enough to write to Caesar and endeavor to reconcile Caesar to Quintus, and Caesar generously permitted the reconciliation. Cicero, however, was deeply depressed by the loss of the affection of his brother, whom he had so warmly loved through all the years and so frequently assisted.

Cicero's loss of hope for the Republic resulted from the strife between Pompey and Caesar. Those rivals both acted in defiance of the traditions of the Republic. Their strife destroyed the last vestiges of the ancient order, and the force of their war was, moreover, so all-encompassing that it disrupted old alliances. Cicero was too prominent to remain neutral. His adherence to one faction was displeasing to the other, and the loss of old friendships accompanied the loss of the Republic. It is necessary to examine Cicero's conduct in connection with the events.

The ebbing life of the Republic had been dependent on the balance of power established by the First Triumvirate. But the coalition of Pompey, Caesar and Crassus came to an end with the end of Crassus. His unfortunate and unwarranted military expedition against the Parthians had resulted in a staggering defeat to Roman arms and the slaughter of both Crassus and his son. Crassus was not a military commander, and it was a mistake for him to try to rival the reputations of Caesar and Pompey. He had distinguished himself by amassing a fabulous fortune. He should have been content with financial success. His overreaching ambition caused even that accomplishment to be made a mockery. His inordinate avarice was recognized in a scornful and gruesome ceremony, when his head was sent to the Parthian king by his victorious military opponent. The king had molten gold poured into the mouth in a post-mortem attempt to satisfy the Roman's greed.

The disaster to Crassus is of import to this study because it destroyed the principal basis of peace between Caesar and Pompey. At the same time all personal bonds of attachment between those two generals became severed. Julia, Caesar's daughter and Pompey's wife, had died, and the death of her child, which soon followed, broke the last strand between the great rivals. The atmosphere of the whole Roman world became charged with the impending crisis. Caesar had completed his subjugation of Gaul and Britain, and his proconsulship was drawing to its end. During his absence he had maintained a party of supporters in Rome, and he wished to be re-established there before surrendering his position in Gaul. Pompey had been consul and was the most powerful figure at the capital. Moreover, as proconsul of Spain he was the commander in chief of the Roman legions maintained in that province. He was determined that Caesar's return should not disturb his supreme position.

The conditions at Rome made it apparent that some form of dictatorship was inevitable. Constitutional government had come to a standstill. Tribunes prevented the regular election of consuls by the people. Consuls prevented tribunes from presenting measures before the Comitia. The resolutions of the Senate were nullified by the vetoes of the tribunes or by the refusal of consuls to give them effect. The only semblance of government was carried on from day to day by the provisional expedient of an interregnum. Mobs interrupted assemblies, and neither persons nor property were safe from violence. The soldiers of Pompey were necessary to insure the orderly process of public trials. But even Pompey was unable to maintain complete order. With his rival constantly playing for popular favor, Pompey was unwilling to exert an efficient force against the people of Rome. It was due, however, to such force as he did exert that the city was saved from complete anarchy.

Caesar did not wish to relinquish his military command until he had gained a corresponding civil control. He was unwilling to submit himself to the power of his enemies in Rome. Since it was unlawful for a proconsul to bring his military forces upon Italian soil, the Rubicon was the limit of Caesar's proconsular influence. To cross the Rubicon with his army would be a violation of the constitution, an act of treason. He asked for permission to be a candidate for the office of consul while absent from the city. He refused to disband his army until after his election, unless Pompey also surrendered his military command. Caesar needed the authority of office or the power of his army to checkmate Pompey. Pompey, knowing that Caesar's proconsular government would expire soon by force of law, exerted his influence in the Senate against any extension of privilege to his opponent. Since a master of Rome was necessary, he was determined to be that man. A proposal to recall Caesar from his province had been vetoed by Caesar's friends, the tribunes. It cannot be said that Caesar deliberately planned to subvert the constitution and establish a dictatorship. He offered to lay aside his military command if Pompey would do the same. The obstinacy with which each of these characters refused to yield to the other brought on the civil war and destroyed the remaining foundations of republican government.

Caesar, with his usual perspicacity, understood the situation and acted with characteristic dispatch. With his usual courage he accepted the challenge contained in the refusal of his terms of peace. He was a master of events and knew how to dramatize the situation before him. He called his soldiers together and explained conditions in a spirited speech. He then asked whether they were willing to protect their general against the designs of his enemies. They answered with loud acclaim that they were ready to follow him. He moved into Italy with his legions and began the occupation of strategic points. The consuls and senators at Rome called upon Pompey to defend the Republic and intrusted to him the command of such military forces as were then available. But such forces were no match for Caesar's seasoned legions.

Rome was in consternation. The consuls, the Senate, and Pompey left the city in such haste that they forgot to remove the money in the public treasury. The report that Caesar with his veterans was at the gates of the city terrified them. Pompey was criticized for abandoning the capital, and he cited the example of Themistocles, who left Athens in order to meet Xerxes at Salamis. Cicero, however, contrasted this with the example of Pericles, who had brought the population of Attica within the walls of the city and saved the state. The truth is, Caesar's audacity astounded the leaders of Rome. They had thought he would not dare to march against the city. In spite of the imminence of danger, they had failed to prepare. A disintegrating republic is never prepared.

The Romans, moreover, were unable to understand Pompey's plans. It is questionable whether he had any definite plans. The general was past his prime. At a time when energy and decision were required, he lacked these qualities. A general levy of troops was ordered, but with indifferent success. The recruiting officers themselves were afraid of Caesar's approach. With only two legions available in Rome, Pompey and his party retired to Greece with the hope of adding to their forces some of the legions located in the east. Caesar entered Rome and promptly took possession of the public treasury. He then directed his army to pursue the retreating forces of Pompey.

When Pompey finally gave battle at Pharsalus he had acquired a definite advantage in number of soldiers. He also had the advantage of elevated location. But these were not sufficient to save him from complete defeat. He had put his trust in his cavalry under Labienus. His infantry was ordered to stand firm while the cavalry turned the flank of Caesar's army. But Caesar had prepared for this strategy. Eight cohorts with spears had been stationed for such maneuver. They put the cavalry to flight, and then outflanked Pompey's infantry. The Pompeyan army fled to its camp. When Pompey saw the rout, he retreated to his tent and sulked. Caesar's soldiers, in spite of the heat and their severe exertions, pursued the Pompeyans, headed them off, and forced a surrender of all the infantry. Pompey, when he saw Caesar's soldiers coming over the ramparts of his camp, discarded his military insignia, took horse, and fled to the sea. He still had a considerable fleet under his command. He sailed to Egypt. When he landed, he was stabbed to death by Achillas, an agent of the Egyptian government, and two Roman officers.

Cicero has been severely criticized for his conduct during this struggle. Some critics think he was vacillating, and some intimate that he was cowardly and disloyal. Some of his actions seem to give color to these charges. Cicero had declined to join Caesar in Rome when the general was trying to assemble enough senators to assume control of government there. Cicero gave his support to Pompey, and followed him into Greece. His loyalty, however, was not unquestioning, and he was absent from the battle of Pharsalia on account of illness. After the death of Pompey he declined the command of the republican forces and proffered his allegiance to Caesar. There were, however, reasons for this apparent inconstancy.

Let us not forget that Cicero had urged most earnestly that Caesar's early offers of peace should be accepted. He recommended that Caesar be allowed to stand for the consulship while absent. When Caesar had offered to abandon his army if Pompey would abandon his, in order that the Senate and the people might assume the government as usual, Cicero urged acceptance and was severely critical of the ultimatum which Pompey issued. After the Rubicon had been crossed, however, he gave what support he could to the existing government. He adhered to Pompey because Pompey was the champion of the established government at Rome, even though that government had become a mere shell of the ancient Republic. Caesar was an invader, leading his proconsular army against Rome in violation of the constitution. For personal as well as state reasons Cicero was impelled to Pompey at the first. Pompey had been his benefactor and had exerted a compelling influence for his recall from exile. Pompey, moreover, seemed to inspire the most hope for the Republic. He had been less dictatorial in matters of general government and more favorably inclined to the counsel of the leaders of the senatorial party. It is altogether to Cicero's credit that he joined the republican ranks in spite of the fact that he knew it to be the weaker side. In a letter to Atticus he said it would be better to be vanquished with Pompey than to conquer with Caesar.

It was not long, however, before he realized that the outcome would be fatal to the republic and to free government whichever side won. He was horrified when he learned of Pompey's plans for a general proscription in case of victory. Cicero's correspondence asserts that he had gained personal knowledge of Pompey's intention to lay waste the whole country with fire and sword and confiscate the property of the rich. Pompey told his soldiers that his largess to them would be more bountiful than Caesar's and said that plunder would be the means of fulfilling that promise. In a letter to Atticus Cicero said: "You remind me, with approval, that I once said I should rather be vanquished with Pompey than victorious with the other side. Well, I should rather; but with that Pompey as he then was, or as he seemed to me to be; not with this man, who flies before he knows from whom he is flying or whither, this man who has betrayed our cause, has abandoned our city and is now abandoning Italy." When Cicero was criticized for still clinging to the man after such revelations, he said: "I think he has deserved so well of me that I dare not incur the charge of ingratitude. When I recall his kindnesses and bear in mind his position I think his services deserve the price of my life." He adhered to Pompey as long as Pompey lived, although he saw from the first how utterly unfit the general was for the crisis.

Cicero lost his faith in the cause before the cause was lost. But, impelled by a sense of personal obligation, he followed Pompey to Epirus. He stood with him to the end of Pompey's life. He lent money to Pompey to carry on the campaign, and continued to attend the councils of war. His advice was not always gratefully received, however. His admonitions were frequently scorned. Pompey became irritated by the old lawyer's criticisms and witticisms. Adversity of fortune creates asperity of mind. Cicero again gave offense by his caustic remarks. He indulged in what today would be termed "wisecracks."

When he was reproached for coming late to camp, he answered: "I am not late, for nothing is ready here." Cicero's son-in-law Dolabella was with Caesar, and when Pompey tauntingly inquired: "Where is your son-in-law?" Cicero replied, "With your father-in-law." When Pompey promised citizenship to some Gauls who had deserted Caesar, Cicero remarked: "This is a fine fellow to bestow citizenship on Gauls when he cannot restore to us our own." When someone remarked, after a temporary defeat, that they should not be discouraged because there were still seven eagles left in Pompey's camp, Cicero replied, "That would be a good reason for encouragement if we were fighting jackdaws." He was not happy and was not inclined to laugh, but he would stalk around the camp with sour countenance, making jokes which would cause others to laugh who were in no jesting mood. He made his noble sacrifices for Pompey with such poor grace that he received no credit for them from the general or his followers. Pompey is reported to have said: "I wish Cicero would go over to Caesar in order to become afraid of us." Although, as stated, Cicero took no part in the battle of Pharsalia, his son, who held a command in Pompey's army, acquitted himself valiantly. But after that battle it was apparent to Cicero that Caesar was the master of Rome and its dominion.

Upon hearing of Pompey's death, a conference of the republican leaders was held. Cato asked Cicero to take command of what remained of the republican army. But Cicero knew that he was ill fitted for such a position.

Furthermore he recognized that the cause itself, as well as its general, was lost. When he declined to accept the command, Pompey's eldest son called him a traitor and he and his friends drew their swords to kill him. They were soldiers, ready to do or die. They had no understanding of the feelings of the old lawyer. Cato, however, interposed and enabled Cicero to withdraw from the camp. Poor Cato, noble and uncompromising, followed Pompey to Egypt and committed suicide in 46 B.C. at Utica, in what is now Tunisia. Pompey's son Gnaeus was tracked to the wilds of Spain and slaughtered like a beast of the fields. Pompey's death canceled Cicero's personal obligation to him, and Cicero was then free to renew friendly intercourse with Caesar. Such a policy afforded brighter prospects for service to his country than he could have found by following the shattered remnants of Pompey's army. Cicero was now old enough to know that he was not a military commander. He was devoted primarily to the establishment of law and order. His conduct is not inconsistent with his principles. He realized that only on Caesar's terms could civil order be re-established.

Cicero now longed to return to Italy and the retirement of his villa. He at last dismissed his lictors and other proconsular attendants whom he had retained up to that time with the pathetic hope of a triumph when he entered Rome. His pride at last was crushed. His soul now thirsted for what he called "adversity's sweet milk, philosophy." He turned again from the sword to the pen with the hope that something might yet be done to persuade men to a more reasonable course. It is the tragedy of such characters that they know human nature, know how unreasonable men are after centuries of sad experience, but must try to persuade them to guide themselves by reason rather than passion, and yet be ever failing in their attempt.

Who can say, however, how much worse the world might be were it not for their efforts?

Cicero's imminent concern was Caesar's attitude toward him. Antony, Caesar's commanding lieutenant in Rome, had said that none of the Republicans would be permitted to return to Italy without Caesar's consent. Cicero received word from another source that such consent would not be refused. He still had grave doubts, however, as to what terms might be imposed. Although he had joined the forces opposing Caesar, he had nevertheless always been honorable in all his dealings with Caesar. When he had determined to align himself with the opposition, he took considerable pains to pay his debt to Caesar.

It is cause for wonder how, in the midst of all the uncertainties and difficulties of his life, Cicero was able to find the money necessary for his needs. The sum which he had lent Pompey was from a fund which he had garnered in anticipation of his triumph. No doubt that fund had also enabled him to repay Caesar. Through most of his life he carried a heavy burden of debt, but he was strictly honorable in all financial transactions. He practiced no short cuts. Since he consistently forbore to practice any form of extortion, he was deprived of one of the general sources of income to men in his position. In later years, in accordance with the growing custom, he received some substantial gifts or fees for his professional services. In addition, he received rent from properties which he owned. It was moreover the custom of that day for wealthy persons to remember prominent men and public benefactors in their wills, and Cicero received many substantial bequests. Yet he always lived well, and that entailed heavy obligations.

But his financial worries were not his greatest troubles. In addition to his domestic difficulties and his apprehension concerning Caesar, he was torn at this time by doubts of himself and pangs of conscience. No man of ancient times has left a more complete record of all his feelings. To his abiding friend Atticus he unburdened his heart without reserve. The publication of this private correspondence revealed to the world Cicero's innermost thoughts. The letters of Atticus to Cicero have never been found. We know, however, that he was a loyal friend through all the trying times. He was a man of calm temperament, keen perception, and sound judgment, especially well qualified to direct a safe course. He had great wealth and considerable influence, and lived to an old age without being embroiled in any of the factional fights of his time. He was prompted by prudence, while Cicero was motivated by principles. If Cicero had followed in the course of his friend, his life might have been spared much trouble and brought to a calm end. But Cicero was not content to be prudent.

It is painful to read the self-censure which Cicero suffered after his return to Italy. Even his country estate could not enable him to forget. He felt that he had made a mistake by following Pompey to Epirus, and he felt that he had made a mistake by returning to Italy. He was too generous to blame any one else. He said he was lost by his own fault and blamed only himself for his sorrows. He knew that he had followed Pompey in spite of Caesar's advice, and contrary to Caesar's request that he at least remain neutral. He feared the condemnation of Caesar and Caesar's followers. On the other hand, he felt that the republican leaders who remained in Greece or had followed Pompey to Africa would consider him a traitor. He had no heart to go back, and no encouragement to go forward. It was dangerous to go to Rome, and it was dangerous to stay away.

This depression was finally relieved by his meeting with Caesar. Caesar, upon his return from Egypt, landed at Tarentum; and when Cicero learned that he was on his way to Brundusium he hastened to meet him. Cicero confessed that it was with grave apprehension that he went to meet the conqueror in the presence of so many witnesses. But the meeting was another demonstration of Caesar's magnanimity. When he saw Cicero coming, he halted his forces, dismounted from his horse, and went to meet him. He saluted Cicero and then conversed with him privately. Caesar's generous and kindly disposition in spite of Cicero's opposition is a strong indication that Caesar must have had a sympathetic understanding of Cicero's great problem—a better understanding than many of the historians and critics of later time. Caesar must have perceived him as a courageous character trying to maintain exalted principles amid trying times—principles of peace in a military age. The only point of sympathy between them was their kindred literary traits. And while such kindred sympathy had been the basis of many reconciliations, yet the indications are that Caesar's conduct at this time was prompted by deep understanding and genuine magnanimity. Their meeting is a compliment to the nobility of both characters. They exchanged expressions of good will, some general hopes as to the future of Rome, and Cicero then graciously accepted Caesar's generous invitation to Rome.

Under Dictatorship of Caesar

After his meeting with Caesar, Cicero proceeded to his Tusculan villa for a brief stay and then went on to Rome. He made no triumphal entry, however. His return was as unostentatious as his departure had been when he was exiled. But he no longer wished a triumph. He was now a disillusioned man. He said, however, that in one way good had come out of evil, for in the ruin of the Republic he was made to feel that death was a thing rather to be desired than dreaded. He nevertheless reopened his city house and took part in formal affairs. He wished also to make peace with his old friends, his books. He said he had felt some reluctance at returning to them, not because he had quarreled with them, but because they made him feel ashamed for having become submerged in the turbulence of life and for having given too little heed to their precepts. He said he would thenceforward devote himself to study and, like the wisest of the ancients, render what service he could to the state by writing. The desire to write, to compose, as he expressed it, had always been present in his mind, and the opportunity at last to gratify that urge was some compensation for his other disappointments.

It is the lawyer's fate to grow weary of life because of its contention and strife. Life becomes in time a sordid experience. As the infirmities of age increase, the illusions of youth disappear. Disappointments, embarrassments, and discouragements increase with age, and he wearies because of the dissension which his profession imposes. The real glory of life exists in the spirit which transcends it. The retreat of the learned lawyer has always been the library. There through the years he has found consolation and inspiration. Cicero, however, could not quit Rome entirely to pursue his studies lest he be suspected of unfriendliness. His relations with the controlling forces were still too strained to be neglected. His absence might have been interpreted as fear or ill will. Many of the republican leaders were still alive, and Caesar had to be vigilant against their connivance and intrigue. Cicero knew that

Caesar and his followers felt safer while he was in Rome. He wished to do all that he could honorably do to ingratiate himself with the leaders of the victorious party. He said that one should try to be of service to his times, and that it was a mark of good sense not to offend unnecessarily those who were in power. Again he temporarily sacrificed his ideals to expediency—there are times when a public man must do so. Ideals are not categorematic. If they are advanced too rigorously or out of season they only beget antagonism. In statesmanship there are degrees of truth and value, and their boundaries overlap. The superior mind makes its choices under the broadest aspects and does not allow resentments to interfere with ultimate goals.

Caesar's favor gave Cicero a sense of security and relief. He was tired of the doubts and fears that had afflicted him. Although he was deeply depressed by the loss of the Republic, he found repose in the order which was being established by the Dictator. Mob violence was suppressed. When the people are unable to maintain self-discipline they must suffer superimposed discipline. Society, like the individuals that compose it, must have discipline of some kind. Cicero was encouraged by the existing civil order to enter again into the social life of Rome. But the insincerity of the social set, the inanity of their conversation, wearied him. He kept his house open to his clients nevertheless, and attended the fashionable dinners of his prosperous friends. He rested on his reputation and ceased to be a contentious advocate or reformer. He resolved to be silent during heated debates in the Senate and tried to avoid the appearance of being in eternal mourning for the Republic. He said he had already mourned for his country more heavily and longer than a mother would mourn for her only son.

His fondness for a joke and display of wit served a better purpose at this time than ever before. Caesar relished Cicero's quips and quirks and tolerated them even when they were at his expense. Cicero was in a delicate situation, and his wit helped him to maintain his position while he also maintained his self-respect. That he could be humorous and self-sufficient when others were morose or obsequious proved that he was a master of himself, if not of Rome. His wit maintained liberty of speech after liberty of action was gone. Wit is not always a trivial thing. It is at times essential to sanity. It helps the mind to transcend great disaster. When events tend to make men silent, downcast and discouraged, a sense of humor serves to maintain human poise and affability. The old lawyer, with his hand at chin, as he uttered his cynical or humorous comments, became a favorite at the capital. He enjoyed temporarily this play as a man of the world. He had been the champion of righteousness, had been looked upon as a moralist and treated somewhat as an obtrusive reformer. He now found some relief in this pleasanter and easier pose.

In his letters Cicero described his mode of life at the time. He received visitors and clients in the morning, and such conferences were well attended. Afterwards he turned to his studies, either writing or reading for some time, and then devoted the rest of the day to bodily exercise and the good dinners given by his friends. He said in jest that he had turned epicure and that plain dishes and simple fare would no longer satisfy his taste. When declaring his intention to call on a friend who was confined with gout, he slyly remarked that he hoped his friend's cook did not have gout. He enjoyed the company of the young men of Rome and said they were his pupils in the art of speaking well, while he was their pupil in the art of dining well. We are surprised, however, to find Dolabella, Cicero's worthless son-in-law, in this company. We hardly know whether to interpret his presence as evidence of Cicero's magnanimity or merely as evidence of the decadence at Rome of all the finer feelings. That he could be gracious and civil to one who had so mistreated his beloved Tullia is certainly proof of his great urbanity.

Cicero was not able, however, to maintain this pleasant mask continuously. It did not represent his habitual state of mind. He at times despised himself for falling into ways for which he had so little liking. When writing to some of his trusted friends he did not hesitate to pour forth his grief. He longed to leave Rome, where there was so much that offended him. Since he could not practice his eloquence in the Senate or Forum, his mind became restive. He wished to retire to literary pursuits and the study of philosophy. He wrote that he had more cause to complain of life than to rejoice that he still lived. Whenever he deemed it safe to do so he would return to Tusculum, his favorite country estate.

While at Tusculum Cicero received news of Cato's death at Utica. It was especially tragic because self-inflicted. To Cato's noble but intransigent mind death seemed less destructive of self than a continuation of life under the conditions that confronted him. Cicero was urged by Atticus and others to write a eulogy of their illustrious countryman. His own sentiments prompted him to do so. But the project was fraught with danger lest praise of Cato should give offense to Caesar. By their very natures and by events those two Romans had been made bitter enemies. Cato had opposed Caesar at every turn and had lost no opportunity to utter his relentless hatred. Cicero and Cato, on the other hand, had been in close association during their lives. They were drawn together by their devotion to the Republic and their respect for the same code of honor. It is true, however, that they had not always been in complete harmony. Cato was uncompromising, while Cicero was more pliable, more practical. To Atticus Cicero had written, "Cato speaks and votes as if he were in the Republic of Plato, not in the scum of Romulus."

Their relations had become strained when Cicero, after his return from exile, had destroyed the tribunicial tables which recorded the acts of Clodius, for they were also the record of Cato's administration at Cyprus and Byzantium, of which Cato was justly proud. Cicero attempted to justify his act upon the ground that Clodius, because a patrician, was not a legal tribune and that all his acts were therefore invalid. Cicero considered the adoption of Clodius by a plebeian a subterfuge and nullity. There was much merit in Cicero's argument, but it did not justify his act of violence. He should have had the adoption and election nullified by law. His conduct was another aberration from that orderly legal procedure which he generally championed. Cato therefore had a just complaint. But the later co-operation of Cicero and Cato under the leadership of Pompey had served to mend their estrangement, and Cicero, after Cato's death, felt a deep sense of obligation to his former associate. His usual courage sustained him and he wrote a strong encomium which he entitled, "Cato."

Caesar's reaction to this panegyric is another proof of the great commander's magnanimity and literary inclination. He entered the controversy not with sword but with pen. He wrote a reply which he entitled "Anti-Cato." He had the generosity to praise Cicero while he endeavored to refute his words. It is by such acts as these that Caesar's greatness is proved in spite of his faults. Such magnanimity makes us feel as Cicero felt when Caesar ordered Pompey's statues, which had been pulled down during the civil war, to be erected again: Cicero remarked that by erecting Pompey's monuments Caesar had established his own.

In spite of all efforts, however, Cicero was unable to gain repose. His recollection of former times made him discontented with public affairs. Nor could he be contented at Tusculum, because his happy memories of former life there were a part of his misfortune. He wandered from place to place like a lost soul. He said, in his response to the beautiful letter of consolation which Servius Sulpicius had written him, "There is no Republic now to offer me refuge and a consolation by its good fortunes when I leave my home in sorrow, as there once was a home to receive me when I returned saddened by the state of public affairs; hence I absent myself from both home and forum, because home can no longer console the sorrow which public affairs cause me, nor public affairs that which I suffer at home."

While he was at Puteoli his mind was diverted by a visit from Caesar. The Dictator was evidently not content to leave the orator unattached. While Cicero was flattered by such attention, still he was irked by the call. Caesar was attended by about two thousand soldiers, and Cicero therefore referred to the call not as a visit but a billeting. Cicero was honored and pleased, yet he remarked that Caesar was not such a guest as would prompt one to say, "I shall be glad to see you again when you come this way." But the incident served Caesar's purpose to revive Cicero's interest in public life, for soon thereafter he returned to Rome.

While at the capital he called on Cleopatra. She received him at her villa across the Tiber. The young queen had come to Rome after Caesar's Egyptian campaign in order to devote her time and attention to her lover, Julius. The interview with Cicero was not a pleasant one. Cicero complained afterward of Cleopatra's imperiousness when he wrote of the incident to Atticus. The ex-Consul was a thoroughgoing Roman and did not like the growing influence of this Egyptian woman any more than he liked the haughty manners of the Asiatics, Spaniards, and Gauls, who strutted about the Forum. Her seductive beauty, her blue eyes that matched her ever present amethyst ring, her golden hair (which marked her as a Macedonian and not an African), her soft voice, left him cold; and evidently the royal lady was no more impressed by the old commoner who had become Consul. He had asked for some valuable old books which had been saved from her Alexandrian library, and although she had promised to send them, she sent instead some Milesian tales which, as intended, shocked Cicero's sense of propriety. It was a jest he could not appreciate. Neither felt complimented by the experience. They had nothing in common. Their outlook on life was from opposite poles. He was rational; she was artful. His dependence was in the mind; hers in personal appeal. His ratiocinations, his studied phrases, were but affectation to her. She was unmoved by them. Her haughty manner was to him but mere superciliousness; her erotic ways were to him exotic. He should not have gone to see her. His curiosity and intellectual vanity misled him. The accomplishments of each were lost on the other. He stooped but did not conquer. She would not stoop. Each retained an unpleasant memory of the meeting. But the incident affords a striking contrast between the old Roman and the daughter of the Nile, between the Roman statesman and the Egyptian dynast, between the laborer in the law and the lady of intrigue.

Such was the meeting between the man to whom Byron referred as "Rome's least mortal mind" and the woman of whom Shakespeare said, "Age can not wither, nor custom stale, her infinite variety."

Cicero was painfully conscious at this time of a desire to do all that he could for the republicans who were still in exile. Because he had formerly been their confederate he was now diligent in his efforts to relieve their misfortune and obtain for them Caesar's favor. Some historians seem to think that this activity on Cicero's part was prompted by fear and remorse. They think he was uneasy so long as any of the republican leaders were at large and unattached to the government at Rome. It is only just, however, to attribute this conduct to Cicero's deep sense of loyalty, the lawyer's essential virtue. That Cicero had this virtue is made manifest again and again throughout his entire life. Cicero was deeply sensitive to any charge of disloyalty. Probably the only letter in his voluminous correspondence that shows intense anger and stern resentment is his reply to a letter from Fadius Gallus reproaching him for forgetfulness of former services. Cicero had suffered too much for his friends, clients, and the Republic to brook such insinuations. Through his zeal and devotion so many republicans had been restored to their positions in Rome, at the risk of his own, that he thought his loyalty was established beyond question. His inclination to serve them was so well known that the republicans came to feel that they had a right to command his services, not merely ask for them.

Cicero's effort in behalf of one of these militant republicans was the occasion of a great forensic triumph. It was one of the greatest tributes ever given to his ability as an advocate. Ligarius had been indicted for bearing arms against Caesar in the African campaign. He had stuck to the republican cause after most of its champions had been killed or had retired. Cicero had written to him to mollify his attitude toward Caesar and had represented Caesar as disposed to clemency. He had also interviewed Caesar in behalf of Ligarius, but because of the excessive and obstinate character of the activity of Ligarius, Caesar was firm and relentless. In spite of Caesar's attitude, however, Cicero undertook the defense. It was a matter of no little delicacy to defend Ligarius against a charge which bore so many implications to himself. When Caesar heard that Cicero had undertaken the case he said, "I have already made up my mind as to the guilt of Ligarius. He is clearly a bad man and my enemy. But why should we not give ourselves the pleasure of hearing Cicero speak again?" He therefore attended the trial and presided as judge.

There was no dispute as to the facts. The case permitted nothing but an appeal for mercy, and such an appeal was never more dexterously made. Cicero cited his own pardon as proof of the goodness and mercy of the presiding judge, and asked for his client the same clemency that had been extended to himself:

All that I have said I have addressed to your humanity, your clemency, your compassion. I have pleaded many causes, Caesar, and some with you as my co-counsel, when you were paving the way to your future honors by practice in the Forum; but never did I adopt this tone for my client: "Pardon him, judges; he has erred; he is guilty; he did it unwittingly; if ever again." That is the language to be addressed to a parent, but to a court of justice this: "He did not do it; he never contemplated the act; the witnesses are forsworn; the charge is false." Tell me, Caesar, that you are sitting as a judge to try Ligarius on the question of fact, ask me in whose garrison he was found—and I am at once silent. I care not to plead in excuse that which might perhaps avail, even with a judge: "He went there as a lieutenant before the war. He was left in the province during the continuance of peace. He was taken by surprise when war broke out; he showed no animosity while it lasted—even then he was in his heart, and in his wishes, on your side." Such would be the line of defence before a judge; but I am speaking as to a parent: "I have sinned; I acted unadvisedly; I am sorry for my fault; I throw myself upon your mercy; I ask pardon for my offence; I pray you to forgive me." If no one had obtained forgiveness from you, it would be presumption for me to ask it; but if very many have, then you, having encouraged hope, should likewise bestow favor.

Caesar was greatly moved by Cicero's appeal. The orator's pathos and irresistible charm caused the judge's face to color. It was evident that his mind was torn by conflicting emotions. And when the orator touched on the battle of Pharsalia, Caesar was so affected that he actually trembled and let some papers fall from his hand. Ligarius was acquitted. The conqueror was conquered by eloquence.

The incident seems to prove, as Cicero had asserted, that Caesar had a hearty respect for superior mental attainments. It serves to refute the charge that Caesar's generous attitude toward genius was nothing more than a desire to have a brilliant court, a wish to be surrounded by brilliant followers. Caesar's change of mind toward Ligarius was a sincere tribute to Cicero's ability. It was also another instance of Caesar's far-seeing statesmanship. His magnanimity toward his republican opponents was a definite policy. After the Battle of Pharsalia he declared that he would not imitate Sulla. There would be no proscriptions. "Let us," said he, "introduce another way of conquering and seek our safety in clemency." To those who promptly sought pardon, it was freely given. As Cicero said, he triumphed over victory. It was only the prolonged obstinacy of some of his enemies that made Caesar cruel. When his proffers of peace were spurned he became merciless. He declared that those who would not lay down their arms should be put to death. It was this determination on his part and the desperation of his active enemies that led to the terrible massacre of the Battle of Munda.

Cicero's counsel against such desperate strife had been unceasing. He labored diligently to bring the opponents together. To those who supported exile too courageously he wrote in high praise of Caesar and of the conditions at Rome, and begged them out of consideration for their families to allow him to ask for their recall. On the other hand, when suppliants for Caesar's favor exhibited too servile an eagerness, Cicero with infinite tact would prompt dignity and self-respect. For those who properly asked pardon he interceded. He went to see Caesar and Caesar's friends. He feared that he would weary them with his applications. He was generally successful, however, for Caesar was anxious to draw him and his friends into the support of the government at Rome.

Cicero's greatest achievement in behalf of the exiles was no doubt his obtaining of pardon for the former consul Marcellus whom Caesar really had much reason to dislike. A prolonged negotiation was necessary both with Caesar and with Marcellus. Cicero conducted the negotiations with tact and skill. When his efforts were finally crowned with success—a success that had seemed so remote—he was delighted. His joy was so great that he again broke his resolution to be silent. He delivered his famous *Pro M. Marcello* in the Senate. For this oration also he has been both praised and censured. It has been referred to as the perfection of eloquence and as base flattery. Considering the character and customs of the times, the language does not seem greatly excessive. The praise which he spoke was mild compared with the flatteries heard daily. Many of the remarks are not as forthright and plain as we should expect today, but still, in view of the courtesies and deference shown by Caesar, we cannot say that Cicero's remarks were insincere. The speech was not an affectation for a special occasion or a sinister purpose. He was truly overjoyed by the prospects of peace. He said in a letter to one of his friends that the day seemed so glorious to him that he thought he saw the Republic rise again. The speech, moreover, was not all praise. Cicero had the courage to utter some plain truths and offer some sound advice. While he acknowledged that Caesar had done much to gain the admiration of men, he urged him to do a little more to deserve their praise.

The conduct of Cicero as well as the conduct of Caesar was prompted by principles of sound statesmanship. Cicero was not actuated by remorse and a desire for personal safety. Neither was Caesar motivated by vainglory and the mere desire to bring his enemies into subserviency. Their conduct was prompted by a sincere hope that a firm government might be re-established at Rome. Cicero was not unmindful that even the republicans had found it necessary to establish Pompey as Dictator in order to preserve some semblance of civil government prior to Caesar's return from Gaul. Nor could Caesar forget the terrible conditions he found in Rome after it had been abandoned by Pompey, the consuls, and the senators. The moment control had been relaxed, the mobs broke loose. Civilians hid themselves in their houses, knowing that they would be killed if they should be seen. Women had their clothing torn from them in the streets. They fled to the temples, where their hopeless moaning could be heard, and children wandered aimlessly about the city. The most terrible crimes went unpunished. All those men whose sensibilities were wounded by such sad spectacles were anxious to create a strong and durable government. They were not concerned about the kind of government; any authority that could give security to life and property would be welcome. The exploits of the conqueror of Gaul were the only accomplishments in recent years that Romans could look to with pride. It was natural, therefore, that those concerned for Roman honor should turn to Caesar as the source of relief. The devolution which delivered Rome to a Dictator had been accomplished before Caesar assumed control.

Caesar was not permitted to live long enough to demonstrate what kind of government he would have established. But his conduct after Pharsalia indicates a clear desire to draw nearer to the republican party. He was not satisfied with the adventurers who had flocked to his standard. He desired men who could command respect. He did not show that repugnance for liberty which is so often instinctive in hereditary princes. He respected the free institutions of Rome. Caesar not only recalled the exiles; he encouraged them to take part in public affairs. He gave commissions in the government to prominent members of the republican party. He made Cassius his lieutenant. Brutus was made governor of Cisalpine Gaul, and Sulpicius proconsul of Achaia. Caesar not only provided for participation in public affairs; he encouraged public discussion. He knew the enervating effect on the commonweal of indifference to politics. He and Cicero shared a common desire to preserve public life and nurture civic interest. Cicero wrote of the period following Caesar's ascendancy: "We enjoy here a profound calm; I should prefer, however, a little honest and salutary agitation; I see that Caesar is of my opinion."

It was not absurd or base for Cicero to attempt a compromise between Caesar and freedom. It was quite natural for him to expect, as he said, that one who had been so clement and generous to individuals would not be wanting in liberality to his country. However thin the hope of accomplishment might have been, so long as there was no other hope it was commendable of Cicero to make the most of it and to encourage Caesar to its fulfillment. The course of a demagogue and soldier of fortune like Antony, who gave himself up entirely to the conqueror, is easily understood; and the course of an uncompromising patriot like Cato, who resisted obstinately, is also easily understood; but the course of Cicero, a middle course, is easily misunderstood. If Cicero, at a time when some despotism was inevitable, was honestly trying to revive free institutions, then his conciliatory attitude toward Caesar does not seem so abject. It is but another instance of his general devotion to peace and order. He at all times was frank about his preference for the balanced government of the Republic. But when that balance was lost, he tried to be expedient about its restoration. Expediency is always necessary in politics, because government is itself a compromise between ideals and actuality. If one is firm and forthright about his ideals, it is not base to temporize and negotiate for their acceptance. Cicero's conduct exemplifies the precept of Protagoras that one should always support the law when it is attacked. Even the intransigent Cato had said that any government was better than anarchy.

Whether the usual cycle of governments could have been arrested or retarded if Caesar had lived longer and he and Cicero had been drawn into closer co-operation is a question which history does not answer. Although man's hope is perennial, his efforts against that cycle seem futile. History creates the impression that it is inevitable. It seems almost as irresistible as the cycle of the solar system, a veritable cosmic tendency which no man nor party can fight against with any chance of success. Rome had had her kingdom, her tyranny, her republic, and the Republic had slipped into democracy and anarchy, and then came the Dictatorship and Empire (or kingdom). Whether by the united efforts of Caesar and Cicero the course of events could have been reversed, the Republic restored, is quite doubtful. Man's progress is never so abrupt as that. The undulations of change are never arrested. Evolution is accomplished by the gradual increase of the surge and decrease of the backwash. Both the high and the low watermarks of civilization are gradually elevated, but the waves or cycles of change do not stop. Improvement is detected only in distant perspective. The efforts of one man or one generation are always discouraging. It seems that society at large learns only by experience, its own experience. There is always enough variation in the circumstances and enough selfishness in individuals to prevent one generation from profiting by the experience of preceding generations. Those who reason are few and their influence is slight. Caesar and Cicero even together could not have done much. The force of events that had created the need of autocratic power at Rome served also to maintain it. Caesar, having taken hold, could not have let go, for fear of a return to the horrible conditions which had immediately preceded his rule.

That condition, however, did not induce the republican leaders to support autocratic government. The Empire could not be firmly established as long as men lived who had known the Republic. Romans still yearned for the conditions which they had been unable to maintain. Those who at the reign of terror had desired only life and peace, now wanted more. They began to lament their lost liberty. Although they had honors and offices, they grieved for the freedom of the Republic. Not only the governors of the provinces, who were appointed by Caesar, but also the officers elected by the people felt the necessity of conforming their conduct to the will of one man. They resented this feeling of restraint. In spite of the public security which had been gained under Caesar's rule, those who had been leaders under the former order could not now be content. The very favors which they received oppressed them. They could not enjoy what they had for lamenting over what they lacked. The exercise of freedom has a lasting attraction. It cannot be forgotten after it has once been enjoyed.

Tusculan Villa and Literary Work

The discontent at Rome of course affected Cicero. In spite of all efforts, the feeling of dependence oppressed him as it did the other republicans. Although he had praised Caesar's clemency and rejoiced over the return of Marcellus as a sort of restoration of the Republic, he soon changed his mind. His correspondence reveals an increasing bitterness. He became a victim of the very feelings which he condemned in others. When he censured others because "after having disarmed their hands they did not disarm their hearts," he indicted his own emotions. His gratitude for Caesar's clemency gradually turned to resentment because he felt humiliated by it. Cicero preferred his memories of the glorious past to any participation in the compromising conditions of the present. He liked retirement at his villa better than activity in Rome. He wrote from his Tusculan estate, "Rome has no longer any attraction for me; I am happy only here. This is the only spot where I am quite content with myself." When he felt that he had appeased his critics, he spent his days there in study, in cultivating his domains, and in praising the simplicity of former times.

Cicero's Tusculan villa had formerly belonged to Sulla. It was a place of some pretensions before Cicero acquired it, and he had made extensive improvements. He constructed a library which contained many valuable manuscripts; and a gymnasium which was supplied with water from the near-by aqueduct. The home contained many rare pieces of furniture, Greek statues, and other ornaments which he had acquired in his travels or had received from friends abroad.

The order of his living there has been preserved in his letters. In the morning he would attend to his extensive correspondence. He had to write not only to his numerous friends, but to and for his numerous clients whose affairs were pending before officers of state and provincial governors. Even his business letters received critical attention; they are noted for their literary style. With professional patience he yielded to all importunities and declined no opportunity to be of service to friend, client, or servant. But when he had to give attention to his own affairs, he complained of the annoyance which his property caused him. After such work he would receive in the atrium those visitors and clients whose affairs demanded personal attention. When these had departed he would enter his library and spend happy hours in reading and writing.

With the approach of evening he sought the refreshment of the bath, which was a thing of great importance to the cultured Greek and Roman. Cicero had made elaborate provision for it in his home, because he deplored the immodesty of the public bath. He was a man of innate modesty. He had expressed the opinion that "nudity is a beginning of prostitution." Personal dignity was considered an essential part of virtue. For this reason some thought him fastidious. He belonged to that class of Greeks and Romans who did not deny and did not neglect the body. But, on the other hand, they did not humor it or make it the chief concern of life. They accepted it as the temporary habitation of the soul, and they tried to make it a worthy habitation. The body was nourished temperately and exercised moderately in order that it might be kept in health. They recognized that a healthy body afforded the mind the greatest freedom. They groomed the body once each day so that it might be forgotten the rest of the day.

After the bath came the principal repast of the day, and during dinner and for some time thereafter Cicero's attention was devoted to the members of his household, such relatives as were with him after the divorce of Terentia and the death of his daughter Tullia, and to the more intimate guests of the home. At the time of retirement there was imposed upon the entire villa an utter silence, another condition highly esteemed by cultured Greeks and Romans.

Out of his enforced partial retirement from active life came Cicero's great literary masterpieces. His mental energy throughout life was marvelous. In addition to the effort given to current affairs and the composition of his great orations, he wrote a series of essays on oratory, including *De Oratore,* which some able critics consider his greatest literary work, *De Claris Oratoribus,* a history of Roman eloquence, and *De Partitione Oratoria,* an analysis of oratory; he also wrote *De Finibus Bonarum et Malorum,* an inquiry into man's chief good and evil, or theories of ethics; *De Officiis,* dedicated to his son Marcus, on moral duties; *De Amicitia,* his tribute to friendship; *De Senectute,* "the most complete treatise on old age that ever was written"; *De Natura Deorum,* which portrays his conceptions of divinity; *De Legibus,* on laws, and *De Re Publica,* known as *The Commonwealth,* which has been preserved only in part, and other compositions like *Hortensius* which have been lost entirely.

These works prove the value of an avocation in a lawyer's life. It affords the best kind of recreation, and the time spent is not lost. What one gains in one's avocation is carried over into one's vocation and life is given a richer content. Cicero's practice also proves that it is best to make one's avocation as much of an art as possible. Artistic production affords the most complete relief because it gives the freest release to one's spirit. It takes one furthest from the too stern reality of life. In the pursuit of artistic truth one rises above the hurly-burly of life to serene and lasting things. Cicero might have said, as Gladstone said years later, that his rest was a change of work. That work, the accomplishment of his avocation, proves again the value of the by-products of effort. His writings are to many his most valued accomplishment. Cicero himself paid a high tribute to such pursuits as a recreation: "Such studies profit youth and rejoice old age; while they increase happiness in good fortune, they are in affliction a consolation and a refuge; they give us joy at home and they do not hamper us abroad; they tarry with us at night and they go forth with us to the countryside." It is not only the merit of these works that moves us to praise; we are stirred to the highest commendation of the spirit that prompted them. That Cicero, after all his disillusionments and sorrows, his disappointments (even with himself), should still have the inspiration and devotion to complete such exalted compositions is proof of faith and fortitude of the most admirable quality.

In view of Cicero's elevated way of life, his devotion to philosophy and literary effort, it is difficult to understand his remarriage late in life. The truth is it was a serious mistake. He soon realized that it was, and promptly did what he could to correct it. The new wife was the daughter of a client who had died, leaving his daughter and her fortune in Cicero's care. Publilia was her name. Terentia, who had also remarried, and to a man considerably younger than herself, said that Cicero took Publilia for her beauty. Cicero's freedman, Tiro, said that he married her for her wealth. It is difficult to believe either statement. It is not likely that a man of Cicero's age and attainments would be beguiled by either beauty or property. Whatever the spell, it did not last long, and we know that Cicero restored to Publilia all her property when he divorced her. It is more probable that Cicero felt the yearning for sympathy and companionship which every sensitive mind must endure. A man of Cicero's wisdom, however, should have known that it was futile to expect a kindred feeling where there was such disparity of ages.

It is not the physical consequences of such disparity that make a happy marriage impossible. Between a man of sixty and a girl in her teens are all the mountains and forests of life and whole oceans of experience. They cannot come to each other in sympathy. Their outlook on life is from opposite poles; one is bright with the health and hope of youth; the other, suffering the aches and disillusionments of age, feels the futility of all things. Publilia's want of sympathy and understanding for Cicero's terrible grief at the time of his daughter's death caused an irreparable estrangement, though they had been married little more than three months. Cicero's grief was not alone for Tullia; it was prompted by all the experiences of life, the unutterable woe of the world. How could Publilia, so young, so full of hope, be expected to understand? And how could Cicero be expected to forgive indifference to grief so profound? But these questions do not explain what prompted the unfortunate venture. Charity impels us, however, to remember how few philosophers have regulated their lives by their precepts. Except in the case of an Epictetus or a Marcus Aurelius, there is generally marked difference between philosophical dissertations and ways of life. Cicero, moreover, was as much artist as philosopher, and some allowance must be made for artistic temperament. It probably best accounts for his belated emotion and delicate sensibility.

Cicero's sorrow over the loss of his daughter was the source of his essay on "Consolation," which has been lost. That essay grew out of the letters which he wrote to himself in an attempt to assuage his grief. But the hopelessness of his grief is disclosed in his statement that, "Even if I could allay it, I would not." The peculiar effect of great love and great sorrow is that they make their victims resent all cures. A cure seems to them at the time worse than the affliction. We may be grateful, however, that Cicero did not allow his sorrow to make him mute, and we are glad to know that the writing of his essay on "Consolation" at least afforded him some distraction. His experience has been a source of comfort to many other sorrowing hearts. He gave expression to some of the noblest aspirations of the soul of man.

The lack of sympathy which Cicero felt in his own home was supplied to some extent by the many expressions of condolence which he received from his numerous and illustrious friends. Among these was the famous letter from Servius Sulpicius, whom Byron referred to in *Childe Harold* as "The Roman friend of Rome's least mortal mind." It comforted the mourner by thoughts regarding the vicissitudes and decay of all earthly things and attempted to drown Cicero's sorrow for Tullia in his sorrow for the Republic. The sentiment "that her life and the life of the Republic passed away together" must have been pleasing though bitter to Cicero, for they were the two objects of his greatest devotion. The exchange of letters between these great Roman lawyers is a high-water mark of the comity and courtesy which have generally prevailed among leaders of the legal profession. It is remarkable that the members of this profession, who are so often required to oppose one another, have generally shown less jealousy and envy than members of other callings. Probably this is true because lawyers give honest expression to their feelings in their contests and thus put all poison out of their hearts and are thereby enabled to show greater charity when occasion requires.

In order to protect his son against current evils, Cicero set before him a practical and well balanced code of conduct. His instructions reveal his own standards for life. Pleasure was not prohibited. The contemplation of beauty and the enjoyment of the senses were recommended, with the admonition, however, that that enjoyment is harmful which must be paid for with pain. He taught his son to respect others and to respect himself, to avoid questionable companions, to avoid the dissipation of his patrimony and the strangling effect of usury, and to honor virtue and innocence and feminine chastity. He cautioned against any attack upon the family or personal reputation of others and against any part in any homicidal project.

Cicero acted as preceptor not only to his own son, but to many of the brightest young minds of Rome. When he retired to his villa at Tusculum they followed him. There he continued to receive them until their visits became an institution, and the record of their conferences became *The Tusculan Disputations*. Cicero was the grand old man of the Republic. By his teaching he aroused in youth an interest in literature, a devotion to philosophy, and a respect for the constitution. The fact that he was a master of oratory, a model in letters, a philosopher and a teacher, enabled him to inculcate his political theories without suspicion.

Cicero translated many of the Greek philosophical works and created Latin terms for many Greek words which formerly had had no Latin synonyms, examples of which are set forth in Plutarch's *Cicero*. Not only did he give the Romans a philosophic and scientific language, he helped to bring to the Romans the spirit of Greek philosophy and culture. The Greek philosophers found their way to the Romans largely through Cicero, just as later generations found their way back to the Greek philosophers through him. He did much to perfect Latin prose and was a source of encouragement to some of the best literary minds of the time. Gaston Delayen implies that Virgil may have been among the visitors to the Tusculan villa. A tall, dark, young man of delicate constitution, shy and reserved in manner, but sincere in character and gentle in disposition; his full name was Publius Virgilius Maro. His *Aeneid* and his *Georgics* have made him one of the world's greatest poets. Some of the sentiments of the *Georgics* may have had their inception in Cicero's discourses on the benefits of agriculture and the contentment to be found in rural life.

These Tusculan conversations afford a pleasing interlude to the general tragedy of Cicero's life. It was gratifying that so many able young men would follow him to the country to enjoy his company and counsel. To them he was a hero of historic forensic engagements, a veteran of great political and military campaigns. He was, moreover, the oracle of a system of government which they cherished with all their hearts. They were deeply worried about the trend of events in Rome, and their groping thoughts needed to be ordered by philosophical analysis and directed by a mind of vision.

The picture of these social visitations is in happy contrast to the cruelty of the political and military conditions of the time. Here we see Roman life at its best. The elderly lawyer-statesman, with his white hair immaculately combed, clothed in flowing senatorial toga, would sit in his favorite chair of heavy marble, and about him the young Romans would repose on marble steps, lean against marble pillars or recline on seats of bronze and rare wood. Around them were the artistic furnishings which Cicero had assembled to decorate his villa. Their conversation would begin with the posing of some philosophical question, such as, "What is the supreme good of life?" or, "Is virtue sufficient for happiness?" But no matter how detached or remote the beginning, soon they found themselves discussing what was uppermost in their minds—the principles of just government and the events of the day. Even these remote and peaceful gatherings became pregnant with tragedy.

As Cicero listened to the passionate expression of the ideals of youth, he would recall with sadness the lost enthusiasm of his own early life and the bitter disappointments of his later career. In historic perspective the world presented a dreary picture—the eternal principles of justice and reason, championed by lonely sages and saints, being ever and anon sacrificed for ephemeral advantage to gratify the pride and passion of men of the world. And then as he caught the enthusiasm of the young men about him, his own heart would swell with renewed hope. What could a man of reason and honor do but follow his ideals? To give in to the ways of the world was the worst form of suicide. Only by adherence to ideals could one hope to transcend the world. And in the lives of the young men before him his principles might yet be realized, or at least advanced toward realization. In the sanctuary of his own home, he was free from fear; in the presence of these serious youths he could drop the jester's mask; his hand could leave his chin; with no self-centered ambition, no personal advantage to gain, he could abandon all hampering thoughts of expediency; and from his own burning zeal he could enkindle in the minds of his young disciples the sacred fire of freedom.

> Of what avail [he would ask] are all our Roman conquests, if we have not freedom of life in Rome? To a person of character, what can compensate for the loss of the right to live according to reason and conscience? We have discussed the things that differentiate us from the animals and other forms of life about us—memory, mind, thought, the power to keep hold on the past, foresee the future, and comprehend the present. This nature which has the power to feel, to know, to create, to invent, to order its existence by an interior principle of life, we hold is heavenly and divine. It is divine because of its godlike properties. And God can only be understood as mind, unbound and free.

Among Cicero's disciples was another notable person, Brutus, the son of Servilia, sister of Cato and paramour of Caesar. He was a youth of fine character and unusual talents. Cicero greatly admired him. Turning to him, Cicero would lament, "You were destined to be the master of the Forum. What a pity that the Republic should be lost to you, and you to the Republic! I deplore the wounds to our liberty!" "Yes," Brutus would reply, "and our forebears believed that we should not endure a tyrant, even if he were our father!"

Here was the inception in thought of that fateful act which wrung from Caesar his last sad words: "And you, Brutus!" Yes, certainly, for in Brutus was the blood that could not endure a dictator. Every conqueror sows dragon's teeth. Caesar must suffer the proverbial fate of those who live by the sword.

UNDER SECOND TRIUMVIRATE

The assassination of Caesar caused conflict and confusion not only in Rome but throughout the Roman world. His death dissipated all civil discipline. His personality had been the magnetic force that held the parts of government together. But the master hand of Rome performed its last act when it drew the folds of its toga over the dictator's face to shut out the sight of Brutus's treachery. When Caesar fell, the government broke into fragments. The military forces that had conquered the world for Rome then engaged in internecine struggle to conquer Rome for themselves. The senators who had not participated in the assassination were struck dumb with horror and retired to their private estates for safety. The populace, in a frenzy of emotion, first followed the assassins. They were led by Brutus, with the cap of liberty on a bloody sword, acclaiming the restoration of the Republic. But, after they heard the reading of Caesar's will and Antony's flamboyant speech, they turned against the murderers of their benefactor. They seized brands from Caesar's funeral pyre, fired the building where he had been murdered, burned the houses of the conspirators, and in the streets tore to pieces citizens who happened to bear the family name of any of the assassins.

Cicero was not a member of the conspiracy. The conspirators, though they had the greatest regard for Cicero and the utmost confidence in his principles as a republican, had concealed the conspiracy from him. When they considered the inclinations of men to determine whom they could trust, they excluded Cicero because of his age and because of his general opposition to violence. Although Cicero had inveighed against the despotic conditions, he had generally spoken of Caesar as gracious and courteous. He knew too much to blame one man for the conditions which he deplored.

There is no doubt, however, that after the murder Cicero approved the act. Not only did he approve; he exulted. He so rejoiced over the prospect for restoration of the Republic that he not only condoned the crime, he acclaimed the conspirators. His gratitude to Caesar as friend had become submerged in his detestation of Caesar as despot. Even though at times men may concede autocratic power to be necessary, still they soon detest the man by whom it is exercised. In one of his letters at this time Cicero wrote, "Though everything goes wrong, the Ides of March console me. Our heroes have done gloriously and nobly." In another letter he wrote, "Our saviors will always be illustrious, blessed in the consciousness of their act."

It seems that Cicero's only regret was that Antony had not also been killed. He understood better than the conspirators the dangerous propensities of that demagogue. He was Caesar's chief military commander, and Cicero knew he would use his power for selfish and evil ends. The conspirators had thought that the people would acclaim them for having destroyed a tyrant and would support them in their efforts to restore the Republic. Cicero, however, was not so sure of the support of the masses. He had learned by sad experience that the body politic was fickle and corrupt. The people were careless of the fate of the constitution. They wanted free grain and extravagant shows.

Cicero exerted his utmost influence to draw the leaders of the people into co-operation for the establishment of order and a balanced government. He knew that it was as futile to blame or to hope to change the people as it would be to blame or to attempt to change the weather. He knew that society acted only through leaders; that leadership was necessary for social order. But those who should have been leaders had grown corrupt, and their corruption had made them selfish and fearful. Rome had lost her character. It was too late for reason. Although Cicero gave sound advice, the men in the positions of leadership lacked the courage to follow it. That his advice was not followed is proof that the destiny of Rome was fixed. He told Brutus and Cassius that they, as praetors, should promptly summon a meeting of the Senate and assume control. The consuls were, of course, the proper officers to convoke the Senate, but one of them was dead and the other fled when Caesar was murdered. If the praetors had acted promptly and firmly, Antony could have been prevented from staging Caesar's funeral so effectively. The praetors could have assumed sufficient authority to act in such an emergency if they had had the courage. With the support of a courageous Senate government might have been stabilized and with the support of virile citizens the Republic restored. The conspirators, however, temporized, the Senate deferred, and Roman citizens were submerged into an emotional mob.

Although Cicero spoke publicly in favor of a general amnesty and declared that the acts and orders of Caesar should be confirmed by the Senate, yet when the conspirators asked him to endeavor to persuade Antony to come forward as a defender of the Republic, he declined. He knew that such an arrangement would be merely the installation of another tyrant. He was too familiar with Antony's character to place any trust in him. He said frankly that no reliance could be placed in Antony, even if he professed the cause of the Republic. Cicero tried diligently, however, to avoid unnecessary affront to Antony. He realized the conditions and was aware of all the dangers. He therefore tried to avoid Antony's open opposition. His public utterances were at first conciliatory. He wrote complimentary letters to Antony and made concessions at Antony's request, but all his efforts were useless.

When Antony found his life was safe he began at once to play for the favor of the people, and advanced in rapid strides. The conspirators, instead of assuming the control, as directed by Cicero, also played for popular favor, but were outplayed by Antony. Through sheer audacity he then assumed the authority which the conspirators and the Senate had declined to exercise. He seized the reins of government which Caesar had dropped and took possession of the treasury. He paid his private debts with Caesar's money and made lavish expenditures of public funds to pander the people. With the co-operation of Caesar's secretary, Faberius, he forged edicts and decrees to make it appear that his plans were in accord with Caesar's will. In order to gain military support he made an alliance with Lepidus, who was in command of a detachment of Caesar's veterans near Rome. He gave his daughter in marriage to the son of Lepidus and promised Lepidus the office of Pontifex Maximus, which had become vacant at Caesar's death. He next usurped the governorship of Cisalpine Gaul in order to get control of the military forces there. With that army he knew he would be master of Rome. In spite of the fact that Caesar had named Brutus as governor of that province and that Caesar's appointment had been confirmed by the Senate, he appealed to the people and obtained their confirmation of his own appointment, quite contrary to the constitution, which conferred upon the Senate the authority of naming provincial governors.

But Antony's course was not unopposed. His usurpation

of power was severely challenged. His chief opponents were Decimus Brutus and Octavius. They, however, were not united and there were, therefore, three contestants for the dominating position. Brutus treated Antony's appointment and the confirmation by the people as invalid and prepared to hold control of Gaul by the sword. Octavius was the grandson of Caesar's younger sister Julia, and Caesar's will gave him three-fourths of the decedent's property and declared an intention to adopt him as heir. The will did not attempt to direct the succession to Caesar's political power, but Octavius, in spite of his extreme youth, made claim not only to his grand-uncle's property but to his position. Many of Caesar's veterans rallied round Octavius, called him Gaius Caesar, and urged him to avenge his uncle's death. With this following, the young man hastened to Rome to take possession of his inheritance and assume his uncle's influence. Quite naturally he had to oppose Brutus and the other men who had assassinated his uncle, and otherwise his position made him at first a bitter rival of Antony. Brutus, Cassius, and their confederates naturally resented the claims of Octavius because they were champions of the Republic and did not wish to see Caesar's autocracy continued. Antony at first also opposed Octavius. He disputed the adoption of Octavius by will and asserted that the property bequeathed by Caesar was a part of the treasury of the state, although, as we have seen, he had not hesitated to use it freely for his own personal needs.

This was the conflict that confused and confounded Rome. The conspirators, through suspicion of one another, were unable to complete their plans for the reestablishment of constitutional government. The Senate was without courage, and divided into factions. The consuls-elect were opposed by the ex-consul Antony. Antony's legions were besieging Decimus Brutus in one of the chief towns of Gaul. Every province was divided into parties, and the contenders for control there, as in Rome, bid against one another for popular favor, for support of legions, and for the influence of pro-consuls. Couriers from distant provinces could not travel to Rome without being intercepted and robbed of their messages. All the functions of the state were corrupted by fear, suspicion, and intrigue.

That was the setting of the stage for the last act of Cicero's public life. With forlorn hope he again came out of his retirement and offered his counsel and services for the re-establishment of constitutionalism in Rome. By the force of his own personal influence he persuaded the Senate and the consuls to oppose Antony's plans. It is easy to understand why he would oppose Antony more actively than he had opposed Caesar. In the world of thought, of letters, and of principles of decorum, Cicero and Caesar had been congenial. They entertained mutual disdain for mean conduct. Although Cicero found it difficult to maintain his complacency during the last years of Caesar's autocracy, still he recognized in Caesar a skillful politician, an able administrator, a soldier of the first rank, a statesman. But Caesar's nobleness, refinement of taste, and commanding intellect were wholly wanting in Antony. Cicero could make no compromise with such a coarse and unprincipled mountebank. He therefore opened a campaign against Antony and delivered or published fourteen orations, known at the time as *Orationes Antonianae,* but subsequently known as the "Philippics."

In these virulent speeches he declared Antony a traitor and a public enemy, and opposed all suggestions that the Senate should treat or negotiate with him. He called Antony's activity an insurrection (*tumultus*) and resented any reference to it as a war (*bellum*). He pilloried Antony as an unprincipled politician and a disgusting debauchee. "I again assert," he said in the seventh oration, "that I who have always been the panegyrist and counselor of peace, am against peace with Antony." To him Antony was the personification of the arbitrary forces that would destroy the established order and free institutions. His slogan was, "No peace with Antony." "We have stood against the weapons of traitors," he said, "but we still must wrest those weapons from their hands. If we cannot do this," said he, "I will speak as becomes a senator and a Roman—let us die."

Cicero did not confine his invective to Antony but, when occasion presented, extended it also to Antony's wife, the former wife of Clodius. Antony, in one of his feeble replies, attempted to discredit Octavius, whom the Senate was inclined to support in opposition to him, by a slighting reference to the mother of Octavius as a provincial. Cicero seized the opportunity to influence the senators more strongly against Antony. He called attention to the fact that nearly all the senators had sprung from provincial stock, and in that connection he referred to Antony's wife, Fulvia, as the daughter of a nobody from Tusculum, whom the natives referred to as Bambolio—a booby, a dunce.

While most of the orations were given over to invective, there were in some of them very fine expressions of exalted sentiments and noble opinions. In the first oration, which shows the most restraint, he declared that he had lived long enough, both as to age attained and glory acquired. If life were prolonged, he said, it would afford no advantage to himself but only an opportunity for service to the state. The sincerity of that sentiment, coming from one of Cicero's years, experience, and avowed principles, can hardly be doubted. In noble phrases Cicero defended the constitution and the law, the dignity of the Senate, and the sanctity of government. He exposed the futility of that selfishness which sacrifices the public weal for personal gain. He thundered against the traitors to the Republic and called attention to the fact that they had all been his enemies. He tried to animate the Senate and people to dare everything for the sake of their country. In the last oration, the last that he ever delivered, so far as we know, is his beautiful apostrophe to soldiers who die for their country.

His sincere admiration for the devotion of soldiers, however, did not deter him from denouncing the Senate's abject fear of Caesar's veterans. Nearly every measure that had been proposed for the advantage of Brutus and Cassius and the other champions of the Republic was opposed by the reiteration of grave apprehensions as to its effect upon the soldiers. While the opposing military leaders were bribing the veterans for their support, the senators were inactive through fear of displeasing them. When it was proposed that Brutus should be given the command of the republican legions, Cicero frankly admitted that such an appointment would be distasteful to Caesar's followers. But he called upon the Senate to perform its duty to the Republic regardless of the wishes of the army. What is meant, he asked, by always bringing up the thought of the veterans? He was ready to praise their valor and good conduct, but he would not brook their arrogance or assumption of unwarranted power. When we are endeavoring to break the chains of slavery, he asked, shall we be stopped because our conduct is displeasing to the veterans? Are there not thousands of others who would take up arms to defend the common cause of liberty, whom a noble indignation impels to cast off the yoke of slavery? Let us say what is true and what is right.

If the members of this august body are to be dominated by the fear of soldiers and all our words and actions regulated by what pleases them, it would be better to choose death, which Roman citizens have always preferred to servitude. Let us concede the point, said he, that the issue of war is uncertain and fortune fickle, still we must fight for liberty even at the hazard of our lives. Life is not mere breath—it has no existence in a slave. How long, he asked in conclusion, are we to deliver our opinions to please the veterans? Is their arrogance such that we must select our generals at their dictation?

If the Senate had shown the courage, character, and devotion to the state which Cicero expounded and exemplified, the Roman Empire and the world at large might have been spared the later disgrace of having the imperial throne sold by the Praetorian Guard at public auction.

The energy and courage of Cicero at this time were remarkable. In spite of his excessive invective he was grander in this last year of his life than ever before. He was the very soul of the opposition to autocracy. He represented the moral order—Antony the will to power. As between Caesar and Pompey, Cicero had had doubts. But now all doubts were gone. The issue was between law and license. His course was clear, his duty manifest. There now could be no compromise. If Antony were not destroyed he would destroy the liberties of Romans. The last of Cicero's vital energies were devoted to the safety and freedom of his countrymen. He gave his life to that cause.

But before the end of Cicero's life three things happened to remind him of his former glory. It seems that Providence must have pitied him for the fate that awaited. It allowed him to experience again his success as quaestor, his return from exile, and his grand triumph as consul. These three experiences came to pass in this way. When

Cicero had seen the trend of things following the death of Caesar, he at first determined to take refuge again in Greece. Mindful of his age, he felt that the destiny of Rome should be left to younger men. He sailed from Pompeii and stopped at Sicily. There he was warmly welcomed by the citizens of Syracuse, who still honored him for the justice and humanity of his quaestorship. While he was in Sicily, however, he received word from Rome that indicated a favorable attitude on Antony's part toward the Republic. He thereupon abandoned his plan to go to Greece, a plan which had never been free from misgivings. Upon his return to Rome, the citizens, whose appreciation of him had always grown with his absence, were so cordial and demonstrative that he said his reception reminded him of his glorious return from exile. But soon thereafter the hope of Antony's favor had been dispelled. That soldier of fortune was found in the military alignment against constitutional Rome. Then came news of the Battle of Mutina. The victory of the republican forces was exaggerated in the reports, and the populace was overjoyed. They marched to Cicero's house and asked him to accompany them to the Capitol to return thanks for the victory. As he traveled again along the Via Sacra with the jubilant throngs, he experienced again the triumph of his consulship when he was proclaimed "Pater Patriae." These events were fresh in his mind when he said, during the delivery of the Philippics, that his life had had enough, both of years and of honors.

Cicero was not deceived, however, by the news of Mutina. He cautioned the people against overconfidence. He said the war was not won if Antony was at large. He encouraged them to renew their efforts for a continuation of the struggle, asserting that no sacrifice was too great for their noble cause. While the struggle lasted, Cicero devoted his efforts day and night to the encouragement of senators, consuls, and people. He strove diligently to incite Brutus and Cassius to more effective activity and he labored to bring all the forces of the Senate, the consuls, and the conspirators into harmony of operation under the control of a strong central government. He wrote to his friend Pollio in Spain and to his friend Plancus in Gaul and entreated them to stand by the Senate and hold their legions in readiness to oppose Antony. In order to offset Antony's appeal to the veterans and friends of Caesar, Cicero was forced to favor the cause of Octavius and tried to bring him into co-operation with those who championed the constitution.

Cicero had grounds for hope. Octavius had lived with his stepfather near Cicero's villa at Puteoli and, while neighbors, they had become friends. Octavius had always shown Cicero the greatest respect and deference. It was quite natural for Cicero to sponsor his cause against that of Antony. Cicero encouraged him in his efforts to levy troops and spoke of him in high praise to the Senate. He became his sponsor in the fullest measure in order to bring the Senate to his support and to prevent him from making common cause with Antony. Cicero proposed that Octavius be invested with military command and allowed to sit in the Senate as a pro-praetor. To the objection that Octavius was under legal age Cicero replied that his excellence had anticipated the march of years. When some doubt was expressed as to whether Octavius would always be faithful to the Republic, Cicero replied that true glory consisted in the esteem of the Senate and the respect of the people, and that no man who enjoyed that would yearn for other glory. He pledged his sacred honor to the Senate and the Roman people that Octavius, whom he now referred to as Gaius Caesar, would always be such a citizen as he then was. Cicero staked all on this young man—and lost. He misplaced his trust. The conditions at the time, however, not only warranted but required some reliance in Octavius. Cicero paid for his mistake with his life.

While Cicero was laboring to bring the support of the Senate to the cause of Octavius, he in turn was doing all he could to make the Senate unpopular with his army. The personal ambition of Octavius proved greater than his love for the Republic. The thought that he was Caesar's adopted son swelled his ambition to inordinate proportions. He was bitterly aggrieved by the Senate's appointment of Brutus as commander of the army in Italy. The fact that he was looked to as avenger of his uncle's death prevented his entering into cordial relations with Brutus and the other conspirators. Whether he really hated them or merely feigned a hatred, it is impossible to tell. It is probable that one so lacking in permanent principle held all such feelings in subjection to his selfish ends. He demanded of the Senate that he be elected a consul in spite of the fact that he had attained hardly half the required age. When the Senate refused its consent to this plan, he turned against the Senate's cause. It no doubt seemed to him that if he co-operated with the senatorial party to crush Antony, he would thereby strengthen the republican forces and would make it more difficult to establish himself in autocratic power. If, on the other hand, he joined Antony, he might share the chief power for a while even if he could not enjoy it alone, and in time might dispose of Antony.

Pollio and Plancus, in spite of their previous assurances to Cicero, like Lepidus, went over with their legions to Antony. Treason to the commonwealth was in the air that Romans breathed. They considered only their selfish ends.

Devotion to the Republic was dead. While the Senate under Cicero's direction was mustering all available forces in order to place an army in the field under the consuls-elect, and while Brutus was training his new recruits, Octavius abandoned Cicero and the Senate, and entered into negotiations with Antony. Antony, the enemy of all legal authority, depicted Cicero to his followers as a master of gladiators, trying to pit two armies of the same country against each other. In order to deflect Octavius and his followers from the senatorial party, he had invited negotiations for a triumvirate.

As soon as Octavius had arrived at an understanding with Antony and Lepidus, he turned his forces against Rome. The Senate had under its command only two legions of infantry which it had recently brought over from Africa. Octavius had under his command eight legions of infantry and some seasoned cavalry. The Senate, moreover, had bartered away its influence. It had nothing left with which to appease the soldiers' greed for gold and lust for power. Corruption had sapped its strength. The supreme power had passed from the Senate to the military commanders. Rome was no longer greater than the greatest Roman. Cicero had cried out with his whole soul, "Let audacity yield to authority!" But there was no authority. The character which had given the ancient government its authority had been undermined. Loyalty to authority was superseded by jungle instincts. Force and deception had supplanted reason and conscience. Octavius entered Rome as a conqueror, and the spineless senators proceeded at once to propitiate their master. They did by compulsion what they had declined to do by negotiation. They made him consul at once in spite of the fact that he was only twenty-one years old. His adoption as Caesar's son was promptly confirmed and approved by the people. The name

"Gaius Julius Caesar Octavianus" was legally established. The Senate then at his dictation repealed the act by which it had declared Antony and Lepidus public enemies.

Octavius, Antony and Lepidus then met on an island in the Reno River near Bologna, and completed the arrangements for the Second Triumvirate. After dividing the dominions of Rome, they proceeded to the dastardly business of preparing their proscription lists. Friends, relatives, and followers were sacrificed with the most ruthless disregard of obligation. Each surrendered victims to satiate the vengeance of the other two. Antony sacrificed his uncle, Lucius Caesar; Lepidus sacrificed his own brother, Paulus, and Octavius gave up Cicero. Historians agree that this was one of the basest compacts ever made. It is a disgrace to humankind. The participants allowed their fury, lust, and fear to deprive them of all the sensibilities by which humanity is distinguished from beasts. The conspiracy for the Second Triumvirate was the crest of that tidal wave of evil which followed the submergence of personal character and constitutional government at Rome.

Antony and Lepidus might have been forewarned of their own subsequent fate by the treachery of Octavius to Cicero. But, dazzled by the prospect of immediate power, they were blinded to the future. It is easy to condone the sin in others that serves one's selfish purpose. Those whom perfidy presently favors can never see themselves as its ultimate victims. Octavius proceeded at once to plot the destruction of the other two Triumvirs. It was not difficult to reduce Lepidus to a nullity. With the aid of Cleopatra's sinister influence, to which Antony had succumbed while on his campaign against the Parthians, Octavius was enabled to effect the destruction of his chief rival. He then assumed all the important offices of Rome. He became Sole Consul, Pontifex Maximus, Perpetual Tribune of the People. His will was the supreme command. He took the title Augustus. The Empire was established. It was fortunate for society that Octavius was one whom power improved. The performance of his later administration greatly exceeded the promise of its perfidious beginning.

The favors which the Emperor subsequently extended to Cicero's son indicate some inclination to make amends. There is no doubt that he always held the elder lawyer in high regard. Plutarch relates an incident which shows that such regard continued into late life. When the Emperor found his grandson reading Cicero, he commended the author in these words: "A learned man, my boy, a learned man, and a lover of his country." To Augustus and many of the prominent men about him Cicero was the representative of that cultivated influence which came from the commingling of Greek and Roman civilization. The Ciceronian culture of the last days of the Republic became the ideal of the early Empire, the Augustan Age.

But that prospect is beyond the purview of this study. All that remains to be recounted here is the tragic fate of the last champion of the constitution. When the Triumvirate was established, Cicero realized that his cause was lost. He did not remain in Rome to witness the degradation of the Senate. He took no part in its obeisance to Octavius and his confederates. He and his brother Quintus, who had been reunited by common misfortune, fled from the capital. They first sought refuge at Cicero's Tusculan villa. As they traveled toward Tusculum, they gazed back across the campagna to the former capital of the Republic. Quintus lamented the prospect of desolation—their beloved Rome now subject to the complete domination of Octavius, for whom Cicero had pledged his honor only to be betrayed, and of Antony, whom he had denounced as the basest of demagogues! But, while Quintus saw only their blighted aspirations, Cicero was given a more distant vision. His distress was alleviated by that prophetic insight which comes to men who live by eternal principles. He caught the prospect of distant generations, in lands then undiscovered, studying his writings as models of classic literature; the founders of new republics quoting his statements as authority for just government; honorable politicians citing him as a model of decorum; statesmen turning to his compositions for instruction and inspiration; old men, men weary of life's strife, finding comfort in his philosophy; and the legal profession being led by his spirit in the evolution of that beneficent institution, the Law.

That conception of Law, in its eternal struggle against anarchy, had to encompass the world before it returned to Rome. Two thousand years were to elapse before constitutionalism would prevail in the world over despotism. Cicero's triumph—the triumph of his principles—was to occur in A.D. 1944, when the forces of the United Nations returned to Rome a "government not of men—but of law."

Cicero and Quintus tarried but a short time at Tusculum. When news of his proscription reached Cicero, he again set out for Greece. He reached the coast at Astura and took ship, but doubts, fears, and seasickness assailed him, and he turned back. The prospect of foreign lands was not inviting. He wished to die on Italian soil. He thought of going to Rome for the purpose of entering the house of Octavius and committing suicide before the domestic altar in order to bring the vengeance of heaven upon his betrayer. But, after going a short distance, he turned and went to his villa at Formiae. Weary, worn, deserted, and desolate, he sat down to await the end. He knew there was no escape. His household servants learned that a reward had been offered for his head and that his murderers were on the way. With affectionate regard they forced him into a litter and started to carry him again to the shore. Cicero had once taken credit for having made a friend of a slave. His slaves were now his only friends. As he moved along to his unknown destination, he no doubt wondered why all his plans had failed, why unjust men prevail. He was "weary of flight and of life." But he was comforted by the thought that many great and good men had faced a similar fate. Socrates' noble resignation sustained him: "I suppose these things are destined so to be; and I think that it is all for the best."

His pursuers reached the villa soon after Cicero's departure. They were under the leadership of a centurion, Herennius, and the military tribune Popillius Laenas, whose whole family had an ugly reputation for violence and brutality. Cicero had once defended Popillius successfully against a criminal charge of parricide. When the pursuers learned their victim had left, they took up the trail in hot haste. Cicero heard the approaching footsteps and ordered his attendants to put down the litter and seek their own safety. He commanded them not to defend him. When the assassins arrived at his litter he threw back the curtain and put out his head. We can imagine the old lawyer's feelings when he beheld his former client. He burned with contempt for the ingratitude of Popillius, but masked his emotions with characteristic sarcasm. With hand at chin he looked up at the leader of the murderers and asked, "Popillius, have you come to thank me for your acquittal?" That ironic jest was all that remained to set the fatal blow in action. The heavy sword descended, the head and hand were severed.

The lifeless body was left to the faithful servants, who came out of their hiding to possess it. Cicero's heart was buried, as he had wished, in the country he had "so often saved." But the assassins took the head and the hand to Rome. They bore them directly to the Forum. Antony was there, shamming the administration of justice. When he saw the murderers coming, he terminated the proceedings. He could not restrain his delight. He promptly paid the promised reward and gave an additional sum. He carried the head and the hand as a present to his wife, whose hatred was more intense than his own. Fulvia, the plebeian, then exulted meanly. She laid the head upon her lap and addressed it in words of bitterest insult. She took a bodkin from her hair and stuck it through the tongue that had uttered such scorn for her and her husbands. Antony then had the head taken back to the Forum and affixed to the Rostra. A more revolting spectacle Rome had never seen.

That head upon the Rostra is one of the most arresting scenes of history and a most tragic instance of the irony of Fate; that which had been the living head of the Republic was now the death mask of the Republic; that head which had drawn to itself the admiring gaze of multitudes, the praise of Caesar, now an object of loathing and scorn; those eyes that had flashed the light of reason and the glint of humor now dark in death; the lips that had uttered deathless sentences now still in death; that tongue which had been so piercing with its vain jests now pierced by the bodkin of vain revenge; the voice of the law silenced by lawlessness in the law's own Forum; literally and figuratively that head was given to the country that would not accept its counsel. The Forum of Rome had been to it the center of life and the apex of existence; there it wanted to be in life and there it was in death, pilloried for all time on the Rostra of the Eternal City—the head of the eternal lawyer.

Cicero's restless soul continued its quest for the divine

law of which he spoke, the eternal justice, the universal harmony. At last his worldly doubts were all dispelled, his apprehensions quieted. He, as he had said of his daughter, had been permitted to exchange the pain of life for the painlessness of death. He had followed his beloved Tullia and the Republic. The sacrificial victim of the Roman Republic became the high priest of future republics—the inspiration of all those who struggle to maintain the difficult balance of that most equitable form of government.

Qui vivens laedit, morte medetur. While it is true that one who does wrong in life atones for it by death, it is also true that one who suffers in life is comforted by death.

VIII

THE MAN AND HIS PHILOSOPHY

Of Life

What a man is depends on his philosophy of life. And what kind of lawyer a man is depends on his philosophy of law. His temperament and talents are of course part of his make-up and largely affect his action and the reaction of life on him. But his basic character as lawyer, the weight and color of his influence, depend on his idea and ideal of the law, its origin, function and purpose. His conception of the law is affected moreover by his conception of government, his theory of the state, its nature and purpose. And all these ideas, conceptions, and attitudes are controlled in last analysis by his belief as to man's essential nature, his relation to his fellows, and his place and purpose in the world.

A man who has no philosophy of life is hardly a rational being; he is the victim of primitive instincts and impulses. His acts have no consistent plan or conscious direction. Most men have a philosophy, even though it be unannounced. In such case we must discover the man's philosophy by analyzing his acts. But in Cicero's case we can come to his philosophy more directly. He gave it ample expression. Furthermore he gave it exemplification. While the philosopher is usually a man of thought only, Cicero was a man of both thought and action. We therefore can compare his principles and his performances.

Cicero was a success in his own day largely because of

his oratorical talents and psychological perceptiveness, but what makes him great for all time—and particularly for our time—is the fact that he was a seer, a philosopher. Perhaps he lacked the originality and thoroughness of the pure philosophers, the founders of our philosophic systems, but he was that more rare character—a practical philosopher. Certainly he did not lack curiosity and the courage to face all questions. The remarkable thing is that his experience in the harsh and confused world did not submerge him or his principles or destroy his faith in the human race and its reason. The weight of his influence today supports reason in its desperate struggle against force.

Cicero liked to refer to himself as a philosopher. We find such references in his letters, addresses, and essays. He frequently recommended the study of philosophy to his friends, and his gratitude for its consolation is a refrain that runs through all his writings. He quoted philosophers frequently. He said of Socrates, "Surely I should rather have had this man's soul than all the fortunes of those who sat in judgment on him." As lawyer, however, Cicero indulged in no confusion of thought. He recognized the place of positive law as administered by the courts. He defined a practitioner as one who must be "skilled in the laws and the usages of private citizens and trained in giving opinions and bringing actions and guiding his clients aright." But Cicero did not stop there. The thing that distinguishes him as the truly great lawyer is the fact that he recognized a higher law (*summa lex*), the principles of which he considered the science of the just and unjust. It is no great accomplishment to be a master of the formulary and statutory part of law, but it is an accomplishment to be a champion and master of the "science of justice."

Cicero has high standing in that science for having

helped to raise legal knowledge to a broader and higher plane. He said that "the study of law must be derived from the depths of philosophy, and that, by an examination of the human mind and of human society, principles may be discovered in comparison with which the rules of positive law are of but trivial importance." Cicero said repeatedly that justice was the object of the law. Furthermore he listed it as one of the cardinal virtues and said that the harmony of all social relationships was dependent on justice. He quoted Plato to support the statement that knowledge divested of justice deserved the appellation of cunning rather than wisdom. He acknowledged that man's conception of justice depends on his moral code, his fundamental beliefs, his acceptance of standards, duties, and obligations.

Cicero based his philosophy principally on the nature of man and the nature of the cosmos, and it led to a belief in a divine creator. To him all creation was the handiwork of a divine intelligence, and it was designed according to plan and for some good purpose. He ridiculed the assertion that the sky and the earth were formed through the accidental concourse of a number of particles without the intermediation of any organizing principle. He asked ironically, "Why do not those who maintain that the blind swerve of the atoms in the void produced the beauty and the order of the universe also maintain that this blind concourse of atoms produced a temple or a city—things far less elaborate than the order of the universe?" With something of the inspiration of the psalmist he said that only those who had never gazed upon the sky could talk such nonsense. And his views seem to be supported by the great astronomers and physicists of our day, like Millikan, Jeans, and Eddington.

Since the universe was created by an intelligent power

according to some plan and for a good purpose, then to Cicero's mind it followed that there was necessarily a moral order of the universe. He further supported that view by stressing the ornament and beauty of the universe and by reference again to man's inherent nature. To him man's moral nature and free will denied absolutely that man was the victim of blind fate. If everything were subject to an eternal nexus of cause and effect, he argued, then morality would be impossible. Because he thought man the highest order of creation, Cicero held that his welfare was the purpose of creation. To him the excellency of man over all other types of being was apparent from the fact that in addition to a wonderful body man had also a mind. For whose sake, he asks, was the *mundus* formed? For the trees? For animals? No! But for the sake undoubtedly of those animated beings that exercise reason (*quae ratione utuntur*).

In the *Tusculan Disputations* he says: "Not without design nor by chance were we created, but surely there was a power considering the good of the human race; nor would this power produce and nourish a being which, when it had finished its labors, should sink into eternal misery of death. We should rather believe that a haven and a place of refuge have been prepared for us." Cicero was of course too well informed, too philosophic as well as scientific, to be dogmatic about matters as to which there was no positive proof. His religious insight did not submerge the critical attitude. His experience had taught him that truth, in philosophy as in the courts, was not easily discovered, and less easily formulated. But on a number of occasions he affirmed his faith in immortality. As Professor H. M. Poteat suggests, his initiation into the Eleusinian mysteries "planted a seed which later, watered by his tears for Tullia, grew into a noble tree of hope and faith—of which the finest fruit was Book I of the *Tusculan Disputations*." But he also gave expression to that faith in *Pro Archia*, *De Natura Deorum*, *De Amicitia*, *De Senectute*, and *Consolatio*.

Religious practices and ceremonials were of interest to him because of their political importance. As to them he maintained the attitude of the lawyer and statesman of that time. Educated Romans were profoundly skeptical regarding their conglomerate lot of gods, but they did not abandon them. They had always had a bargaining tendency in their *pietas* and they still observed certain ceremonies for the chance of ultimate benefit. To Cicero the *ius divinum* was a part of the *ius civile*, a serviceable portion of state activity in order to maintain a good public spirit and salutary conditions between citizens and deities. He knew that moral standards in man or state do not long survive the abandonment of the religious attitude. Upon that attitude depended the *pax deorum*.

Cicero's personal belief however was derived from Stoic philosophy after it had been softened of some of its asperities by an admixture of Platonism. He was something of an eclectic, borrowing from all the schools, except the Epicurean. But the important fact is that he accepted the Stoic theory of a world-soul, identifiable with Jupiter, the ultimate sanction for law and morality. In his defense of Cluentius he said: "The favor of Heaven may be gained by duty done to God and man, and by righteous prayers, not by base superstition and victims offered for the success of crime."

Is it not remarkable that the culture of Greece and Rome should produce moral and religious opinion so similar to Biblical scriptures? When stripped of all ceremonial, dialectic and mythology, the Hebrew religion, Greek philosophy and the Roman humanities (*humanitas*) teach essentially the same truth. The Christian church drew heavily from all three sources. But is it not sad that the world should be so slow in giving practical application to truth so expounded and so exemplified, with such wonderful promise for a better and happier world?

George Gissing, writing *By the Ionian Sea* in 1900, said he retired for a half-hour to the eucalyptus grove and tried to shape in fancy some figure of old Pythagoras who had died there in 497 B.C. of a broken heart because of the failure of all his efforts to make mankind gentle and reasonable. Such efforts had not made much headway in Cicero's time—nor in Gissing's time. And the world today has suffered the cruelest and most destructive war of all time. Such reflections enable us to understand why Cicero said, "Wisdom is sad—Plato was a sorrowful man."

But the glory of great lives consists not in denial of human depravity but in transcending it; not in ignoring men's proneness to evil but in affirming their potential goodness. Cicero, in spite of the fact that his life was caught in a great retrogression that destroyed the Republic did not allow it to destroy his faith and philosophy.

Of Government

Based upon his observations as to man's nature and his belief in a moral order Cicero constructed his theory of government and man's obligation to the state. Man was by nature sociable. This sociability, said Cicero, is the outcome of what we are, a concomitant of our being. And, said he, it is reason and language that make this sociability possible. Because of the existence of this common tie between all the members of the human race, and because man was the object of creation, the obligation rested upon every human being not only to have a care for his fellows but to spare himself no toil or trouble in his efforts to help others. Failure to promote the universal sociability and well-being he thought a violation of our nature (*repugnante et adversante natura*). It is remarkable how closely his theories approximate the doctrine of charity (*caritas*) of the Christian teachers whom succeeding generations were soon to hear in Rome. No wonder that Erasmus felt that "a divinity inspired the man."

His deliberate observations regarding the nature of society and his theory of the state are found in *De Re Publica,* a treatise written in the form of the Greek dialogue. Though it comes to us in mutilated form, and the opinions are presented as those of the participants, still from the introduction, in which Cicero speaks in his own person, and from the probability that Scipio represents Cicero's own views, we gain a very reliable presentation of the author's persuasions and beliefs. The state (*civitas*) is "an arrangement of the people" for their mutual interests. It acts according to law and custom through its agents, the magistrates, and the deliberative bodies who give form and expression to the popular will.

At the very outset of *De Re Publica* Cicero points out that without a sense of public duty Rome's great generals would not have endured hardships and sacrificed life to save the city from her enemies, nor would her political leaders have ridden the storms and tempests of public opinion to serve the interests of state. As a very theme-note he says: "I content myself with this one assertion: The need and love for noble actions, which nature has given to men that they may defend the commonweal, are so compelling that they have overcome all the enticements of pleasure and of ease." Based upon that fundamental social obligation he built his theory of politics, his philosophy of government.

The phrase *res publica* did not signify a form of government. The phrase is properly translated *Commonwealth,* meaning the affair of the people, the public welfare or commonweal. It is not an artificial creation, said Cicero, but it exists as a part of and an outgrowth from man's very make-up. It is the source and object of government, and indicates the scope of governmental authority. It is conserved by the exercise of justice in the broadest meaning of the word, and requires of every man an unselfish support. The author said that the administration of justice alone justified the state, and acknowledged that various forms of government might serve that end. Although he discussed the various forms and recommended a composite of the simple or basic forms, yet he was concerned more with the underlying philosophy of political life than with political organization.

His work on the *Commonwealth* and on the *Laws* is the only Roman contribution of that period to the philosophy of politics. The Romans were essentially realistic. Although they had extended their government into world dominion by aggression and compromise, and by an aptitude for law and its administration, yet they had shown no enthusiasm for theoretical discussion of the state. But the popularity of Cicero's work indicates that he stimulated a lively interest. It was through Cicero that Greek political theory came to Rome. In his works were the basic principles which influenced the great jurists of the imperial age and the political theorists of the Middle Ages. And his fundamental theory of the state has been accepted by the most profound writers of modern times. Pope Leo XIII said: "The right to rule is not necessarily bound up with any special mode of government. It may take this form or that, provided only that it be of a nature to insure the general welfare."

Cicero recognized three basic forms of government—monarchy, aristocracy, and democracy. He knew however that these forms were not fixed and unchanging, but like everything else in life were in a flux and succession. Each had in it an inherent weakness—monarchy tended to tyranny; aristocracy to oligarchy; and democracy to ochlocracy. He accepted the theory of a natural cycle of governments. When a monarch became a tyrant, the aristocrats expelled him; when the aristocrats became an oppressive oligarchy, they were expelled by revolution and democracy was established; and when democracy degenerated into mob rule or anarchy, a dictator became necessary and monarchy was again established, completing the cycle. This cycle or succession of control was variously phrased by various writers. Cicero knew that the actual succession might not follow so logical a pattern as the statement of the principle; he likened it also to the passing of a ball from one group to another; but he did acknowledge the tendency to continuous change and tried to provide against it.

Permanence and security being one of the chief objects of government, Cicero hoped to attain this end by establishing a balance among the shifting forms of state organization. By combining the best elements of each of the basic or unmixed forms he would obtain for government the virtue of stability. It was his wish "that there be in the state a supreme power, that another part be reserved for the authority of the chief citizens, and that certain things be left to the judgment and will of the people." This arrangement was to be obtained by agreement (*pactio*) among the otherwise discordant elements in order to maintain peace. They would all fare better by subordinating their selfish interests to the commonweal than by continuing the factional conflict.

Cicero was no champion of the plebeians or knights or nobles as such. He had no special love for the common people; there was nothing about their commonness to appeal to his informed and cultured mind. He said right reason would ever have more weight with him than the opinion of the multitude. On the other hand, he was repelled by the arrogance of the aristocrats and the avarice of the knights. He was too sincere a character to pamper the masses or truckle to the classes. He recognized that classes existed; but the interests of every class were subject and secondary to the *res publica.* This devotion to the state as a whole accounts for that wavering conduct between parties which so many historians interpret as evidence of irresoluteness, vacillation, and want of firmness. It caused them to rate him a failure as politician. If he failed as politician it is because he adhered to his principles as patriot. To carry an election by force or by the tricks of the demagogue was to him not success, and he did not care to see any party prevail at the expense of the public weal.

What Cicero championed in theory was constitutionalism, that is, government of law as distinguished from fiat government. He was the first to use the word "constitution" in its modern sense of public law of the state or law by which government itself was limited. Such a constitution insures justice against power. As Cicero said, "This constitution [*haec constitutio*] has a great measure of equability without which men can hardly remain free for any length of time." He recognized that just as man has a higher self that controls his ordinary self, so the state should have a higher or permanent self, embodied in a constitution that would set bounds to its ordinary self as expressed in the government or the popular will at any particular moment.

The men who gave the United States of America

its charter and character of government—"aristocrats prompted by democratic principles"—were students of history, particularly Roman history and Ciceronian principles. The English constitution was of course their model; but they knew that it was the grand example of Cicero's theory of *balance*. The central argument of John Adams's preface to *The Defence of the Constitutions of Government* was that the English constitution had demonstrated the practicability of Cicero's ideas of a commonwealth. Said he, "As all the ages of the world have not produced a greater statesman and philosopher united than Cicero, his authority should have great weight." He quoted the famous Roman to the effect that a stable constitution must maintain a balance of the functions of king, nobles, and people. Adams refers to such a government as a balance of the "authority of the one, the few, and the many." In the English and American constitutions this balance was made more secure through the separation of executive, legislative, and judicial functions and the application of such balance to them.

It might be well for the British Commonwealth of Nations and the North American Republic to consider the Ciceronian theories and examine present trends in the light of his political philosophy. In recent times those governments have been so desperately challenged by modern dictatorship, a revival of despotism in its most violent form, that they may have been forced out of their normal balance. War always requires a concentration of power, an increase in the executive authority (*imperium*), and in modern times that requirement has been intensified by the despotic nature of the enemy and because war has been mechanized and now demands total mobilization of strength, economic as well as military. Such disturbance of balance, however, would not be so alarming if that were all. That condition would no doubt be corrected by the restoration of peace and normal life. But there is another departure from balance in the opposite direction. It is more subtle, more general, more in line with the proverbial cycle of governments, and therefore more threatening.

Because democracy has been assailed there has been a rush to its defense. Its champions are legion. The character of the war has caused an accentuation of the virtue of democracy in the popular mind. The undiscriminating use of the word by the opponents of despotism creates a tendency to think of democracy as a panacea for all social ills, even the evils of democracy itself. There was moreover even before the war a strong inclination to extreme democracy. The great movement for economic freedom, following in the wake of political freedom, weighted the balance in favor of *the many* instead of *the few* or *the one*. As a part of that movement the opposition to imperialism, national, corporate, and individual, increased the popular trend. And then there was as always the tendency of those who seek popular favor to flatter and pander the populace. The effect of all this was to disintegrate the central, unifying, or executive force of government. That was manifest in the failure of constitutional government to prepare for its own defense in the face of dictatorship's open and violent threat. It did ultimately prepare and prosecute a world war with vigor, but only after it had restored the *imperium*, the unifying power of government. If the preparation had been timely it would not have been so costly.

It might now be profitable for those who champion stability, justice, and the commonweal, as opposed to those who champion class, bloc, or special interests, to remind themselves and others that Cicero and those who established constitutionalism, reposed their faith in a *balance* of the powers and classes found in society. As between the different forms of government they had least confidence in democracy, because its tendency to degenerate into mob rule was more pronounced and rapid than the tendency of other forms to their attendant evils. The world needs to be reminded that there are still physical limitations to rule by *the many*. In spite of all inventions facilitating communications, government by plebiscite is impossible. Conference and deliberation are necessary. A referendum may properly be used to determine a popular preference, but the functions of government cannot be exercised by wishful-thinking. And there are still limitations in the very nature of humanity and social life. Talents are not equally distributed. Truth is not revealed first to all. It comes first to those who diligently seek it and discipline themselves to receive it. Specialists serve in other fields, why not in government? The *res publica*, the commonweal of all, should have the services of those who are best qualified by nature and training to exercise the varying and exacting functions of government. But absolute democracy does not provide such services. Representative government provides better by the processes which Madison referred to as "filtration."

There is also occasion to re-emphasize the need for over-all devotion to the public weal which Cicero expounded and exemplified. Such devotion is necessary in order to dissolve the selfishness, factionalism, and class bickering which threaten the balance of constitutional government. Industrialism and commercialism center human attention on gains and profits, and beget a disdain for politics. It seems moreover to be an attendant evil of liberty to make men self-centered and narrow in their interests. They forget their common dependence on the *res publica*. Freedom from oppression by government is then construed as freedom from obligation to government.

Liberty can release men's bonds, but it cannot of itself elevate their plane of life. They must accomplish that by devoting themselves to high standards of service. The relaxation of outer control increases the need for inner control. Only that man who looks up is worthy of being looked up to, and only that man who devotes himself to the commonweal is worthy of other men's devotion. Leadership of that type is the only effectual substitute for that of the imperialistic superman.

While Cicero championed the highest devotion to the state, it should be noted that he did not advocate *state-ism.* Although he considered distinguished public service the highest expression of life, and the work of the statesman the highest calling in life, still his principles are definitely opposed to state socialism and communism as we have known them in recent years. He had too high a regard for the worth of the individual, the dignity of humanity, the divinity in personality, and the usefulness of reason to consent that they be subjugated by any exterior control. While he said that it was glorious to sacrifice life for country, yet he recognized that it was degrading to consent to its subversion. One who freely gives his life for the commonwealth becomes a patriot, a martyr, a saint; but one who submits to the suppression of his reason and conscience becomes a serf, a slave, a brute. For, as Cicero pointed out, it is reason and conscience that distinguish men from animals. Cicero believed in private ownership of property, but subject, however, to regulation for the commonweal. He acknowledged the state's interest in natural resources and their conservation, but he definitely rejected communism of property. Individualism in ownership and freedom of enterprise would not be so threatened today if those who sought private wealth had always respected Cicero's principle of obligation to the *commonwealth.*

Cicero also rejected the communistic arrangement regarding wives and children which Plato had proposed as a method for insuring eugenic offspring. Cicero considered monogamous marriage the only proper relationship for the procreation of children. The family was the basic social unit, and the chief source of that permanence which the ideal state embodied. He taught that children must be educated in order that they might render intelligent service to the state. Such education should provide for both physical and intellectual training. He stressed the need for instruction regarding ethical problems and the inculcation of moral principles. The recent revival of interest in the humanities and religion is an acknowledgment of the soundness of Cicero's views. Modern educators might also note that he cautioned against exposure of the naked body and intimate association as tending to moral impairment. To his perceptive mind privacy, modesty, continence, and reverence were virtues worthy of inculcation.

He is at least one champion of decorum who cannot be dismissed by the modern pagans as being Puritan and Victorian. Cicero did not approach such problems with the attitude of the reformer or uplifter. He bore no grudge to pleasure. And the urge to save souls was not within his ken. He was concerned with functions of state and public discipline that would preserve the commonwealth. He had seen the subtle disintegration of the republic through the relaxation of moral fiber and the consequent weakening of the social fabric. He had witnessed the tendency of the democratic influence to create demagogues, and the tendency of demagogues to undermine discipline by indulgence. He had viewed with alarm the steady encroachment of easygoing expediency upon that stern resolve which is so necessary for the day of ordeal. But his reaction was that of the practical philosopher concerned ultimately for men as rational and moral individuals. He knew however that individual lives could not realize their highest possibilities unless the social order was arranged to that end.

The religious recluse of later ages, concerned only with salvation, could well declare that "the rule of souls is the art of arts, the highest form of knowledge." But that was not the attitude of the lawyer-statesman of Rome. Cicero's feeling was more like that of the socially conscious student of modern times who asks, "Is not the creation of a fair society the supreme and inclusive art?" To that question Cicero would have answered, "Yes, and the supreme purpose of government." In order to gain a more thorough understanding of Cicero's philosophy of government, however, it is necessary to consider his philosophy of law.

Of Law

A striking presentation of the function of law is given in the defense of Cluentius. The language is rather oratorical, but it portrays Cicero's views: ". . . For law is the bond which secures our privileges in the commonwealth, the foundation of our liberty, the fountainhead of justice. Within the law are reposed the mind and heart, the judgment and the conviction of the state. The state without law would be like the human body without mind—unable to employ the parts which are to it as sinews, blood, and limbs. The magistrates who administer the law, the judges who interpret it—all of us in short—obey the law to the end that we may be free."

From this, from other statements in his orations, and from assertions in the *Commonwealth* and the *Laws* it is clear that Cicero considered the law the most important aspect of government. He considered it indeed a reflection or imitation of divine and eternal law, the moral order revealed to man through his reason and conscience. Since the state was a group of individuals united by law, since it was necessary to have in the state some common factor affecting all men in the same way, law was the necessary bond that held political society together. It could not be provided that all citizens should have the same character and ability, nor could they wisely be constrained to the possession of the same wealth; only the law could be shared by all citizens on equal terms. The essential quality of law therefore, according to Cicero, was that it be just and grant no special exemptions or dispensations. This conception of the equality of men before the law was a definite advance of Roman legal and political theory over the Greek.

This seasoned Roman lawyer had practiced too long in the courts and had acquired too much experience in politics and public administration to have any confusion between the civil law and the philosophy of law, between the law of nature and the positive law. He knew that in every state clashes of legal rights and interests were inevitable and that some practical legal system was therefore necessary if such disagreements were to be adjusted in an orderly and peaceable way. The maintenance of peace by process of law, he stated repeatedly, was the only decent procedure for civilized beings. It seems impossible that an observation made so long ago, so patently true, and so generally accepted in theory, should still be considered impracticable for world affairs! Only recently and inadequately has an effort been made to implement that theory for industrial disputes! But two thousand years ago Cicero acknowledged the practical function of the law as a substitute for force.

Even if Cicero's work on the *Laws* did not specifically embody "the modern idea of a written constitution"; even though it does not, in its present incomplete condition, treat of what is termed criminal law, and deals with civil procedure only vaguely; still there is no doubt that Cicero recognized the general division of the state's legal system into public law, criminal law, and civil law. There is no doubt that he accepted such legal system as the positive law of the land; that is, the law administered by the magistrates and interpreted and applied by the courts. He knew the sources of such laws; that it took actual form in custom, legislation, decree, agreement, and judicial opinion. But the important fact is that he saw underlying that positive law a fundamental law or law of laws which had its origin in man's nature as a rational, social, and moral being.

That conception was of course not altogether original with Cicero, but he gave it most adequate and beautiful expression. His words, according to respected authority, are "among the most memorable in political literature": "There is in fact a true law—namely, right reason—which is in accordance with nature, applies to all men, and is unchangeable and eternal. By its commands this law summons men to the performance of their duties; by its prohibitions it restrains them from doing wrong. Its commands and prohibitions always influence good men, but are without effect upon the bad. To invalidate this law by human legislation is never morally right, nor is it permissible ever to restrict its operation, and to annul it wholly is impossible. Neither the Senate nor the people can absolve us from our obligation to obey this law, and it requires no Sextu[illegible] Aelius to expound and interpret it. It will not lay d[illegible] one rule at Rome and another at Athens, nor will it [illegible] rule today and another tomorrow. But there wi[illegible] law, eternal and unchangeable, binding at all [illegible] all peoples; and there will be, as it were, [illegible] master and ruler of men, namely God, w[illegible]

of this law, its interpreter, and its sponsor. The man who will not obey it will abandon his better self, and, in denying the true nature of a man, will thereby suffer the severest of penalties, though he has escaped all the other consequences which men call punishment."

This idea of true law (*vera lex*) had been advanced by the early Greek philosophers and was an established part of Stoic doctrine. It accepted human nature as a part of universal nature and therefore subject to nature's law; but because human nature possessed reason it was unique among the creations of the world-soul, and sustained a special relation to the divine being. For the same reason there was a special relation between all rational beings; they were social. The animals were invested with impulses and instincts for their preservation. But man, because he was endowed with reason, had to live a rational life in order to enjoy a complete life. In order to live as part of a moral world order and develop an endowment which is rational and social, it was necessary to live according to the law of his nature. It followed that law and justice upon which social life depended existed by nature and not by convention. This conception came to be known as *natural law,* but of course it must be distinguished from the law of the physical sciences. Natural-law philosophy was founded on human nature, not the nature of the physical world.

This Stoic idea found ready acceptance at Rome because a similar conception had already been developed by Roman law itself. World dominion had forced on the Roman praetors and propraetors the necessity of administering the law of foreigners. Peregrine praetors had been established at Rome. Because foreigners presented to the Roman judges every variety of law and practice, the judges were impelled to decide cases upon common ideas of fair dealing.

As a consequence of this practice there developed the conception of *ius gentium,* or law common to peoples of different countries. A similar evolution occurred in English history when the law merchant was developed as a part of the common law. It was inevitable that Romans familiar with the legal notion of *ius gentium* and the Stoic conception of natural law should unite the two.

When the ideal law of the Stoics came into contact with the positive law of the Romans, intelligence and enlightenment were brought to bear on traditional practice and mechanical formulas, and a sense of fairness and sound judgment succeeded mere ritual. It tended to abolish the arbitrary distinctions of class and privilege, it recognized the uniform application of law to all men, maintained the divinity of personality which made man sacred to man, and adjusted the law's needle to the magnetic pole of justice. It established the law as a rational process, and recognized the exercise of the ethical will as a part of reason. It was not a substitute for the positive law, but served, and has served throughout the years, as a *critique* and norm of positive law. It operates not directly on positive enactments, but indirectly through the minds of men; but that which controls the minds of men will in the end master their institutions. Cicero was a vital influence in such legal evolution.

In spite of the fact that it was never universally accepted, still natural-law philosophy gave an indelible impress to Roman law. The great lawyers and jurisconsults of the republican era favored the Stoic philosophy and supported its moral and legal principles. The legal system of the republican period, except public law, survived and continued under the Empire. The tyrant emperors were of course not restrained by natural-law principles. Under Nero educated Romans realized the suffering from which

Cicero had tried to save them. Despots and dictators, as the world has again learned, never favor natural law or any other moral restraint. But the most tyrannical Roman emperors did not interfere with the development of private law. During the classical period of legal evolution the great jurists of the Empire were free to refine and elaborate that law in accordance with natural law concepts. Their work has had a profound influence on the legal systems of the civilized world.

The early Christian church accepted the basic principles of natural-law philosophy. The church Fathers sponsored and expounded it. Its principles were incorporated in the canon law of the church, and it was elaborated by the scholastic philosophers. Augustine and Aquinas were both champions of its principles. And it might well be noted in passing that the Roman Catholic Church has the oldest government in the world today. It represents, in theory at least, not only natural-law concepts but also Cicero's theory of government. It is a hierarchy not hereditary or plutocratic, the authority being vested in *the one* and *the few* who are devoted to the welfare of all. If "God maintains his church," still it is worthy of note that He does so by principles which civil governments might emulate.

Through the influence of the canon law and the ecclesiastics, who were the first justiciars of the law of England, Roman law and its principles of natural law were carried into England and made part of Anglo-Saxon jurisprudence. It is strange but true that Roman law had a greater impress on the law of Britain than on the law of the Continent. It was so completely accepted in England that Englishmen thought it their own. It never was foreign after the twelfth or early part of the thirteenth century. It had an extensive influence on Bracton and through him on Coke. While we think of Coke as particularly a champion of the common law, his basic principles were the same as those of the Roman law and natural law.

Through their acceptance into the common law of England natural-law principles became a part of the constitutional history of England. They inspired and supported the Petition of Right and the Bill of Rights, and they finally found fruition in the Constitution of the United States and its Bill of Rights. England's colonizing success has been due largely to the existence of natural-law principles in the system of law which has obtained in all her settlements. In spite of the arbitrary conduct of early monarchs and the mistakes of her imperialistic policy, the basic principles of England's law have been carried around the world. And here in this country our history and our high level of life bear testimony to the beneficence of natural-law principles.

Natural-law doctrines, however, have never been free from opposition. There have always been minds that seemed to have an aversion to such principles. Their acceptance has been impeded, moreover, by overzealous champions. For instance, some enthusiasts over the rationalism of natural-law philosophy thought that a perfect system of law could be worked out by abstract reason alone. This extreme in time produced its opposite, and the rational basis of the law was then denied entirely. But the rejection of law as pure logomachy, as a mere legal formalism, does not require its acceptance as an *arational* development. Because logic alone cannot lead to it, rationality need not be abandoned as a test for it. The true basis of law is, to borrow a phrase from Justice Holmes, "reason working on experience," or, as Dean Pound says, "experience developed by reason and reason tested by experience."

During recent years a school of legal thought emerged

and became popular which opposed any attempt to hypostatize the law. To it the principles and concepts, ideas, and values, which support the notion of true law, were only illusory and deceptive images; the law was simply governmental fiat, administrative command, threat of state force. Such theory of law was prompted by a desire to carry over into the legal and social field the scientific methods which had been accepted in the physical and exact sciences. It attempted to reduce life to fixed patterns of conduct or classifications of what was called behaviorism. Moral intuitions, ideals, and standards were excluded with the expectation that law could be made a positive science. Many who supported this trend had been influenced by Marx and other social reformers. They were moreover encouraged by the modern cynicism and sophistry which resulted from the crass materialism of the times. They advanced the same old arguments, slightly rephrased, which we know Cicero answered in his *De Re Publica,* although we do not have the complete text of his answers. They abandoned reason and logic and proclaimed experience as the only criterion of legal adjudication. To them everything was derived from experience, and they ignored man's capacity to interpret experience. The processes that express the synthetical function of sensibility and understanding were overlooked as a part of the phenomena of human nature. They took pride in their classification as realists. But the error of their "realism" was their rejection of the insights of human nature, the natural and empirical reality of ideals and standards, those beliefs and wishes which Justice Holmes accepted as having "a transcendental basis in the sense that their foundation is arbitrary."

The most recent trend in legal philosophy however has been away from such "realism" and back to natural law concepts. It was discovered that the effect of such realism was inimical to constitutionalism and entirely too similar to the *Realpolitik* of the modern dictators and militarists who with destructive force were impinging more and more upon the United Nations and their vital standards of life. In last analysis the war that has rocked civilization to its foundations was a struggle for supremacy in the world between the champions of two opposing conceptions of government, between those who champion government by law (*ius naturale*) and those who champion government by arbitrary command. When the crisis came the champions of liberalism and idealism seemed to hear again Cicero's assertion: "I declare that no importance is to be attached to anything which, as we suppose, has hitherto been established about the state, and that no further advance is possible, unless we shall prove both the falsity of the view which regards injustice as a necessary part of government, and the truth of the view which regards a high degree of justice as essential if the state is to function at all." When free men were put to the final test they again fought for their ideals. They would rather die than give them up. The statements of dictators and cynics that liberal governments had failed to realize those ideals made no difference. The fact that justice had not completely prevailed over privilege, class interest, and imperialism, did not warrant its abandonment as an ideal. The value of ideals does not depend on their complete triumph; they afford the moral incentive, the rational guidance, the intelligent restraint, without which—the world has again learned—society becomes entirely debased and brutal. The true and worthy memorial for the military heroes of World War II will not be in stone or trees but in the maintenance of those ideals as a vital force in the civil and business life of the world.

Cicero's conceptions of government and law served well the transition from the Greek city-state to the Roman world-state. The world-state broke up in time into nation-states. His conceptions can now serve well the transition from independent and warring nation-states to an international organization of states for world order. It is true that Cicero did not give the outlines of that form of state which would maintain the balance of social classes of his day—as Tacitus said, that is more easily praised than realized. Neither has Cicero given us the form of a world organization. He has however given us the philosophy, the norm and *critique* for such an organization. And that philosophy teaches that no special form is essential, a *sine qua non*. Various forms may serve, and any is better than none. Paraphrasing Cato, it can be said that any world government would be better than international anarchy. That philosophy teaches moreover that a balance of the political forces that exist should be established, leaving the way open for adjustment of that balance as future developments require. Such balance should of course, in light of subsequent experience, be extended to legislative, executive and judicial functions, and also to individual, local, and international interests.

That philosophy should deliver the world from the bogey of national sovereignty. It teaches that sovereignty is not in men or nations, but in the law. It should also keep men from making a fetish of democracy. While it inculcates the highest devotion to the commonweal, it also enjoins the acceptance of human nature as it is. Nature creates leaders. But the tendency of both despotism and democracy is to thwart the influence of such leaders. Man's welfare and evolution depend on his acceptance of such leaders in their various fields. That necessitates representative government. Human nature is such that men must trust one another—and therefore must be trustworthy. The selection of public officers must be more of a drawing-up and less of a playing-down. The method must not favor demagogues, but recognize character. Ability is included in character, for a man of character will not assume an office for which he has no talents, and within the range of his talents his ability grows with responsibility assumed. The *Commonwealth* requires the best, and government should afford the means by which it is obtained. The purpose of law is not to favor any faction, even though it be a majority, but to allay the friction of all factions.

But of course the deepest significance of Cicero's philosophy lies in its noble insistence on the duty of all men to serve the commonwealth—a duty generally accepted only in wartime; in its recognition that while the commonwealth exists for the greater freedom and welfare of the individual, still its interests are superior to any selfish, class or factional interests, because any selfish advantage at the cost of the commonweal could be but temporary; in its inculcation of the principles of justice and fair dealing; and in its acceptance of a universal society, founded on reason, including all rational beings within its influence. Cicero saw clearly that the acting bond of society's diverse parts, the social solvent, the political catalyst, was the law. Its object, and the justification of government, was justice. With poetic insight he likened justice in society to harmony in music. Recalling his observation that melancholy is the lot of intellectual men, we can imagine his wistful pleasure if he could have read Justice Holmes's tribute to legal philosophy:

> It opens to the forlorn hopes on which we throw ourselves away, the vista of the farthest stretch of human thought, the chords of a harmony that breathes from the unknown.

CONCLUSION

CICERO's social and legal philosophy made him quite naturally a champion of high professional standards. At the very inception of the legal profession he inspired it with fine ideals. As the science of jurisprudence was developed the legal profession was formed. When reason supplanted ritual the jurisconsults succeeded the priests as directors of legal affairs. The passing of the practice of law from pontiffs to public brought forth a body of men who made it their calling. Men experienced in public affairs and learned in the law were looked upon by their neighbors as counselors and champions. They took pride in their calling and developed standards of practice. The profession was not recognized legally until after the Empire was established. But it was during the last years of the Republic that the world's great legal system was founded, and it was then that it was animated with a professional spirit.

That professional spirit is evident in the attitude of lawyers toward the law and its function, and toward their calling and its purpose. In the service of the law they are ministers of court. As attorneys at law they are agents of clients. They have very definite obligations to the courts, to their clients, to the public, and to one another. They must respect the confidence which they invite and be worthy of the trust reposed in them. A profession should be distinguished from a guild or union by the absence of self-interest, and differentiated from a trade by its desire to serve rather than to profit or gain.

That Cicero expounded and practiced the highest professional principles there can be no doubt. That he considered the love of money one of the most sordid of motives is evident in his conduct and in his expressions. In his famous letter to his brother Quintus on the duties of a magistrate he called attention to the selfishness of men who gave their lives to the making of money and pointed out that it was seldom that one could be found who considered anything except his own interest. He said, "There will be no class in your acquaintance more to be avoided; because they know all the arts of getting money, they do nothing but for money, and they are indifferent about the opinion of any man except as it affects their selfish ends." He counseled his brother in the virtue of moderation and continence, and admonished that by checking the passion for money he would be better able to restrain the dishonesty and rapaciousness of others. It would be impossible for a man of such convictions to allow his professional conduct to degenerate to the practice of a trade.

His letter to Trebatius is as fine a portrayal of a lawyer's obligations as can be found in brief compass. Though written in a pleasant, half-bantering style, it contains the very substance of the professional attitude. It emphasizes the importance of principles, the necessity of reconciling tenets to profession, the duty of acting for clients' interests and conserving the welfare of the people, and it contains the statement, "For neither truth nor trust can there be in those who professedly govern themselves upon motive of absolute selfishness." And it revealed again Cicero's belief that man's sense of moral obligation was dependent on his conception of God.

Cicero recognized the impersonal authority of the law. He said, "It can be truly affirmed that the magistrate is law made vocal, while law is a voiceless magistrate." But while the law is impersonal he saw clearly that the relation of lawyer and client is personal. He accepted all the delicate implications of that relationship. He concluded that the professional relationship, being one of trust and confidence, could not be forced. In his oration against Q. Caecilius, he said, "Will anyone be found so impudent as to dare to assume or to aspire to conduct the cause of others against the will of those very people whose affairs are involved in it?"

True, he practiced the arts of the advocate, and, like other great lawyers and good men, was led by the very diversity of his cases into inconsistent positions, and was carried away at times by the emotional force of his own arguments. But those results were inherent in the nature of trial procedure and in the conditions of his time. A learned Italian lawyer of recent times, Professor Piero Calamandrei, has made clear the necessity for latitude of judgment regarding practicing attorneys. He points out that it is the assumption of the law that truth is best attained by hearing the opposing sides of an issue. Truth, he says, has three dimensions and can appear differently from different points of view. Lawyers, although sustaining contradictory positions, do so in good faith because each presents the truth as it appears to his client. The lawyers present the two profiles of truth, only the judge in the center looks it full in the face. The scales, says he, are the mechanical representation of the judicial function; as each lawyer presents the most favorable case for his client, they create between them the equilibrium which the judge is seeking. He who would blame the lawyers for their partiality, he concludes, should also blame the weights on the scales.

The evolution of trial procedure is no doubt away from such adversary limitations; it tends toward the attitude of the laboratory rather than that of the arena. The judicial function should become a search for truth, rather than the mere determination of a contest. But that evolution had not progressed far in Cicero's day. A case in court had many characteristics of trial by battle, brain having been substituted for brawn.

Cicero knew that the world had not yet realized the ideal state and that the administration of the law had to be tempered to the needs of his generation. He helped to develop the science of jurisprudence, the object of which is the adjustment of the law to varying conditions. He had no respect for those men whose devotion to the law consisted simply of blind adherence to precedent. On the other hand, he knew the danger of constant change. He wrote: "All confidence was banished from the Forum, not by the stroke of any new calamity, but by the general suspicion entertained of the courts of justice, and by the disorder into which they had fallen, and by the constant reversal of previous decisions."

Cicero like a true Roman was conservative. He looked to the law for preservation of stability. Still he knew that man's social evolution required a corresponding evolution of law. The eternal principles had to be translated and rephrased into the language of each new age. It was the recognition of this principle of growth as well as the permanence of the professional ideal, a living system of law, that enabled the jurisconsults of Rome to expand the law of a city to the needs of an empire. Cicero's ideals and principles remain constant through all vicissitudes—they are still the inspiration of the profession. Through devotion to those ideals the function of the lawyer is elevated to the status of statesmanship.

It is of course useless to have professional principles if one lacks the moral courage to assert them. Throughout his life Cicero demonstrated that he possessed such courage. He defended unfortunate people whom the aristocrats oppressed under Sulla. Thirty years later he defended the republican refugees under the dictatorship of Caesar. He spoke out vehemently against the bad practices of popular leaders and did not hesitate to prosecute influential members of the Senate. His voice was ardently championing a government of justice up to the very day the army of the Second Triumvirate marched against Rome. He accepted death rather than sacrifice his principles in any kind of compromise with Antony.

Cicero's life at first seems to have ended in failure. But the standard of a lawyer's success is not, Did he win? but, How well did he present his case? If he has analyzed the facts and the law thoroughly and presented his arguments clearly and courageously, the responsibility for the decision rests not with the lawyer but with the court. Cicero presented his cause to the Roman senate and to the Roman people in a masterly manner. He was answered not by reasoned arguments in the open forum of the law—his opponents dared not meet him there. He was overcome by the violence and force of the perfidious Triumvirate. His cause was lost temporarily, but he was eternally justified.

The very things for which he is criticized are evidence of Cicero's finer qualities. Politicians frequently succeed through their defects and want of character. When evil times demand evil men it is a compliment to say that a man is unsuccessful in public life. Cicero's natural uprightness was a handicap. If he had been less scrupulous he might have temporized for party success and then he would have appeared more consistent. Not only his moral and professional standards but his openness to impressions, his delicate and almost irritable sensitivity, the breadth and vision of his understanding, his perspicuity, made him appear impractical and wanting in zeal. Because of these very qualities, however, he should be given credit for constancy and courage greater than that required for ordinary success. When he suppressed the Catilinarian conspiracy he was mindful of the vengeance to which he was exposing himself. During his opposition to Clodius he had a premonition of his exile. He followed Pompey though he foresaw his failure. He was mindful during his struggle with Antony that his life was at stake.

Such constancy and courage were the result of Cicero's intellectual honesty. He had the scientific spirit, faced facts squarely and followed their logic to its natural conclusion. This intellectual insight is revealed by the fact that while he was augur, an office which he held in high esteem because of its ancient implications and political influence, he had the temerity to write his *De Divinatione,* denying the significance of omens. He issued this pronouncement against the superstition of divination in spite of the fact that his views were contrary to historic precedent, against the practices of honored statesmen, and also against the temperamental attraction of mysticism to his own nature. Voltaire said that we honor Cicero because he taught us to think. We should honor him also because he had the courage to say what he thought, even to a hostile age.

Cicero was confronted by four great crises in his life: The Catilinarian conspiracy, the First Triumvirate, the Civil War, and the contest with Antony. Probably he was too prideful over his suppression of the conspiracy. His zeal to suppress lawlessness led him into temporary neglect or misinterpretation of a fundamental principle of Roman policy. During the First Triumvirate he lacked the equanimity which his philosophy would lead us to expect. We read with regret his bitter lamentations at the time of his banishment. During the Civil War his course wavered. He vacillated between opposing forces. Probably he was too complacent about Caesar's dictatorship. One of his French biographers, Boissier, says that he seemed to be abasing himself when he was only bowing. Probably he should not have bowed. In his final struggle with Antony he may have been too vitriolic in his utterances and not vigorous enough in his command. But at no time was he faithless to his professional principles. He was devoted to the maintenance of law and order and justice. It is consistent with his principles that he did not resort to force or practice the arts of the demagogue.

We see Cicero in true perspective only when we consider the permanence of the principles which he espoused. Against that background how selfish and vain are the standards of commercial success; acquisitive impulses are futile when there is no stability of government! By that measure, how ephemeral was the success of his opponents! Their triumphs were of short duration. He outlived Pompey and Caesar, who both suffered violent deaths. Antony, who died by his own hand, did not long survive Cicero. They all were—as men always are—the victims of their times. But as Tenney Frank has said: "Cicero's work has been a living force from that time, not because of the accident that he was murdered for advocating a policy that his world rejected, but because he had faith in ideals, the worth of which will always be recognized by men of sanity, since they lie at the very root of human nature."

Cicero was human and had faults and foibles. A mundane pride made him wish for temporal success. When he failed of that success his pique was in proportion to his pride. He was vain, and loved acclaim; and that vanity made him vulnerable to scorn. He did not have the benefit of Christian teaching and did not know the power of humility to forestall humiliation. Sarcastic affectation concealed his lighter wounds; but when he was banished from his beloved Rome, like the psalmist by the rivers of Babylon, he sat down and wept. As advocate he extenuated the culpability of clients; as orator he glossed and colored facts to win his cause; as politician he sometimes temporized to meet emergencies. And that personal pride, that adulation of Rome, those little tricks for temporal attainment have served to discredit him. At the last, however, he displayed a noble disdain for ephemeral success. And in the main the force of his life was spent for things that transcend time and place. As philosopher, as literary artist, as lawyer, he was constant to truth, to beauty, to justice. And the more he sacrificed in his day for these eternal verities the more we glorify him in our day. Because he endured against odds and withstood the hostility of life; because he labored wisely and was clear-headed in spite of prejudice, and fair-minded amid cruelty; because he was kind and generous to the undeserving; because he was influenced not by personalities, but by principles; because he obeyed his convictions regardless of the cost and gave up life itself on the chance that his faith was true; because in a word he was not the victim of his vanity or passions but ordered his life according to reason and the law of man's better nature, we consider him a great man. What he said of Gaius Aquillius might well serve as his own epitaph:

> "So just and virtuous a man that he seems to be a lawyer by nature."

AUTHORITIES AND NOTES

CHAPTER I

Delayen, Gaston, "Cicero" (Translated by Farrell Symons), New York, E. P. Dutton & Co., 1931, pp. 14, 15, 29.

Sohm, Rudolph, "The Institutes" (Translated by James Crawford Ledlie), Oxford, The Clarendon Press, 1901, pp. 93, 94.

Hunter, W. A., "Roman Law," London, William Maxwell & Son, 1885, pp. 34–43, 58.

Frank, Tenney, "Cicero," London, Humphrey Milford, Amen House, 1932, p. 23.

Plutarch's Lives (Translated by John and William Langhorne), New York, Harper & Bros., 1854, Vol. IV, pp. 95, 98.

Boissier, Gaston, "Cicero and His Friends" (Translated by A. D. Jones), London, A. D. Innes & Co., 1897, p. 249.

Gibbon, Edward, "The History of the Decline and Fall of the Roman Empire," Boston, Phillips, Sampson & Co., 1853, Vol. I, p. 46.

Rolfe, John Carew, "Cicero and His Influence," Boston, Marshall Jones Co., 1923, p. 23.

Page 9. There was so much conflict and confusion in the historic references to the Roman Rostra that Dr. George Karo, the noted archeologist, was appealed to for the latest reliable information. His valuable report follows:

The Republican Rostra

From very early days, the civic life of Rome centered in the *Comitium,* the Assembly Place at the northern end of the Forum, in front of the Curia, the Senate House, said to have been built by King Tullus Hostilius. The Comitium was an open area, not a *templum* or precinct with fixed limits. But one of the most venerable shrines of Rome lay near its southern end: the legendary sepulchre of Romulus (or of another prince of his house) which our earliest literary sources mention repeatedly.[1] It was apparently marked by a sacred Black Stone (*niger lapis*), and the older Rostra are said to have stood near by, on the border line between the Comitium and the Forum. When this region was excavated in 1899, a square pavement of black marble slabs came to light and was promptly (though I think erroneously) identified with the *niger lapis*. Some five feet below it lay the remains of a shrine of characteristically Etruscan type, whose main features are a small rectangular base between two much longer ones. In all probability, a pair of couchant lions once occupied these twin bases, while the central one would have carried the real *niger lapis,* one of those black volcanic stones, rounded like a huge pebble, which frequently appear in Etruscan sanctuaries and cemeteries. Their religious importance is shown by the fact that they were often taken over by the Church in Early Christian times, and supposed to have been used for stoning martyrs.

Close by the bases just mentioned, another one supports the truncated remnant of a square pillar, inscribed on all four sides with the oldest Latin inscription on stone known to us. Its badly mutilated text seems to be a sacrificial law. Small votive offerings found around the shrine date from the eighth century B.C. to the sixth century B.C. The small sanctuary was evidently destroyed, probably during the Gaulish invasion of

[1] Pompeius Festus (based on Verrius Flaccus, a contemporary of Augustus), p. 177 M.: "the black stone in the Comitium marks an ugly spot: according to some it was intended to serve as the grave of Romulus, but this intention was not carried out, and in the place of Romulus his foster father Faustulus was buried; according to others, it was the grave of Hostus Hostilius, the father of the third king Tullus Hostilius." The contemporary Greek historian Dionysius of Halicarnassus adds, X, 57: "Many people think that the stone lion, which is in the noblest place in the Roman Forum, close to the Rostra, was a monument for Faustulus, who was buried on the spot where he fell in battle." The scholiast (annotator) to Horace's *Epodes,* XVI, 13/14, quotes Varro as saying that Romulus was buried behind the Rostra, and adds: "It is known that in memory of this two lions were erected there."

390 B.C., and covered over with the black marble pavement. The extant remains [2] corroborate descriptions of the Tomb of Romulus, by writers of the time of Augustus who had never seen the ancient shrine, long hidden underground and declared an unlucky spot. But its memory lived on through the centuries.

The original site of the speaker's platform or *suggestus,* from which magistrates and orators addressed the citizens assembled in the Comitium, is determined by its proximity to the Tomb of Romulus, opposite the Curia.[3] It was thus closely associated, in early republican times, with that sacred memorial of Rome's origin, and gained added importance by such a connection, though it was not itself a consecrated place. Otherwise its site could not have been changed several times, as the scanty excavated remains of republican date can show. It must have been a platform of considerable size by the middle of the fifth century, since the Twelve Tables of the Law, engraved on bronze, were placed there in 450 B.C., as well as, a decade later, the statues of three Roman envoys killed by the Fidenates, in 438 B.C.[4] But the name *Rostra* was not applied to the structure before 338 B.C., when six beaks (*rostra*) taken from captured ships of Antium were fastened to its front wall.[5] Remains of a spacious tufa platform, with five broad steps leading up to it, were discovered in the area of the black pavement mentioned above, and some eight feet below it.[6]

This earliest structure was superseded by a later one at a higher level; parts of a large curved platform, nearly sixty feet in diameter, have survived, with steps leading up from the Comitium and a straight wall more than twenty-four feet behind these. It is impossible to ascertain the exact shape or date of this structure, which has plausibly been connected

[2] See Chr. Huelsen's standard work, *The Roman Forum,* pp. 103 ff., with figs. 46 and 52. Also Pauly-Wissowa, *Real-Encyclopaedie d. Klassischen Altertums,* s. v. Rednerbuehne.

[3] Varro, *De lingua latina,* V, 155; Diodorus Siculus, XII, 26; Dio Cassius XLIII, 49.

[4] Diodorus, XII, 26; cf. Dionys. Halicarn., X, 57; Cicero, Philipp., IX, 4; Livy, IV, 17, 6.

[5] Livy, VIII, 14, 12; Pliny, *Nat. Hist.* XXXIV, 20.

[6] Huelsen, *l.c.,* pp. 9 f., 69 ff., 110 ff., with plans and illustrations.

with Sulla's renovation of the Comitium. By that time it had become customary for orators to turn toward the citizens assembled in the Forum, a practice first introduced by the Tribune C. Licinius Crassus in 138 B.C., and followed by the democratic reformer C. Gracchus.[7] In the old aristocratic days the Comitium had sufficed for the assemblies of privileged citizens; by the turn of the second century it had become practically part of the Forum. The ancient Tables of the Law and the fifth-century statues must have been replaced upon the new platform, while the *rostra* (beaks) now adorned the wall turned toward the Forum. In Cicero's time several other statues had been added; he mentions those of the ambassador Octavius, of Servius Sulpicius Rufus and the gilded bronze statue of Sulla on horseback, inscribed *Corn*(*elius*) *Sulla imp*(*erator*) *fel*(*ix*).[8] Of the successive changes which the Rostra underwent after Cicero's death, the earliest is commemorated by a coin of Marcus Lollius Palikanus, struck in 45 B.C.; its elaborate arches appear to be an innovation. The great remodeling of the early Empire, when Augustus moved the Rostra to the middle of the Forum, does not concern us here.

Pages 23, 24. Delayen, *supra*, p. 53: "Hewn from the rock of the hill and decorated, as at Rome, with rostra, was the colossal tribunal, the Bema."

In note 23 at p. 280, Delayen adds: "However, the bema of Pericles was not that of Demosthenes; in early days the tribune faced the sea, while that of the time of Demosthenes was turned toward the north, the orator having on his right the Areopagus and the Acropolis. (Duruy: *Historie des Grecs*)."

Professor Louis E. Lord, Chairman, American School of Classical Studies at Athens, after reading the manuscript of this work, wrote that he was so doubtful about the statement that the Bema in the Pnyx at Athens was adorned with the beaks of ships like the speaker's platform in the Forum at Rome,

[7] Cicero, *Laelius de amicitia,* 96; Plutarch, *C. Gracchus,* 5; Varro, *De re rustica,* I, 2, 9.

[8] Cicero, Philipp., IX, 4, 13 and 16.

that he wrote to Professor Homer Thompson of the Department of Archeology at the University of Toronto, who conducted the excavations of the Pnyx. He received the following letter in reply to his inquiry: "I have no knowledge of beaks of ships in connection with the Bema of the Pnyx. Had such been dedicated in the period of which the Bema remains, one would expect to find the appropriate cuttings in the face of the great cube of living rock, but none of the cuttings on that bema would seem to be appropriate for beaks. The Greeks, however, appear to have carried away the upper ornaments of prow and stern as trophies more commonly than the actual beak or ram such as adorned the Rostra; some of the cuttings on the floor of the familiar Bema may conceivably have supported such an object (on these ἀκρωτήρια see Hesperia 13, 1944, pp. 201 ff.)"

Chapter II

Moore, Frank Gardner, "The Roman's World," New York, Columbia Univ. Press, 1936, pp. 11, 12.

Pellison, Maurice, "Roman Life in Pliny's Time" (Translated by Maud Wilkinson), Meadville, Pa. Flood & Vincent, The Chautauqua-Century Press, 1897, Chaps. II and III.

Haskell, H. J., "This Was Cicero," New York, Alfred A. Knopf, 1942, pp. 118, 379.

McCrea, Nelson Glenn, "Marcus Aurelius Antoninus to Himself," New York, Macmillan Co., 1928, Intro. p. viii.

Taylor, T. M., "A Constitutional and Political History of Rome," London, Methuen & Co., 1899, pp. 204, 205.

Hunter, W. A., "Roman Law," London, William Maxwell & Son, 1885, pp. 44, 45, 56, 57.

Plutarch's Lives, *supra,* IV, 100.

Rolfe, John Carew, *supra,* p. 64.

The Cambridge Ancient History, Vol. IX, The Roman Republic, London, Cambridge Univ. Press, New York, Macmillan, 1932, pp. 337, 338.

Pages 40, 41. Delayen, *supra,* p. 112: "Tullius Cicero was unanimously proclaimed consul and no count of the votes was made."

CHAPTER III

Delayen, Gaston, *supra,* pp. 23, 24, 89, 90.
Taylor, T. M., *supra,* p. 317.
Hunter, W. A., *supra,* pp. 10, 53, 55, 1045.
Sohm, Rudolph, *supra,* pp. 93, 95, 96.
Sabine, George Holland, and Smith, Stanley Barney, "Cicero, Marcus Tullius. *On the Commonwealth,* by Marcus Tullius Cicero." Translated with notes and introduction. Columbus, The Ohio State Univ. Press, 1929, Intro. p. 9.
Liddell, Henry G., "A History of Rome," New York, Harper & Bros., 1872, p. 736.
Windolph, F. Lyman, "The Country Lawyer," Philadelphia, Univ. of Penn. Press, 1938, Chap. IV—Defending A Bad Cause.

CHAPTER IV

Taylor, T. M., *supra,* p. 321.
The Cambridge Ancient History, *supra,* pp. 484–486, 502–505.
Bryce, James, "Marriage and Divorce Under Roman and English Law," "Select Essays on Anglo-American Legal History," Boston, Little, Brown & Co., 1909, Vol. III, p. 799.
Delayen, Gaston, *supra,* pp. 93, 108, 109, 122, 129.
Liddell, Henry G., *supra,* pp. 642, 644, 646, 647.
Rolfe, John Carew, *supra,* p. 41.
Hamilton, Edith, "The Roman Way," New York, W. W. Norton & Co., 1932, p. 117.
Sabine and Smith, *supra,* Intro. p. 55.
Forsyth, William, "Life of Marcus Tullius Cicero," New York, C. Scribner & Co., 1865, Vol. I, pp. 131, 133, 136, 146, 147, 161.

Pages 92–95. In emphasizing that Cicero's conduct regarding execution of the conspirators was that of consul rather than counsel, or, in other words, expedient rather than legal, it is not meant that Cicero's action was entirely arbitrary or without any justification. The crisis presented two alternatives:

1. Cicero as consul could order the conspirators brought to court for trial and sentence according to law, and risk the charge of endangering the city for the sake of legal procedure; or

2. He could order them executed as traitors and suffer the accusation of having put Roman citizens to death contrary to law.

If the first alternative had been chosen and there had been no insurrection, that would have been the most fortunate outcome. But no one can now be certain that there would not have been an insurrection and delivery of the prisoners.

A strong defense of Cicero's action as consul may be found in the *Journal of Roman Studies,* Vol. xxxiii, 1943, page 93, by Professor Hugh Last, of Brasenose College, Oxford. Professor Last says: ". . . society at least tacitly reserves to itself the right, if a situation develops in which its normal means of protection are inadequate, to use abnormal means of any kind whatever which may seem necessary to ensure its survival." He points out "that it was the alleged threat to release the prisoners by force which moved Cicero to convene the Senate for the meeting held on 5th December."

Cicero had been invested by the Senate with the supreme *imperium* for the protection of the city. Professor Last thinks there was good reason to believe that danger had reached a magnitude at which the procedure prescribed by law was no longer capable of coping with it and that consequently the reign of law had suffered an interruption. To his mind the legal procedure of accusation and trial could not have been followed without graver risks to society than could reasonably be run by a magistrate responsible for its preservation. He states the central issue thus: "Were the men under arrest put to death at a time when their legal right to trial could not be respected without exposing the state to dangers of a gravity from which it was the supreme duty of the magistrate to protect it?" He says: "In Sallust's account Cato is made to suggest an extension of established precedent on this point by arguing that, if non-legal measures were justified when taken to suppress civil disturbances of a magnitude beyond the capacity of the law and its legal sanctions to quell, they should be regarded as no less justified when taken as the only means of preventing the outbreak of civil disturbance on such a scale."

Chapter V

Boissier, Gaston, *supra,* pp. 204, 205, 225, 245, 263.
Delayen, Gaston, *supra,* pp. 65, 105, 130, 141, 144, 146, 149, 150, 153, 156, 166, 177.
Sabine and Smith, *supra,* pp. 45, 46, 47.
The Cambridge Ancient History, *supra,* pp. 487, 488, 491, 505, 506, 509, 511, 512, 515, 516, 523, 526, 623, 876, 878.
Liddell, Henry G., *supra,* p. 659.
Plutarch's Lives, *supra,* vol. IV, pp. 112, 113, 117; vol. III, pp. 322, 323, 324.
Rolfe, John Carew, *supra,* pp. 44, 73.
Frank, Tenney, *supra,* p. 25.

Chapter VI

The Cambridge Ancient History, *supra,* pp. 446, 460, 529, note 530, 533, 535, 628, 693, 694.
Boissier, Gaston, *supra,* pp. 219, 224.
Wright, Frederick Warren, "Cicero and the Theater," Northampton, Smith College, 1931, p. 8.
Delayen, Gaston, *supra,* p. 176.
Plutarch's Lives, *supra,* vol. IV, p. 123.

CHAPTER VII

The Cambridge Ancient History, *supra,* pp. 36, 645, 665, 692, 739, 745, 802.
Plutarch's Lives, *supra,* vol. IV, p. 282.
Delayen, Gaston, *supra,* pp. 197, 201, 215, 219, 221, 223, 229.
Boissier, Gaston, *supra,* pp. 266, 291, 293.
Forsyth, William, *supra,* Vol. II, pp. 179, 181, 183, 186, 190, 191.
Haskell, H. J., *supra,* pp. 131, 136, 347, 389.
Poteat, Hubert McNeill, "Selected Letters of Cicero," Boston, D. C. Heath & Co., 1931, note p. 210.
Zane, John M., "The Story of Law," Garden City, N.Y., Garden City Publishing Co., Inc., 1927, p. 183.
Frank, Tenney, *supra,* p. 25.

Professor Hugh Last gives this list of Cicero's most important works in chronological order:

De oratore, 55 B.C.
Partitiones oratorum, 54
De re publica, 51
(*De legibus,* probably begun soon after *De re publica* was finished but still unpublished when Cicero died.)
Brutus, 46 (*De claris oratoribus*)
Orator, 46
De optimo genere oratorum, 46
Hortensius, 45 (famous for its influence on St. Augustine)
Academica, 45
De finibus, 45
Tusculan Disputations, 45
De natura deorum, 44
De senectute, 44
De divinatione, 44
De amicitia, 44
De officiis, 44

CHAPTER VIII

Litman, Alexander, "Cicero's Doctrine of Nature and Man," New York, Columbia University, 1930, p. 15 et seq.

McCrea, Nelson Glenn, "Marcus Aurelius Antoninus To Himself," *supra,* Intro.

Sabine and Smith, *supra,* pp. 21, 23, 33, 37, 39 et seq., 47 et seq.

Peabody, Andrew P., "Cicero's Tusculan Disputations," Boston, Little, Brown & Co., 1886, XXI.

Moore, Frank Gardner, *supra,* p. 113.

Holmes, Oliver Wendell, "Dissenting Opinions of Mr. Justice Holmes" (arr. Alfred Lief), New York, Vanguard, 1929, xvi Natural Law.

Frank, Tenney, *supra,* p. 20.

Haskell, H. J., *supra,* p. 383.

Adams, John, "Works of John Adams," Boston, Little, Brown & Co., 1850–56 (v. 1–1856), Preface pp. 294–295, Vol. IV. Chap. VII, p. 520.

Haines, Charles Grove, "The Revival of Natural Law Concepts," Cambridge, Harvard Univ. Press, 1930.

Pound, Roscoe, "The Revival of Natural Law," XVII Notre Dame Lawyer No. 4, pp. 287–372, Notre Dame, Inc., Notre Dame College of Law, June, 1942.

Northrop, F. S. C., *The Meeting of East and West,* New York, The Macmillan Company, 1946, pp. 254 et seq.

McIlwain, Charles Howard, "Constitutionalism, Ancient and Modern," Ithaca, N.Y., Cornell Univ. Press, 1940, pp. 27, 37, 39, 62, 63, 73, 74, 89.

McIlwain, Charles Howard, "Our Heritage from the Law of Rome," Foreign Affairs, April, 1941.

Calamandrei, Piero, "Eulogy of Judges" (Translated by John Clarke Adams and C. Abbott Phillips, Jr.), Princeton, Princeton Univ. Press, 1942, pp. 51 et seq.

Rolfe, John Carew, *supra,* p. 59.

GENERAL REFERENCES

Select Orations of Marcus Tullius Cicero (Translated by C. D. Yonge), New York, Nourse Co.

Select Letters of Cicero (Translated by G. E. Jeans, J. S. Watson, and others), Philadelphia, David McKay, 1897.

The Letters of Cicero (Translated by Evelyn S. Shuckburgh), London, G. Bell & Sons, Ltd., 1912.

Select Orations of M. T. Cicero (Translated by C. D. Yonge), New York, Harper & Bros., 1888.

Cicero's Tusculan Disputations (Translated by Andrew P. Peabody), Boston, Little, Brown & Co., 1886.

The frontispiece "Rostra from which Cicero Spoke" may be found in "The Roman Forum, Its History and Its Monuments" by Christian Huelsen (Transl. from the 2nd German edition by Jesse Benedict Carter), Rome, 1906.

INDEX